Could It Be Otherwise?

The *Critical Social Thought* Series

edited by Michael W. Apple, University of Wisconsin—Madison

Could It Be Otherwise?

Parents and the Inequities of Public School Choice

Lois André-Bechely

Routledge
Taylor & Francis Group

NEW YORK AND LONDON

Published in 2005 by
Routledge
Taylor & Francis Group
270 Madison Avenue
New York, NY 10016

Published in Great Britain by
Routledge
Taylor & Francis Group
2 Park Square
Milton Park, Abingdon
Oxon OX14 4RN

Printed in the United States of America on acid-free paper
10 9 8 7 6 5 4 3 2 1

International Standard Book Number-10: 0-415-94520-8 (Hardcover) 0-415-94521-6 (Softcover)
International Standard Book Number-13: 978-0-415-94520-2 (Hardcover) 978-0-415-94521-9 (Softcover)
Library of Congress Card Number 2004027390

Library of Congress Cataloging-in-Publication Data

André Bechely, Lois N., 1953-
    Could it be otherwise? : parents and the inequities of public school choice / Lois André-Bechely.
        p. cm. -- (Critical social thought)
    Includes bibliographical references and index.
    ISBN 0-415-94520-8 (hardback : alk. paper) -- ISBN 0-415-94521-6 (pbk. : alk. paper)
    1. School choice--United States. 2. Educational equalization--United States. I. Title. II. Series.

LB1027.9.A77 2005
379.1'11'0973--dc22

2004027390

Taylor & Francis Group
is the Academic Division of T&F Informa plc.

Visit the Taylor & Francis Web site at
http://www.taylorandfrancis.com

and the Routledge Web site at
http://www.routledge-ny.com

For Julian, J.C., and Paul

SERIES EDITOR'S INTRODUCTION

This is a time of what might be called "conservative modernization" in education, a time when we are being constantly told that the *only* solutions to our educational dilemmas are a combination of the neoliberal emphasis on marketization and choice and neoconservative and managerial emphases on standardizing curricula, teaching, and evaluation and on a return to "real knowledge" (Apple, 2001; Apple et al., 2003; Buras, 1999).

All of this has led to some profound political, ethical, educational, and empirical disagreements about the benefits — or lack of them — of these supposed reforms. Choice proponents argue that such plans create institutions that are more apt to be responsive to community concerns because they are motivated and disciplined by market forces, such as the enrollment or withdrawal of students by parental "consumers." Another argument is that reforms based on choice and competition are unencumbered by the bureaucratic mandates that plague most public schools and hence deliver more innovative educational programming. Evidence in support of these claims is thin on the ground (see Buras and Apple, in press).

Ideas of choice often rest on an unarticulated set of assumptions about family-school relations. That is, they tend to want "better" home–school interactions but do not usually raise some important prior questions that might make their proponents uncomfortable. Among these questions are Who does the work of choice and of enhancing the relations between home and school? Are the programs that are meant to establish "better" relations neutral in their effects?

These are among the issues that are at the center of this book. Lois André-Bechely makes a powerful case for a much more socially situated and critical approach. She argues that our understanding of the family-school relationship and of how choice plans work within them must "begin with gendered parents with real lives, particularly with mothers who bear the major responsibility for the work of schooling." She then documents why it is so important for studies of parents' involvement in choosing schools for their children to "openly examine how parents' race and social class intersect with their gendered roles so we can better understand how some parents' children become privileged over others." Such statements point to the engaged and serious nature of the material with which this volume deals.

Like the impressive work of Alison Griffith and Dorothy Smith (2005), André-Bechely wants us to think about the actual labor of choosing. It may at first seem strange to think of choice in this way, but it is a form of labor, and it is often incredibly intense. Furthermore, the specific people who are doing the time-consuming and emotionally draining work associated with choice are usually mothers. And again like Griffith and Smith, she insists that any understanding of these efforts that does not have gender relations at their very core cannot be fully serious. But as the quote from her in the paragraph above indicates, she knows full well that mothers are classed and raced at the same time. How these intersect in complex and sometimes contradictory ways is part of the story she wishes to tell. The story offers some salutary lessons for those who approach choice with an almost religious fervor. For them, criticizing their assumptions or going beneath the surface to examine closely the real and determinate effects of many of these kinds of educational reforms is almost like heresy.

In one of my own books (Apple 2001), I make the point that the neoliberal agenda is grounded in a lack of understanding of unpaid labor and because of this the neoliberal agenda is actually masculinist at its very core. The fact that most educational reforms that have arisen from a commitment to marketization, or from an uncritical sponsoring of choice as the "real" solution to the very evident problems in our schools also seem not to understand this, makes *Could It Be Otherwise?* of interest to an even wider audience.

The book takes seriously a good deal of the critical research in a number of fields that has documented how, by simply following the rules that underlay our daily practice and by employing the sense-making tools that we know "work" in organizing our lives, we may also participate in re-producing the relations of inequality that dominate our society. It demonstrates how what Bourdieu (1984) might call the cultural, economic, and social capital possessed by particular groups enables them to work the system better than others — and how the lack of such forms of capital disadvantages other parents involved in educational choice programs. This process of advantaging and disadvantaging is not necessarily done consciously by the actors involved; nor is it consciously planned by the usually very well-meaning policy makers who have put such plans into effect. And this is exactly the point.

André-Bechely draws upon and synthesizes a wide range of resources to illuminate the meaning of the compelling stories that she tells. These include feminist standpoint theory, feminist policy studies, and critical race theory. Each one enables her to detail how parents who knew how to work the system largely guaranteed that a reform that was supposed to lead to more equitable and democratic outcomes ultimately instead led to the opposite.

Could It Be Otherwise? is a welcome addition to the essential debates about the meanings and effects of educational reform. By taking us inside the process through which choices are made, it challenges us to look much more carefully at the ways such things as voucher plans, tax credits, important elements within *No Child Left Behind*, and similar legislative mandates will work in the daily lives of real people in real communities throughout the United States. Because of this, it will be of great interest to anyone who is concerned with the ways in which school reform goes on.

Michael W. Apple
John Bascom Professor of
Curriculum and Instruction and
Educational Policy Studies
University of Wisconsin, Madison

REFERENCES

Apple, M.W. (2001). *Educating the "Right" Way: Markets, Standards, God, and Inequality.* New York: RoutledgeFalmer.

Apple, M.W., et al. (2003). *The State and the Politics of Knowledge.* New York: Routledge-Falmer.

Bourdieu, P. (1984). *Distinction.* Cambridge: Cambridge, MA: Harvard University Press.

Buras, K. (1999). Questioning core assumptions. *Harvard Educational Review* 69: 67–93.

Buras, K. and Apple, M. W. School choice, neoliberal promises, and unpromising evidence. *Educational Policy,* in press.

Griffith, A. and Smith, D. (2005). *Mothering for Schooling.* New York: Routledge.

ACKNOWLEDGMENTS

Breaking with tradition, I want to thank first my husband, Paul Bechely, for his unwavering love and support throughout this project. I share the accomplishment of this book with him, my awesome sons, Jean-Claude and Julian, my wonderful mother, Elsie Nelson, our lovely daughter-in-law, Sarah, and Ginger, Ph.D (playful happy dog). I am so grateful for their help and encouragement — and for just everything they did to make sure our family's first book got done.

I would like to express my deepest appreciation to the parents, community advisors, and local and district level administrators for sharing their everyday lives and work with me, making this book possible. To the parents especially, I thank them all for allowing me to learn from their experiences. I have tried to remain faithful to their stories, and anything that I did not get quite right, any faults in the telling of their stories, are my responsibility. A critique of Deluca USD's policies and practices was somewhat inevitable in a study such as this, but my respect and support remains for the many fine educators who work in the district and who, as part of their jobs, try to implement the educational policies that continue to challenge us all.

I want to acknowledge the support and guidance provided me at UCLA by Amy Stuart Wells, Kris Gutierrez, Sandra Harding, and David Sears when I undertook the dissertation research on which this book is based — they gave me the freedom to explore my ideas and I am ever so grateful. This project would not have happened without the teaching and mentoring of Sandra Harding who suggested that I read Dorothy Smith's book, *The Everyday World as Problematic,* and then introduced me to Dorothy Smith. Dorothy's suggestion that I contact Alison Griffith about how she uses institutional ethnography in educational studies was most fateful. I cannot thank Alison Griffith enough for her generous gift of knowledge, guidance, and encouragement. She not only showed me how to do institutional ethnography, she introduced me to the institutional ethnography community in Canada and the U.S. I continue to benefit greatly from having her as a colleague and a friend.

My deepest gratitude also goes out to Michael Apple for his ongoing and very patient support of this book. I have been inspired and influenced by his writing since I was a doctoral student. I am honored that he believes in the importance of my project and has included this book in his Critical Social Thought series. His comments on the manuscript pushed my analysis conceptually and helped to make the book more substantive and relevant to the political times we are in. I also wish to thank the editors at Routledge and in particular Catherine Bernard, whose editorial suggestions greatly improved the book. It is her work, and that of my excellent production editor, Jay Margolis, that actually puts this book into our hands and I thank her, Jay, and Brook Cosby for everything they have done.

The wonderful cover art is by Los Angeles artist, Jose Ramirez. I am so excited that Jose allowed us to use his work titled, "Playground" for the book cover. I am also thankful for the help of my graduate student, K. Eric Pohost, soon to be one fine urban teacher. And I very much appreciated the support provided by the California State University Los Angeles Faculty Creative Leave Award, which provided me the time to do additional scholarship for this book. Additionally, there is another group of people I must applaud — the librarians at Young Research Library at UCLA and at the John F. Kennedy Memorial Library at Cal State LA. I have learned that I just could not be a scholar without librarians and the excellent library services made available to me.

A special thanks to Diane Alvarez, Gary Anderson, JC André, and June Behar, for reading and commenting on parts or all of the manuscript at its various stages. Finally, I wish to thank the many other family members, friends, and colleagues who have provided me with encouragement and hugs during the time I worked on this book. I look forward to planning play dates with all of you now.

• • • • •

I would also like to acknowledge and thank Taylor & Francis, Inc., for permission to reprint and use in revised form the material originally published as "The Goals of a Voluntary Integration Program and the Problems of Access: A Closer Look at a Magnet School Application Brochure," *Equity and Excellence in Education*, Special Issue: "Brown +50" (2004), Vol. 37(3). I would like to thank Elaine Whitlock and the editorial team at *Equity & Excellence in Education.* Their assistance on earlier drafts of the parts of the article that are included here improved this book as well. Similarly, I am grateful to Jane Clark Lindle and the editorial team at *Educational Administration Quarterly* for their support and refinements to earlier drafts of some of the material included in this book that was originally published as "Public School Choice at the Intersection of Voluntary Integration and Not-so-good Neighborhood Schools: Lessons from Parents' Experiences," *Educational Administration Quarterly* (2005), Vol. 41(2). I want to thank Sage Publications, Inc., for permission to reprint and use in revised form some material from the *EAQ* article.

CONTENTS

INTRODUCTION: POLICY STUDIES FROM THE STANDPOINT OF PARENTS

It has been a few years now that I have been working on a way to capture what bothers me about how "parents" are presented in the different literature, on parent involvement, school choice, school governance, and reform of grouping practices such as tracking. These are all areas where I have personal experiences as both a parent and an elementary school teacher. My children were already in school when I began teaching, so I had accumulated considerable experience in public schooling as an active parent prior to my teaching studies and practice. Upon entering the research community, I found I continued to look at schooling primarily from the point of view of an urban public school parent, and it was from this position that I always felt that I had some explaining to do.

As an involved, white, and now-middle-class mother of high achieving children, I was sensitive to the variety of ways I was presented in educational literature in the aggregate, from an important stakeholder in building new school communities (Dodd and Konzal, 1999; Epstein, 1995; Henderson and Berla, 1995) to unfairly privileging my children with my cultural capital and place in the dominant culture (Brantlinger et al., 1996; Wells and Serna, 1996). For the most part, I read little that attempted to tell what schooling looks like from the parental standpoint. And, given everything I was reading on the continuous nature of educational reforms that often fell short of their goals to improve education for all students (Anyon, 1997; Sarason, 1990; Tyack, 1992; Tyack and Cuban, 1995) and which my experiences as a teacher could confirm, I admit that at times I felt that parents, especially white, middle-class parents in public schools, were getting a disproportionate share of the blame. I had a hard time reconciling how parents, who had been doing what was asked of them by schools and expected of them by society, could be presented so negatively in some of the educational literature (see, for example, Kohn, 1998).

Yet my own experience as a teacher of African American, Latino and Asian immigrant students in urban schools awakened me to the inequities I had not seen at my own children's schools. The real difference I saw in the subsequent educational opportunities that would be available to my students, compared to those of my own children and many of their white and wealthier classmates, pushed me to search for ways to understand how parents' roles in their children's education were contributing to these inequities.

I began by reflecting on how it came to be that my own actions as a parent implicate me in maintaining the unequal access to educational opportunities of other mothers' sons and daughters. It required that I ask myself difficult questions: How much influence have I had on my children's academic achievement? How can I justify supporting social justice goals for all students, on the one hand, while making sure my children are in the college preparatory courses at their school, on the other hand? Why did I choose to stay at my neighborhood schools versus send my children to magnet schools or private schools like so many other parents I knew?

I tried to reconstruct what and how I learned about schooling through my own schooling experiences as a poor, working-class girl from a single parent household and through those of my two sons. I looked to the social and political contexts of my own learning process as a public school parent and saw the effects of numerous national, state, and local policies on issues ranging from desegregation to whole language instruction to college admission practices. I recalled many teachers' appraisals of my children's abilities and efforts and the report card grades and high standardized test scores which labeled them "gifted." And I realized the advantage I gained from knowledge passed on to me by other neighborhood parents about how to get the best out of our local schools. These many experiences informed how I came to know about parents and schools and provide the standpoint from where I want to begin this book.

After 19 years as an active parent in the urban district where my sons attended school, I learned much from fellow parents with diverse racial, ethnic, social class, and linguistic backgrounds and from talking with them about their children's schools — from parents who were involved at their children's schools and those who were not. Without

disregarding the value of my knowledge and understanding as an edu-
cator, I do believe it is my experiences as a parent that affect how I
approach educational policy research and, of most importance to me,
that form the basis for my insistence on a re-examination of how we
study educational policies and their effects on parents' experiences
with schooling.

MULTIPLE CHOICE QUESTIONS

Imagine with me, if you will, a mother of two school-age children
opening her mail sometime in August to find a letter telling her that her
children's score reports for the standardized tests they took the past
spring are enclosed for her review. Picture also the newspaper article she
sees about the same time that compares her children's schools' standardized test scores to other schools' scores in the district and to the state's
average. When school starts in September the mother will learn that once
again her children's school did not make enough progress raising students' test scores and, as required by the No Child Left Behind Act of
2001 (NCLB), has been designated a low-performing school. Soon after,
another letter will arrive at her home advising her that because her child
qualifies (that her family is poor and her child's scores are low) she can
request to transfer her children from their low-performing school to
a higher performing school. A provision of NCLB (2002) gives parents
that right. Sometime in December a brochure will show up in her mail-
box that advertises the district's magnet schools, which were established
as part of a court-ordered voluntary integration program. The brochure
includes an application for participating in the school choice options of
the district. The brochure also now includes information about public
school choice transfers out of low-performing schools (like the one her
children attend) to comply with the NCLB policy. The letters and documents this mother will receive in the mail offer a hint at the many issues
that now surround public schooling in large urban districts.

Many of the nation's urban school districts have large minority
student populations, and the various choice options they provide for
parents often reflect legal or legislative mandates to promote integrated
schools. These same urban districts often have high percentages of
low-income families living in underserved communities. The NCLB and
specifically its public school choice program requiring that parents be
given the right to transfer their children from low-performing schools
to higher achieving schools has urban districts struggling with how
to provide integrated schooling environments for minority and white
students and ensure that poor and minority students have access to

quality education. Both of these goals have their own histories with the federal government. In 1954 the Supreme Court decided *Brown v. Board of Education* in an effort to bring an end to segregated schooling. The Elementary and Secondary Education Act (ESEA) of 1965 (which in its most recent reauthorization in 2001 became known as the No Child Left Behind Act above) established compensatory education programs to assist schools trying to meet the needs of poor and minority students.

Rodney Paige, Secretary of Education under George W. Bush's first administration, stated: "Equality of opportunity must be more than just a statement of law; it must be a matter of fact .... And factually speaking, this country does not yet promote equal opportunities for millions of children. That is why the No Child Left Behind Act is so important .... we know now because of the 50 years of experience we've had [since *Brown*] that something else is necessary" (quoted in Hendrie, 2004). While desegregation scholars continue to provide evidence of the race- and class-based resegregation taking place in public schools (Cashin, 2004; Clotfelter, 2004; Orfield, 2001; Rossell et al., 2002), some acknowledge NCLB's claims to support reform that will lead to equality of opportunity (Orfield, 2004; Taylor, 2003). Others observe how the debate on equal educational opportunity is shifting from desegregation to improving the achievement of poor and minority students (Love, 2004; Orfield and Eaton, 1996).

School Choice: A Necessity for Change

Today, school choice is a complex issue. Some forms of public school choice have been historically connected to desegregation (Wells, 1993), while others, such as the use of tuition vouchers, are more closely associated with neoliberal and conservative agendas (Apple, 2001). There is a vast amount of scholarship on the desegregation of American schools (Balkin, 2001; Gordon, 1994; Orfield and Eaton, 1996; Rossell, 1990; Rossell et al., 2002; Wells, 1997), the use of magnet schools in voluntary integration plans (Blank et al., 1996; Metz, 1986; Smrekar and Goldring, 1999; Wells, 1991), and current models of both public and private school choice (Elmore and Fuller, 1996; Good and Braden, 2000; Henig, 1994; Marschall, 2000; Saporito and Lareau, 1999; Wells, 1993).

It is important to distinguish between different public school and private school choice options (vouchers) and charter schools, which represent something of a compromise between public and private sector choice programs. Public school choice models include alternative schools and magnet schools historically have been designed and implemented to do more than just offer parents a choice among schools;

they support the social and democratic goals of schooling (Fantini and Young, 1970; Wells, 1993). Market-based choice options such as vouchers and charter schools reach beyond the socially oriented choice options offered by public school districts and incorporate marketplace ideals and strategies founded on entrepreneurial initiative, consumer choice, individual responsibility, and competition (Apple, 2001; McCarthy, 2000).

Consistent with a market model of education, there are now many school choice options from which parents can select: for example, public school choice plans that include magnet programs and open enrollment; voucher plans that transfer public funds to private schools; and a variety of charter school models (Fuller and Elmore, 1996; Meeks et al., 2000). With the conservative judicial endorsement of some forms of voucher programs (e.g., *Zelman v. Simmons-Harris*, 2002) and the legislation of school choice in the NCLB act encouraging transfers to charter schools as well as public schools, school choice in its different forms continues to be used as a means to bring about educational reform. It does so often under the banner of providing poor and minority students access to the educational opportunities that many nonpoor and white students enjoy.

Intending to address the educational opportunities of poor, minority, and low-performing students, NCLB combines neoconservative elements such as accountability, standardized curricula, and testing with a neoliberal position that market-based and choice-driven policies are more efficient and effective ways to serve individual families' needs (Aasen, 2003). However, NCLB's links to private sector producers of curricular and assessment materials, and to providers of private tutoring services welcoming corporate assistance in helping schools meet accountability mandates, suggest that NCLB may be aligning public education more closely to the neoliberal ideals of a market economy than to the equality of educational opportunity goals of the past. Advocates for public school choice programs that address desegregation issues may ultimately find school integration programs operating in the shadow of market-based school choice options.

By and large the literature on school choice makes one thing clear: whatever their racial, ethnic, class, and language background, when mothers, fathers, and guardians make decisions about where their children will attend school (whether for integrated schooling or better schooling or both), they enter into a relationship with schooling institutions known for inequitable organizing structures and practices and unequal educational opportunities (Lightfoot, 1978; Oakes, 1985; Sissel, 2000; Wells, 1993). Parents may or may not understand the nature of this relationship and its effects, but it is still the case that public schools have been authorized by the state (and reauthorized under NCLB) to teach, test, grade, and sort their children, and they thereby exert a powerful influence on families and the choices they will make. While there have been numerous studies on school choice that include parents (David et al., 1994; Gewirtz et al., 1995; Reay, 1996; Smrekar and Goldring, 1999; Wells, 1997), very little is known still about what actually happens in parents' everyday worlds as they choose schools on the ground, so to speak, and how they negotiate the variety of school choice options, and processes organized by school districts with histories of race-based and class-based inequalities between and within their schools.

Reviewing a range of school choice studies from the U.S. and the U.K., Dale concluded that replicating research on the relationship between choice and markets should be less a priority today than a focus on the processes underlying choice and the "institutional and organizational contexts through which it is realized and takes on its meaning" (Dale, 1997, p. 466). The research shared in this book is focused on the institutional organization of choice. Framed within the nexus of neoliberal choice policies that position parents as consumers choosing among schools and the vestiges of choice plans designed to provide families with desegregated and diverse schooling options, discussion throughout the book offers new perspectives on how institutional contexts help construct and organize public school choice.

School Choice Inequities and Inequalities

One of the major decisions that parents make is the decision about where they will send their children to school. As I wrote above, my own experiences with my children's schooling were influenced by the discourses circulated through the institutional policies and practices of public schools, the work of educators, and other parents. The decisions I made or did not make as a parent reflect those influences in many ways. I may not have chosen to escape from our neighborhood schools to magnet schools, but my decision to stay at our local schools was, in a large part, based on the availability of challenging courses and college preparatory programs. The tracking programs already in place, which allowed my children to benefit from those schooling practices, made it easier for me to choose to stay. Whether or not I was initially aware of how my decisions were impacting other students, those decisions, nonetheless, made me a participant in the inequitable opportunity structures affecting other parents' children. With the increase in school choice options that have been made available to parents, the likeliness that parents are making decisions which make them, too, participants in inequitable institutional practices is great. This is the one aspect of public school choice that troubles me most — that parents' involvement in reproducing the inequities and inequalities of public schooling seems "necessary." I want to know why this must be so.

All the many thoughts, feelings, worries, and dreams that mothers, fathers, and guardians have for their children when they send them off to attend school each day are often lost in the scholarship that compares and critiques the roles of parents: elites vs. those less privileged; the choosers and chosen vs. the nonchoosers or not chosen. Since it is not a stretch to assume that mothers overwhelmingly make up (or at least influence) the subject pool for so many investigations that speak of parents and schools, policy analysis needs to make clear that when it refers to parents, it is almost always speaking about mothers (David, 1993). If there is an overriding assumption guiding my thoughts and analysis throughout this book it is this: somehow in the work mothers do (or don't do, or can't do) on behalf of their children's education, mothers become implicated in who gets what in terms of access to quality educational opportunities among the families with school-age children in our urban public schools. I want to know how this happens.

PARENTS AND PUBLIC SCHOOL CHOICE

This book project explores how parents experience public school choice processes and practices in an urban school district. I focus my attention on developing a parents' standpoint for studying educational policy, in this case, public school choice policy. I argue that it is important that our studies of the family-school relationship begin with gendered parents with real lives, particularly with mothers who traditionally have done the homework of schooling. I also argue that studies of parents' involvement in choosing schools for their children must openly examine how parents' race and social class intersect with their gendered roles so we can better understand how parents become complicit in the historical inequalities between and within public schools. The schooling context that parents encounter is complex and confusing. It is not easy to negotiate. If the desired result of critical policy research is to address the inequitable and unequal education outcomes of urban public school students, our analyses will provide more "really useful knowledge" (Jordan and Yeomans, 1995, p. 401) if we learn how and why parents make the decisions they do and in which ways schooling institutions and socio-political forces are helping to shape those decisions.

The book reports on my two-year ethnographic study of a group of urban public school parents engaged in the school choice process. The large urban district that was the site of the study, which I call Deluca USD, has a limited number of magnet schools in comparison to the district's regular schools, huge numbers of applications, and long waiting lists for those who were not selected in the lottery. The district's magnet schools, which were developed in response to a court mandate to establish a voluntary integration program, are perceived by many parents and school officials as some of the best schools in the district. Thousands of parents apply to the magnet school program for their children each year and only a small percentage of the applicants get accepted. Deluca USD also has an open enrollment choice plan, maintains a voluntary transfer program to non-magnet schools, and has over 40 charter schools — all for parents who wish to send their children to schools other than their neighborhood schools. The competition to get into a "good" school in Deluca is high. The competition will only be amplified by the new school choice provisions of NCLB.

Drawing from work in feminist critical policy studies (Marshall, 1997), Feminist Standpoint Theory (Harding, 1991), and feminist sociology (Griffith and Smith, 2004; Smith, 1987, 1990), the study centered investigation on the experiences of these parents, most of whom were mothers, and employed a method of inquiry known as Institutional Ethnography (Campbell and Gregor, 2002; DeVault, 1999; Naples, 2003; Smith, 1987, 1999). The book shares a story of how, through the process of choosing schools for their children, consciously or not, parents became participants in the inequities of the district's choice programs. By showing how these parents accomplished their goals of getting their child into a school other than their neighborhood school and by showing how they actually "worked the system," the story told throughout this book illustrates how school choice policies proposed to be more equitable and democratic for parents, in many ways, still reproduce the schooling inequalities they were intended to reduce.

There are two main ideas about parents and school choice I explore throughout this book. First, doing the work of choosing schools, parents (and this is mostly mothers) become entangled in existing inequitable schooling structures and practices that are historically related to racial and social class issues. The district's overlapping policies implementing a voluntary integration program with other public school choice options will be the context for illustrating this. Second, educational institutions play a powerful role in producing the knowledge that parents use for making school choice decisions — decisions that can contribute to inequalities and inequities — through the discourses and texts circulated by and throughout our public school communities and which continue to support advantages for white and middle class families. An analysis of the district's school choice brochure and application process will help illustrate how this happens in later chapters.

Critical Perspectives on the Parent-School Relationship

The intersection of race, class, and gender is central to an understanding of what happens when parents with different racial and social class backgrounds choose schools for their children. These dynamics bring added complexity to research on parents' involvement in their children's education and require different theoretical tools for studying an educational policy, such as public school choice, and the ways it intersects with parents' everyday lives and the existing structures and practices of local schools.

Some studies have paid closer attention to issues of class and race when examining parents' roles in schools. The research by Brantlinger and her colleagues (Brantlinger, 2003; Brantlinger et al., 1996) reported that white, college-educated women often supported schooling practices that benefited middle-class students and advantaged their children, even when those practices resulted in segregated and stratified school structures. In their study on detracking reform, Wells and Serna (1996) showed the strategies that elite parents used to undermine school efforts to detrack classrooms. Showing parents as participants in the reproduction of schooling inequities, these studies raise new questions about the influence that more affluent parents can have on schools.

Lareau and Horvat show that in the family-school relationship there are race- and class-based "moments of inclusion and moments of exclusion" that result from parents seeking to provide advantages for their children through participation in academically gifted programs or high academic tracks (Lareau and Horvat, 1999). Their work on parents' involvement in such schooling practices also establishes how parents are participating in the resegregation of many schools. Given that advanced academic tracks (e.g., Advanced Placement and Honors courses) and gifted programs are organized, funded, and coordinated through state and local district policies that create opportunities for students to participate in these kinds of programs, educational institutions themselves must be examined to see how the structures and practices that they support essentially require parents' complicity in the continuing inequities and inequalities of schooling.

Over 25 years ago, Lightfoot (1978) articulated the discontinuities and dissonance in the family-school relation, pointing out the tradition in academic literature to blame mothers for their children's inadequacies.

Discussing mothers' relations with schooling institutions, she stated: "The school is the place where *mothers* [italics hers] experience their first public evaluation and scrutiny ..." (p. 62). Today, with increased demands for parental involvement in education, mothers' work on behalf of their children's schooling is again under academic scrutiny but often with an eye on their participation in reproducing educational inequalities (Brantlinger, 2003; Holme, 2002). These studies, like many studies on parents' roles in their children's schooling, are laced with voices of mothers. Whether intended or not, the more critical studies of family-school relations can have the effect of placing blame on parents (mothers) for using the social and cultural capital[1] they possess, for the inequities and inequalities that result. Few have taken up an analysis that explicates how educational institutions position parents in subordinate roles, in race-, class-, and gender-based roles that place parents in a situation in which a decision they make for the good of their own children may result in less opportunity for the children of others (Lareau's excellent analysis of poor, working-class, and middle-class families is relevant to these issues, 2003). I, too, ask questions that probe for those "moments of exclusion" and "moments of inclusion" (Lareau and Horvat, 1999) as they appear in parents' choice work. But I do so with an interest in the institutional context that shapes what choices they can make.

Graue and Kroeger (2001) state that interpretive and critical analyses of home-school relations show that "parental actions are not a matter of individual choice to be involved or not, but are indicative of long-standing cultural and institutional practices that give some people access to school resources while leaving others outside" (p. 471). With school reform policies constantly reshaping notions of good and not-so-good schools (Lightfoot, 1983; McNeil, 2000; Oakes et al., 2000) the resources necessary for making informed comparisons and choices among schools are not available for many parents. There are an overwhelming number of working and single mothers in urban public school districts, and realizing that the work involved in choosing schools only adds to the women's work that mothers already do on behalf of their children's educations, then certainly gender, race, and class relations all become important considerations for any analysis of parents' school choice practices.

A CRITICAL AND FEMINIST FRAMEWORK

When conceptualizing a parents' standpoint for educational policy research, different epistemological issues (the different ways that parents come to know what they know) must be considered. Parents feel a powerful sense of responsibility to ensure the well-being of the children they love dearly. They are not naïve to the changing demographics in urban communities or the changes brought about by increasing competition in the market economy; they understand the importance of education in today's society. Parents probably learned through their own schooling how embedded the notions of meritocracy and intelligence are in the construction of the good student, the smart student. They hear, too, the call for their involvement in helping to raise their children's achievement, thereby supporting their child's performance in school on high-stakes tests. And quite likely, parents who are economically secure and members of dominant groups know that they can advantage their children in schools in ways that poor minority parents cannot.

The intersection of race, class, and gender is central to an understanding of what happens when parents, mothers, with different racial and social class backgrounds go about choosing schools for their children. These dynamics bring added complexity to research on parents' involvement in their children's education and require that I draw from different theoretical and methodological traditions to capture the stories of urban parents who choose schools. Because I am weaving together the work of feminists, legal theorists, and critical education policy scholars to study parents' experiences with public school choice, I am going to spend a bit more time than might be customary in a book such as this discussing the literature that has helped to inform the conceptual framework for this project.

Critical Feminist Theories

Feminist standpoint theory provides an important foundation for the theoretical and conceptual framework that I develop in this book. Feminist standpoint theory starts from the perspective of everyday life and then uses the experiences and local knowledge that help to shape that standpoint to study dominant institutions and discourses (Harding, 1991). Working within the same theoretical tradition, Smith (1987) problematized women's experiences in their everyday worlds to bring into view the links between the particularities of those experiences and the social relations of the society in which they and we live.

Explaining how standpoint theories can be seen as a kind of laboratory, Harding (1997) uses an example of the science lesson that shows how distortion can make a stick in a pond appear to be bent. Walking around the pond to a different location allows the student to see the stick as actually straight. The analogy of the pond is helpful for understanding the logic of standpoint theories, which argue that "distinctive gender, class, race or cultural positions in social orders provide different opportunities and limitations for 'seeing' how the social order works .... for observing and explaining systemic relations between 'what one does' and 'what one can know'" (Harding, 1997 p.384). Harding does not propose that there is one true standpoint, but that it is possible to have "less false accounts" than traditional scientific frameworks have provided in the past (Harding, 2004, p. 38).

The literature I have reviewed on school choice presents different views on how school choice operates as part of the larger social order. Little of the choice research attempts to show how parents are located to "see" schools like sticks in a pond. Consequently, as parents find themselves open to criticism about the decisions they make on behalf of their children, their account of schooling needs to be added to our existing accounts of how school choice operates in urban districts.

Smith developed a feminist sociology from principles of standpoint theory which seeks to understand the social, economic, and political relations that shape and determine women's oppression in society (Smith, 1987):

> my interest is in a sociology that does not displace what people know as the local practices of our everyday/everynight living but, rather, seeks to build on and enlarge it beyond the horizon of any one person's daily experience. I call this .... the problematic of the everyday/everynight world. To take up Sandra Harding's metaphor .... I want a sociology that would seek to discover the shape of the pond that positions the people and their perspectives vis-à-vis one another (Smith, 1997 p. 396).

Smith refers to her work as a method of inquiry that begins from the standpoint of women, with the woman actually "located" as active, thinking, loving, watching television, working, and connected in various ways to other people. Here it is easy to picture a mother located in her world with school-age children. "Activities, feelings, experiences, hook her into extended social relations linking her activities to those of other people in ways beyond her knowing .... Inquiry is directed towards exploring and explicating what she does not know — the social relations and organization pervading her world but invisible in it" (Smith, 1992, p. 91).

Smith is also interested in how power is generated and held in contemporary society. She claims that the functions of organization and control are increasingly vested in distinct and specialized institutional forms of organization like schools, and in relations that are mediated by texts produced by these institutions. This is what she calls the "relations of ruling" (Smith, 1992). Clarifying this further, Campbell and Manicom write:

> Smith has insisted that by the late twentieth century, at least in Western industrialized societies, administration, management, and government are accomplished through work processes that *rely on* distinctively organized ways of knowing those aspects of the world that are to be ruled. Not only does ruling rely on specialized knowledge, but a central task of ruling is *to organize and generate knowledge in a form that is useful for ruling practice.* Thus, for Smith …. "everyday experience," "the social organization of knowledge," and the "work of ruling" are bound together (Campbell and Manicom, 1995a, italics theirs).

Campbell and Manicom say that "The conceptual importance of experience lies in providing a real-life context against which to reflect on administrative practices and their powerful effects on people's lives" (1995a, p. 7). How then could parents' experiences as they choose schools for their children enable us and them to reflect on these powerful administrative practices? And how do these practices help to shape parents' participation in the existing racial, class, and gender inequities of schooling?

Smith proposes a method of inquiry that can help us study these questions. Her method of inquiry begins with the everyday experiences of women outside of the ruling relations of institutions. Women's experiences are a point of entry into an institutional ethnography that can explicate the relations of ruling located, for example, in the power relations operating in the school, in the bureaucracy, the professional world, and the state. Smith's institutional ethnography developed in conjunction with her early work with Alison Griffith on mothers and schools, which will be discussed shortly (Griffith and Smith, 2004; Smith, 1987; Smith and Griffith, 1990).

I quote Smith at length here to capture the importance of her conceptual and methodological framing for a deeper understanding of the ruling influences operating on parents when, as part of the work they do raising their children, they engage with schooling institutions:

> The educational system exercises a huge leverage over parents through their care of children, and over mothers in particular. In the last fifty or seventy years, mothers have been inculcated with an understanding of themselves and their responsibilities that is

all encompassing vis-à-vis their children's fate in school. We have learned a totalizing responsibility for what happens to our children in the school context. It is an ideology, a discourse, that mobilizes our work and care, and that takes no account of the realities of the conditions of that work and care (that we work full time, are single parents, etc.), that takes no account of the way in which resources are allocated within the bureaucratic processes of school governance and within the policy processes articulating educational policy to the interests of capital, that takes no account therefore of differences in the workings of the schools. This is such a major site of anguish and anxiety .... For parents it is the child who is at stake and the child's education is what they work for .... Such strategies of opening up the relations within which women's work as mothers is embedded create possibilities of exploring further the differences in racial and class experience of women in such contexts and of grasping the organization of these oppressions in ways that expand our general knowledge of how these relations are organized and how they work (Smith, 1987, pp. 204–205).

Collins, who also works from a standpoint theory framework, suggests that the concept of intersectionality be used to explain what she calls the interlocking oppressions of race, class, and gender. Her conceptualization is important because it brings into view how the experiences of women of color may present a different standpoint from which to view dominant social institutions. Intersectionality challenges the notion that race, class, and gender can be utilized as additive categories in understanding oppression and instead emphasizes that while always present together in women's lives, at different points in time and under different situations, race and or class and or gender may become the more salient oppressor(s) in women's lives.[2] She warns researchers analyzing how institutional bases of power shape race, class, and gender to remember that "The very notion of the intersections of race, class and gender as an area worthy of study emerged from the recognition of practitioners of each distinctive theoretical tradition that inequality could not be explained, let alone challenged, via a race-only, class-only, or gender-only framework" (Collins, 1997, p. 74).

Equally important for those of us working within feminist and critical frameworks is that we remember that our methodological and analytical projects must be more than well-intentioned, self-interested analyses of the experiences of women of our own race, class, and culture. Feminist standpoint theory focuses attention on the actual consequences of analysis and works to improve the conditions of all women (Harding, 1991), or in the case of my project, all parents, not just those whose everyday lives closely match my own. In this regard, the analysis offered in this book should contribute to a transformative social agenda — one which could help parents from dominant social groups see their school choices differently, to know otherwise so they may *do otherwise*. To achieve this, institutional discourses, cultures, and practices that support the social relations[3] that contribute to differences among racially, economically, and linguistically diverse parents must be made transparent to policy makers, educators, and parents so we can all confront the inequities and inequalities of urban public schooling.

CRITICAL ANALYSES OF DISCOURSES AND TEXTS IN INSTITUTIONAL CONTEXTS

In some of the literature on school reform and school choice, it is now possible to read critical analyses that combine a qualitative research tradition with postmodern and poststructuralist theories about power, knowledge, and discourse. The concept of discourse is defined many different ways because its use overlaps two intellectual disciplines: linguistics and poststructuralism — often associated with the work of Michel Foucault — (MacLure, 2003). Stephen Ball (1994) was among the first to apply Foucault's theory of discourse to his analysis of parents' school choice practices in the U.K.. He used discourse analysis as a tool to deconstruct social relations in the implementation of school choice policy. Ball argues that educational sites are not only subject to discourse but are also centrally involved in the propagation and selective dissemination of discourses, controlling access of individuals to various kinds of discourse. He argues that the effect of policy is primarily discursive "changing the possibilities we have for thinking 'otherwise'; thus limiting our responses to change" (Ball, 1990, p. 3).

Parents, historically, have been called upon or "hailed" (Weedon, 1997) to take up the discourses produced and disseminated by educational institutions. Yet in the U.S. policy literature on parents and school choice, and in parent involvement policies as well, the multiple discourses embedded in the communications between educational institutions and families is seldom studied (see Lopez, 2001, for a study that addresses the discourse on parent involvement). Recall the quote above by Smith, in which she says that "it is a discourse, an ideology" from which "mothers have a learned a totalizing responsibility" for the care of their children. Lemke states that if we want to ask how a particular discourse functions ideologically, "we need to look with both the broader and narrower view of ideology. We need to see how the discourse is situated in the social and political relations of various communities and their interests vis-à-vis one another, and we need to ask specifically what it says about its subject that somehow works to the profit of a dominant social group" (Lemke, 1995, p. 12). Research on parents and schooling very much needs this kind of analysis in order for us to think otherwise about the effects of educational policies such as school choice.

Griffith and Smith have articulated a "mothering discourse" that they show organizing and coordinating the work of mothers to the needs of the school. The mothering discourse "provides systematically developed knowledge, recommendations, systems of categories and concepts, and above all, for mothers, a moral logic of responsibility which subordinates those who participate to a universalized public educational system and the family. *Above all it promotes the responsiveness of parenting practices to the requirements of educational ones*" (Griffith and Smith, 2004, p. 47, italics theirs). They see the concept of discourse as people participating actively in a conversation mediated by printed materials and texts, and with each discourse, there are distinctive production processes, knowledge-producing sites, and means of dissemination (p. 40).

> As we are using it, discourse does not just refer to the "texts" of this conversation and their production alone, but also to the active ways in which people attend to, name and interpret their own and others' doings in relationship to them. As mothers orient towards the texts (whether in books, women's magazines, television, radio, or by participating in "second-hand" textually organized processes such as courses, church meetings, etc.), as they do their work in relationship to their children's schooling, as they measure what they do in terms of its standards, as they interpret and orient to what other mothers do in its terms, they are participating in this discursive process (Griffith and Smith, 2004, p. 40).

Critical Discourse Analysis

Luke's work with discourse analysis is associated more closely to the linguistic strategies used to position readers of texts and discourses. He clarifies the difference between texts and discourses:

> Just as discourses develop to articulate particular fields of knowledge and belief, texts develop to serve institutional purposes and projects. All texts are multidiscursive; that is, they draw from a

range of discourses, fields of knowledge, and voices. They are dynamic, changing in accordance with the demands and needs of the institution or community in question. The texts of everyday life then do not just randomly or arbitrarily proliferate. Rather, they are all tied closely to particular social actions and interests in the contexts of particular social institutions (Luke, 1996, p. 15).

Arguing for different applications of discourse analysis in educational research, Luke points out "how difficult it has been to show how large-scale social discourses are manifest in everyday talk .... at local sites" (1996, p.11). Luke argues that a central task of contemporary approaches to discourse analysis is to theorize and study the micropolitics of discourse, and to examine actual patterns of language use with some degree of detail and explicitness but in ways that reconnect instances of local discourse with salient political, economic, and cultural formations. Luke proposes that critical discourse analysis can be integrated into sociological analysis of education to make transparent how texts manipulate readers and listeners, and can trace how particular discourses create different material sites and shape particular subjects' life trajectories (1996, pp. 19–20). Apple notes that critical discourse analysis "wants to enable people to understand how 'texts' position them and at the same time produce unequal relations of institutional power that structure classrooms, staff rooms and educational policies" (Apple, 1996, p. 131).

My own understanding of discourse emerged out of the work of all these scholars. So let me try to pull some of these ideas together and illustrate how I apply the concept of discourse and show how discourses, when textually mediated, can hail parents (and others) into social actions that sustain unequal relations in schooling institutions. In this study, I suggest that an *integration* discourse constructs, in part, the school district's school choice practices in which both parents and district personnel participate. Moreover, I suggest that an *achievement* discourse similarly helps to construct school choice processes and practices in the district. Here is the way I conceptualize these discourses in relation to the district's choice programs.

An integration discourse. At one time, Deluca Unified School District (USD) (a pseudonym) was under a court order to desegregate its schools, but owing to numerous problems that constrained the mandatory desegregation program, the district resorted to a voluntary integration program. There were historical issues, policies, and practices associated with desegregation in the district, some of which were folded into the new voluntary integration program. Plans were written by the district and approved by the court to use magnet schools as a method for providing integrated schooling experiences to families.

Various organizational practices and application procedures following the court-ordered, racially balanced integration formulas were institutionalized to allocate students to magnet schools by their racial or ethnic identity. The Deluca USD promoted its magnet schools as special places where students received excellent integrated educational experiences. The magnet school application form and brochure included statements, year after year, that described for parents why the integration programs were established. People in school communities learned ways to understand the language and meanings in the magnet school application brochure and application procedures. As a result, the magnet schools developed their own cultures and practices within the district. Magnet schools became identified as and developed reputations for being excellent schools with diverse student populations.

All of these elements — the institutionalized polices, practices, and cultures — help to define the integration discourse I identify in the study and connect back to Deluca's promotion of magnet schools as offering excellent integrated educational experiences through choice in some of its early documents submitted to the courts. As magnet schools became identified with integration goals, they also became identified with having good students and involved parents. As grades and test scores were used as enrollment criteria for some magnet school programs, they carried an increasingly dominant *achievement* discourse, further shaping and defining school choice processes and practices.

An achievement discourse. Beliefs about intelligence and ability historically have been a part of schooling. Tests and reporting practices were developed to measure and compare which students knew what and the academic tasks that different students could or could not perform. Certain characteristics were ascribed to students who demonstrated above-average achievement: they were well-behaved in class, devoted time to studying, and had a strong grasp of language arts and mathematical and scientific concepts. Over time, the practice of assigning grades and giving standardized tests to students institutionalized notions of achievement in school districts throughout the nation. Schools developed local practices in which teachers could discuss students' learning outcomes and report card grades with parents. Parents, who were students once themselves, constructed their own understandings of the meanings assigned to grades and standardized tests and used the information about their children's school performance in ways they best knew how.

Standardized tests increasingly were used to categorize different students. High-achieving students were labeled "gifted," and new school cultures and practices were developed that provided more challenging and enriching learning experiences for gifted students. Low-achieving students were screened for special education services. Test scores were viewed as predictive of students' future academic achievement, so high standardized test scores became criteria for university admissions. Additionally, report card grades, grade point averages, and standardized test scores came to be seen as indicators of good or not-so-good teaching and learning taking place in schools. Newspapers took up the practice of listing the aggregate test scores of students in all the city's schools, thereby contributing to comparisons across school communities. Today, many people — parents, educators, business leaders, and politicians — consider standardized test score results as indicative of school quality and students' academic achievement and use them for recommending schools of choice.

We can see how an achievement discourse is shaping and being shaped by institutional policies, practices, and cultures. When looking at the testing and choice requirements of NCLB, it is not hard to identify the overlapping discourses that could affect (and possibly, overtake) the implementation of the district's voluntary integration program. The texts that are associated with the voluntary integration program and magnet school programs of Deluca USD (e.g., information brochures and application forms) help to the convey notions of ability, discipline, and involvement, all of which are associated with school achievement, thus revealing the way in which such texts are multidiscursive. Like the mothering discourse (Griffith and Smith, 2004), the achievement discourse provides systematically developed knowledge, categories, responsibilities, and recommendations that serve the interests of schools. Those who participate in the achievement discourse (for example, parents and their children) will orient to actions that create "good" students. The integration discourse supports an organization of the magnet school as a "good" school and reorients the actions of those who participate in the integration discourse (people in the district and parents who choose schools) to understand and promote magnet schools as places not just for diverse students, but also "good" students (Lemke, 1995). In the coming chapters I try to illustrate this further.

Recognizing the discourses communicated through schools and the "doings" they organize and coordinate can help to explain how and why language and texts work the way that they do, and when they are put into action, how they often lead to practices complicit with harm and injustice (Gee, 1999, p. 8). If I added to the conceptualization of the integration discourse that the racial/ethnic formulas disproportionately assigned more white students to magnet schools than students of color, and added to the achievement discourse conceptualization that the majority of students who were labeled gifted were white, we can also see how the practices constructed around these discourses privileged white students. Move the analysis one step further and we can see how participants in the integration and achievement discourses could (unconsciously) be oriented to think "white" when thinking of good schools and good students (Staiger, 2004). Do the same exercise with social class, and the power of discourses, language, and texts to shape practices that lead to injustice becomes evident. Therefore the conceptual framework for this study was developed not only to investigate how broader social and institutional relations influence the practical realities of the family-school relationship but also to look for the ways that educational institutions help construct unequal educational opportunities for different parents' children through the discourses, texts, and practices that they produce.

The different theoretical frameworks presented in the literature above help focus this examination beyond what is visible in the everyday world of parents choosing schools and look to the ways in which parents' and particularly mothers' experiences are subordinated to the oppressive structures and practices that they encounter in their children's schooling. Critical and feminist studies bring forth important insights for thinking about how discourses and social and cultural practices position women differently in the social institutions we know as schools. However, to better understand the racial dynamics that historically have privileged white and middle-class parents in the school choice process, particularly in public school choice plans that were developed from desegregation for use in voluntary integration programs, I needed a theoretical framework for analyzing race relations that would be complementary to the institutional investigation that my project takes up. For this, I turn to the institutional analyses of critical race theorists.

Critical Race Theory

Ladson-Billings and Tate were among the first educational researchers to recognize that Critical Race Theory (CRT) contributes to theorizing the problematic relation between schooling inequities and inequalities and race (Ladson-Billings and Tate, 1995; Tate, 1997, 1999) and how educational institutions maintain white privilege. CRT's foundation in the law is helpful for articulating racism in its various forms and for locating racism in "government actions that burden nonwhites more than whites" (Haney Lopez, 2000, p. 1843). Valdes and colleagues explain that CRT[4] challenges the popular belief that racial injustice is about the "bad" acts of individuals and not about our legal and educational institutions (Valdes et al., 2002). Instead, they say:

> Critical race theorists have located racism and its everyday operation in the very structures within which the guilty and the innocent were to be identified: not individual "bad apple" police officers but the criminal justice system; not bigoted school-board members, but the structures of segregation and wealth transmission .... CRT describes not a world of bad actors, wronged victims, and innocent bystanders, but a world in which all of us are more or less complicit in sociolegal webs of domination and subordination (p. 2).

The kind of analysis suggested by CRT moves the focus of critique onto our legal and governmental institutions and to how those institutions address racism, inequity, and inequality.

Incorporating CRT, Tate and colleagues argue that the courts' construction of equality and white self-interest impedes equal educational outcomes for children of color because any definition of equal access is interpreted from the position of the dominant group (Tate et al., 1996). Exposing the irony that many laws and policies intended to address racial inequality do not bring about the racial justice they promised is a powerful feature of CRT analyses (Ladson-Billings, 1999). These researchers give an example of a "model" desegregation plan that although offering special programs for all of its students, white students were more able to access the advantages of those programs than students of color. They follow with this critique:

> What, then, made Buffalo a model school desegregation program? In short, the benefits that whites derived from school desegregation and their seeming support of the district's desegregation program. Thus, a model desegregation program becomes defined as one that ensures that whites are happy (and do not leave the system altogether) regardless of whether African American and other students of color achieve or remain (Ladson-Billings and Tate, 1995, p. 56).

Reinterpreting the results of a desegregation plan in order to make visible white privilege, as Ladson-Billings and Tate do here, opens up the possibility for new approaches to research that examine the institutional structures and practices that maintain ineffective remedies for racial justice. The framework I am building in this introduction not only seeks to conceptualize similar issues around public school choice plans which include a voluntary integration program but also to understand the implications for those who participate in public school choice.

When analyzing why well-intentioned educators continue to produce disparate outcomes among urban public school students, some researchers draw on a theory of institutional racism. Larson and Ovando explain that people who enforce systems that overlook or ignore the inequities of our society can unconsciously maintain racism. They describe institutional racism as "a sedimented system of historical inequalities that are effectively sustained through practices that fail to interrupt established patterns of racial and ethnic hierarchy, exclusion, and discrimination" (Larson and Ovando, 2001, p. 123).

Critical race theorist Haney Lopez developed his definition of institutional racism[5] in the law through an analysis of the exclusionary practices of grand jury selection in which judges' actions choosing grand jury members took the form of in-group prejudice in favor of whites (Haney Lopez, 2000, p. 1814). Demonstrating how judges' understanding of merit is tied to their own white identities and their own notions of what people need to know and be able to do on a grand jury, he shows how judges unconsciously linked qualifications with racial identities (Haney Lopez, 2000). There is a similarity in his line of reasoning to Tate's critique of how merit and high achievement are tied to educators' identities and to the educational standards that are so closely related to white students' performance and the educational opportunities from which they benefit (Tate, 1999).

Ladson-Billings explains that CRT, through the use of storytelling and narrative, can develop "deeply contextualized understandings" of race and provide a way to understand the "taken-for-granted privileges and inequities that are built into our society" (Ladson-Billings, 2003, p. 11). In addition to other applications of CRT, Solórzano and Ornelas state that using CRT in education can challenge traditional paradigms and show how the separate discourses on gender, class, and race intersect to impact students of color (Solórzano and Ornelas, 2002, p. 219). The insights and perspectives found in critical race theory are important tools for educational policy research, and when combined with much of what we know of the race and class resegregation taking place in many U.S. schools of choice, they present us with new issues not usually discussed in the choice literature. To explore these issues we need more nuanced studies and must continue to move educational policy research into more critical frameworks.

I now want to return to the study that is shared in the following chapters of this book, a study of parents in their everyday worlds choosing schools for their children as part of their lived reality with schooling. By linking the theoretical and methodological work of critical policy sociologists such as Ball (1994), of feminists like Harding (1991) and Smith (1987, 1999), and critical race theorists like Crenshaw et al. (1995), Haney Lopez (2000), Ladson-Billings (1999), and Tate (1997), the project I undertake here seeks to bridge the gap between the present body of public school choice literature and critical studies on parents' involvement in their children's schooling and to develop an analytical framework that can contribute new understanding about why *Brown's* mandate for desegregated education and NCLB's requirements for public school choice will continue to challenge the nation's urban school districts.

As you can imagine, such a project is a tall order. Therefore the conceptual framework I apply throughout the book weaves these theoretical traditions together to identify four key principles that I believe are necessary for a critical and feminist analysis of how parents experience the effects of educational policy.

- First, research on parents' participation in educational institutions must be faithful to the real world of parents and their interests on behalf of their children (Griffith, 1995; Harding, 1991; Lightfoot, 1978; Lopez, 2001).
- Second, researchers must recognize that the educational context is socially, culturally, and historically situated for parents just as it is for educators (Apple, 2001; Graue and Kroeger, 2001; Griffith and Smith, 1987; Harding, 1991; Marshall, 1997).
- Additionally, studies of parents' involvement in their children's education must search for how institutional discourses have constituted and positioned parents, and mothers in particular, in roles that reproduce the historical effects of schooling (Griffith and Smith 2004; Smith 1999; Dehli 1996; Luke, 1996).
- And finally, research must not lose sight of how material positions, racial privilege, and dominance still matter in our social institutions (Apple, 2001; Haney Lopez, 2000; Harding, 1991; Ladson-Billings, 1995; Lareau and Horvat, 1999; Lopez, 2003).

I hope to demonstrate that research and analysis attending to such epistemological and methodological issues can strengthen a critique of the ways in which educational institutions sustain the historical inequities and inequalities that they attempt to address through the public school choice options they provide to parents.

AN INSTITUTIONAL ETHNOGRAPHY

The research I write about in this book utilized a method of inquiry known as institutional ethnography (Campbell and Gregor, 2002; Smith, 1987, 1999) which has its foundation in feminist standpoint theory. As Harding (2004) notes, early standpoint theorists recognized that women needed to understand how "ruling" worked, how their exploitation was designed, maintained, and made to seem natural (in the way that "mothering work" is meant to seem natural) by the conceptual practices of dominant institutions (families and schools, for example). Harding states that as standpoint theories began addressing the need for knowledge *for* women, some of the most innovative feminist research "started from particular, culturally-specific, women's experiences, lives, activities, or 'labor'" (Harding, 2004, p. 29). This resulted in research that "'studied up,' focusing its explanations on dominant social institutions and their ideologies," because as Harding describes, "rulers" are at the top of hierarchical social, economic, and political power structures (2004, pp. 30, 41).

Institutional ethnography (IE) was developed as a sociology for women in which the central focus of inquiry "studies up" and looks at how a woman's life is shaped and determined by the ruling relations outside her everyday world (Smith, 1987). IE takes up an exploration, description, and analysis of a set of relations, conceived from a standpoint of some particular person or persons, whose everyday world of work is organized by those relations (Griffith and Smith, 2004). The concept of work as used in IE is not confined to paid employment or housework and is better understood as the doings of people, "what people do that requires some effort, that they mean to do, and that involves some acquired competence" (Smith, 1987, p. 165).

Situating institutional ethnographic inquiry in this way can show how the work women do on behalf of their children is shaped and constructed by bureaucratic structures and practices, so that mothers' work becomes organized and coordinated to institutional relations of ruling (Griffith, 1995; Griffith and Smith, 1987; Smith and Griffith, 1990). In this book, I focus considerable attention to an area of parents' work in support of their children's education that I call choice work. In my definition, choice work consists of the actual activities in which parents engage during the school choice process — gathering information about schools, talking with people about schools, visiting schools, and completing the applications for school choice — some of which is bureaucratically organized and coordinated by the school district and which links parents' activities to the ruling relations of the educational institution.

Local experience is the *entry-point* for an IE investigation into the ways that individuals participate in the extralocal relations that construct their everyday world of experience (Smith, 1987). While an institutional ethnography begins an inquiry by studying people's everyday lives, it does not remain there. The inquiry moves on to study the institutional structures and practices that help to shape and organize everyday experiences (Campbell and Gregor, 2002; DeVault, 1999; Dobson, 2001; Naples, 2003; Smith, 1987). Describing the practice of IE as a method, Smith says: "[The researcher] directs her gaze towards the social as the ongoing concerting of people's actual activities …. [and at] how what people are doing and experiencing in a given local site is hooked into sequences of action implicating and coordinating multiple local sites where others are active" (Smith, 1999, p. 7).

An adaptation of Smith's method helps me shift research on parents into a new direction and explain how parents are positioned within and by educational institutions for participation in school choice processes. Using IE for the research on which this book is based, I could take up analytically the way in which institutional organization and various social relations (gender, class, and race relations) could be seen coordinating and concerting mothers' involvement in their children's schooling. It could show mothers engaged in similar activities for their children — mothers who may never meet or know one another — but whose actions, when linked to and across institutional sites, helped to uncover the racial and class dynamics of public school choice.

An IE project studying parents will differ from other qualitative research approaches because of its focus on exploring "how the institutional practices of the school penetrate and organize the experiences of different individual mothers" (Smith, 1987). Consequently, IE utilizes a nontraditional approach to sampling, site selection, and interviewing for data collection. Participants are not selected in order to generalize to a larger population, but instead for how we can use their experiences as a standpoint from which to investigate further the institutional ruling relations. Describing her research on mothers and schools, Smith (1987) states:

> When we look at the school from the standpoint of women, we do not require a sample; we are not trying to generalize from a small number to the characteristics of a larger population. Rather, we are trying to explore how the institutional practices of the school penetrate and organize the experience of different individual women as mothers. We want to explore this phenomenon from a base in that experience, and we want to "hold" our perspective by moving

from the experience of the women we interviewed to the complementary organization of the school (Smith, 1987, p. 187).

Interviews are important tools for institutional ethnographic methods and include asking participants about the texts they encounter in their everyday activities, and in the case of my research, the texts parents and school people associate with the school choice process (Campbell and Gregor, 2002; DeVault and McCoy, 2001; Smith, 2001). The communication processes of bureaucratic institutions, such as school districts, are primarily textual. Texts often become the links between people working in different institutional activities.

As I will show in the following chapters, when parents decide to participate in school choice, the magnet school application form becomes a major text linking parents' "choice work" to the complementary work done by the school-level and district-level personnel who oversee and manage magnet school programs. The institutional process for implementing the magnet school program also organizes and coordinates the work of different people (mothers, clerical assistants, and district-level administrators) through this text. For example, an administrator at the central office supervises the design of a magnet school application, which is then sent to a local school for distribution to parents, who then complete the application and mail it to the central office, where clerical workers enter the information from the application into a database.

An IE analysis brings into view the textual processes through which an educational policy, such as voluntary integration, becomes implemented through the district, local schools, and families. It brings to light the broader social relations in which school choice is situated by showing what a white mother, for example, does as part of her school choice process and how that is linked to district practices for student school assignments. And it shows what another mother, who may be poor or a woman of color, does as part of her school choice process and how her experiences are different when linked to the same district practices for student school assignments. In this way, IE shows how the texts of schooling — in this case, a magnet school brochure and application — can be "active" in privileging certain discourses, policies, practices, or stakeholder group perspectives while excluding others, thereby sustaining the historical inequalities and inequities of educational institutions.

As can be implied from the literature discussed in this introduction, research on the family-school relationship in the U.S. often begins its inquiry from within the discourses of schooling, from the position of the educational institution, and fails to question the ideological organization and framing that researchers, policy makers, school personnel, and parents take for granted in their understanding of parents' involvement in education (Waggoner and Griffith, 1998). Incorporating critical and feminist theoretical and methodological frameworks, I worked to reverse the trajectory of most educational policy studies which "study down" to the lives of parents in order to explain their decisions. Instead, I began my IE research in the everyday lived realities of parents, mostly mothers, as they chose schools for their children. The standpoint illuminated by the experiences of the racially and economically diverse parents who were participants in the study enabled me to frame the research question that I found most compelling: how do schools and educational institutions themselves place parents in such a position that in making what they believe to be the best decision for their children and their families they become complicit in inequitable outcomes for other parents' children?

The Research Project

This two-year study took place in a high school complex in a large urban district in California during the late 1990s.[6] The Deluca USD was selected because it has operated a variety of choice options for many years, including a voluntary integration program utilizing magnet schools. The district's magnet schools were developed in response to a court mandate to establish a voluntary integration program. At the time of the study, however, the district had a limited number of magnet schools in comparison to the number of regular schools. Thousands of parents apply to the magnet school program for their children each year, and through a lottery system only 18% of the applications are accepted. The competitive element of the district's choice programs was therefore an important reason for selecting the district. The Davis High School Complex (a pseudonym, as are all subsequent names throughout) was one of the district's most diverse complexes and had many schools of choice, thereby allowing for a broad range of experiences for the parent participants.[7]

This study includes 13 parent participants whose children attended elementary, middle, and high school in the Davis High School Complex (see Appendix A) and who were interviewed about the actual work they did as part of choosing schools.[8] The parents were a diverse group. Two mothers were African American, one of them single and on welfare, and the other college-educated and married. There was one divorced Korean mother with a college degree who immigrated to the U.S. as a young teenager. The Latino father was single, an undocumented immigrant who had worked in a professional field in Mexico. The Hispanic mother[9] was born in the U.S. but had spent much of her childhood living in Mexico; she was on welfare and her children's father was not a legal resident. The eight white middle-class parents, seven mothers and one father, all had college degrees. One of the mothers was divorced, another was separated from her husband, and the remaining white parents were married.

Consistent with institutional ethnographic sampling and interviewing practices[10] (DeVault and McCoy, 2001), participants were selected because they helped illuminate the "textual trail" of the magnet application brochure from a parental standpoint, and not because the participants were representative of the parent population or school district personnel in the district. Using this approach, comments by parents about how they understand the magnet application as a text led to interviews with a local school administrator to explain further the application process as it is described in the text. The administrator's comment that the application process was determined by the district's central offices led to an interview with an administrator who helped to design the application text. Moreover, participants were sought who could help to explicate how the magnet school program was organized and coordinated by Deluca USD so that parents would experience the school choice process in the ways that they did.

Incorporating parents' descriptions of their experiences choosing schools and the work they did on behalf of their children's education, principals and community advisors in the local school context were interviewed and observed for the complementary role that they played in shaping the parents' experiences. In order to understand better the way in which the district's structures and practices coordinated and further organized parents' choice work to existing school choice policies and court mandates for the voluntary integration plan, the study moved from the local school context to an examination of the bureaucratic organization of school choice with interviews of administrators at the region and district level. In total, 11 district staff members (central office administrators, local principals, paid community advisors) were interviewed for the study.[11]

THE BOOK CHAPTERS

To support the analysis of the study's findings in subsequent chapters, Chapter 1 includes a brief discussion of desegregation policies and public school choice. I discuss the different choice options of the district and the background of the district's magnet school program. District personnel were interviewed for the study, and some of their voices are used in this chapter to frame a broad and complex picture of school choice in a large urban school district. In Chapter 2, I introduce the magnet school application as an active text, discussing how the district developed a new version of the application brochure that was mailed home to parents. I make a stylistic decision in the chapter to bring the reader, somewhat abruptly, into the institutional context of public school choice through discussion and analysis of the magnet school application text and how it fits into the bureaucratic structures and practices of the district. In this chapter some of the parents from the study are introduced, as are additional district personnel. I show how parents were positioned differently as readers of the text and present the voices of parents of different racial backgrounds as they interpret the magnet application. This chapter illustrates a key aspect of institutional ethnography — the study of texts as part of the relations of ruling — and begins to uncover the ruling relations inherent in the magnet school choice application process.

Chapter 3 captures what was actually the entry point for the research project, the everyday experiences of parents actively engaged in the school choice process, doing what I call choice work. Parents, mostly mothers, are seen networking with other parents, getting information from school personnel, and using what they have learned through various local knowledge systems to help them understand school choice options in the district. In this chapter I present how the choices parents made *happened*, and how parents negotiated the textually-mediated processes the district set in place. Throughout this chapter, the racial relations and the privileging of white students and students from more economically secure families come into focus, as does the way in which key discourses help shape choice in the district. In Chapter 4, the various stages of the institutional ethnographic analysis come together powerfully to make visible the social organization of school choice so that we see how parents become participants in the historical inequities of schooling. By this chapter, all 13 parents and the 11 school district personnel who were participants in the study have been introduced. Several parents' stories about their choice processes and practices are shared. I use a mapping technique to show the textually-mediated and socially organized process of public school choice that the parents encountered. By visually illustrating the choice process put in place by district texts, it is possible to see how some parents are able to advance in the school choice process, while others are not and must pursue alternative choice options.

A primary justification for providing parents with a variety of school choice options is that it is more democratic to allow parents to decide where and in what kind of school they want to enroll their children, particularly when their local school is a not-so-good school. While the stories shared in the book precede the implementation of the No Child Left Behind Act, throughout the book I relate the parents' experiences and the district's practices to the new public school choice provision of NCLB. Chapter 5 explicates how the study's parents came to be the choosers they are. The chapter explores how, in ways not fully visible to the parents themselves, their identities as involved parents were in part shaped and determined by their everyday activities and experiences related to their own and their children's educations. In this final chapter I bring the discussion beyond what parents came to know about the kind of school they wanted for their children, and how to go about getting into such a school, to a discussion of how their roles were constructed in relation to school choice policies and practices and the institutionalized integration and achievement discourses. As the parents' stories are brought to a close, the discussion focuses on how it came to be that the parents did just what they had been positioned to do: become participants in the growing inequities and inequalities of public school choice. I suggest that we do the necessary conceptual work to actually show the discursive shift taking place as school choice is used less as a means for voluntary integration and more for improving school achievement. The book concludes with a discussion of schooling as known and experienced by parents and the issues we must address if parents will one day know and experience their children's schooling otherwise — in more democratic and equitable ways.

Some Claims and Disclaimers

The nice thing about coming of age as an educational researcher today is that a lot of the critical analyses of education that I have read often blend together an interesting mix of theories from different disciplines. As a result, I feel pretty comfortable trying out theories that are new to me, braiding different theories together, and exploring a combination of ways to put forth analyses of my research. But there are limitations I face when following this eclectic and nuanced approach, foremost of which is that I am not able to develop a full and detailed synthesis of the different theoretical frameworks in which I am situating my analysis. I can explore their complementary features but must leave for later work a discussion of their incompatibilities and disciplinary differences.

For some readers, this may warrant criticism, and I accept such a critique. Nonetheless, here is what I have done, while recognizing that I could not cover everything in this introduction, and given the goals and the scope of this book. I selected from theories those concepts that would help me analyze the data I collected and that linked to the institutional analysis I am undertaking. I also tried to be careful not to overdefine the concepts or enter into the internal debates or controversies of the different theoretical traditions (i.e., within and among feminist standpoint theorists or critical theorists). Without meaning any disrespect to the scholars who know these theories so very well, I wanted to give myself some room in how I presented the theories so that I could play with them a bit and innovate a little.

On a similar note, given the topic of public school choice, I necessarily discuss issues related to desegregation, voluntary integration, open enrollment choice plans, and the public school transfer plans of NCLB and the various political and historical contexts associated with these forms of school choice. There is extensive scholarly work on these topics, some of which has informed my thinking, and I have drawn selectively from the vast literature. I do not devote very much attention to the literature on school vouchers and charter schools because these were not the choice options that surfaced in my study. But the arguments calling for caution regarding these choice options put forth by respected scholars like Michael Apple and Amy Stuart Wells were certainly in my thoughts. My primary reason for writing this book is to comment on public school choice from the standpoint of parents, and mothers in particular. It is not my intent to enter the long-standing scholarly conversations about the broader notion of school choice (public or private) or whether desegregation has been successful, though I will have a few thoughts to share about these issues in the final chapter. Consequently, my contribution to those bodies of literature will be a modest one.

In taking a parent standpoint, I did not want to substitute education professionals' realities of school choice or scholars' theorizing on school choice for what parents actually experience with their children and their children's schooling. Institutional ethnographic methods aided my efforts to stay true to a parents' standpoint. Of the many goals I have for this book, two then are worth mentioning. I want those who make or implement school choice policy to have the stories of the parents in this book to think about when they ask the ever salient policy questions: Whose children will benefit? Whose children will not? I also want to generate deeper reflection on how we might better organize our school choice processes and practices so that parents do not bear the blame for the inequitable outcomes that result from those very processes and practices our schooling institutions sustain.

1

INSTITUTIONALIZING PUBLIC SCHOOL CHOICE
IN AN URBAN DISTRICT

Three things — residential segregation, school desegregation as a means to address unequal educational opportunities, and the connection of school choice plans to the excellence movement — all have a place in understanding the historical context of public school choice. Today, school choice is more and more complex. With public school transfers to high-performing schools and charter schools now features of the NCLB federal accountability requirements, the dreams of neoliberal advocates of an open market of school choice could soon become realities as the opportunity to make wide-scale public school choice a permanent part of schooling in the U.S. enjoys a boost from the federal government.

It seems to me that an important question for scholars who study the issues related to school choice should be centered on how voluntary integration and public school choice can be implemented in ways that will achieve the dual goals of integrated schools, as put forth in Brown, and higher performing schools, as required by NCLB. I believe that most urban schooling institutions are trying hard to meet these two goals, carefully designing organizational structures and practices to bring about the social change needed in their districts through choice programs such as magnet schools and transfer-out options. However, I am not so sure how successful they will be. My study of one well-intentioned urban district unfortunately found that the rules and processes that the district institutionalized to bring about access, equity, and equality through school choice often served to hide the very real ways that race and class still supported exclusion in its schools. I suspect that this happens elsewhere too.

My uneasiness with the idea that large, urban, bureaucratic school districts alone can manage such a critically important task comes from an understanding of the historical development of school choice policies and practices, and particularly from how parents' participation in school choice has been constructed over time. Let me contextualize my interpretations, then, by providing an abbreviated history of school choice in the U.S. before I introduce Deluca USD's own history with desegregation, voluntary integration, and school choice.

THE DEVELOPMENT OF PUBLIC SCHOOL CHOICE

One of the oldest forms of school choice developed along with the housing patterns that emerged with the increasing industrialization of urban centers at the turn of the century. Various ethnic communities began to settle outside of the city, and with their move came the need for neighborhood schools to serve the different communities' children (Katznelson and Weir, 1985). Unless parents chose to send their child to private or parochial school, where you lived became where you went to school, the most common form of early school choice. The residential segregation of these ethnic communities impacted where children could attend school and the diversity they would encounter.

The historical research on education indicates that while professional educators, through their increasing control of schooling, were able to reduce community influence on school policy (Tyack, 1974), nothing was done about the development of residential segregation's effects on the schooling available for different children (Katznelson and Weir, 1985). The choice of where you lived and where you could attend school was not the same for minority children. Many black children, due to laws that allowed for racial segregation of schools, could not attend schools they lived close to, but instead traveled past those schools daily, on their way to their separate schools (Wells, 1993b).

As is well known, this situation changed with *Brown v. Board of Education* and subsequent court-ordered desegregation. The courts assigned responsibility for rearranging where parents' children would attend school to bureaucratic, centralized school districts. Although most of the desegregation mandates affected schools in the South or in large urban school districts, which parents could send their children to which schools was from then on a major policy issue for public schools across the nation.

Educational institutions had spent decades convincing parents that educational professionals knew what was best for children, and that they could fairly and appropriately design curricula, instruction, and placement to meet the needs of all students. The schooling institutions had a well-established system of control over public school families and the educational discourses that historically had informed parents' knowledge about their children's schooling. As a result of court action, parents were boldly reminded that where they live, along with their race, had implications for their children's public schooling. The literature suggests that the effects of established patterns of residential segregation on the educational opportunities of students were issues far bigger than any individual public school parent was probably prepared to deal with. I believe a similar context is building for parents today.

School Choice and Voluntary Integration

School desegregation brought about a whole new set of choices for parents and a new set of problems for public school administrators. White parents fled urban public schools in large numbers. The use of busing to integrate schools added to the already cumbersome bureaucracies (Wells, 1993b). Vast numbers of new court orders and federal and state categorical programs were impacting the decisions that could be made in urban school districts and resulted in fragmented and overlapping local policies (Tyack and Cuban, 1995).

In light of these massive changes, different ideas and programs emerged that would result in new and different choices for parents. During the 1970s, many alternative schools opened that gave parents an opportunity to try giving their children a diverse learning environment that was not so tightly coupled with bureaucratic control and mandated compliance. These progressive and humanistic programs, though not widely taken up by mainstream schools, became models for how parents, if given a choice for something special and different from their neighborhood schools, would sometimes voluntarily choose to send their children to schools that were often more ethnically and racially diverse (Raywid, 1985; Wells, 1993b).

As districts struggled with the implementation of desegregation plans, ironically the very parents who had been dissatisfied with the centralized and tracked programs in traditional public schools, and left for other alternative schooling programs, led the way for the development of magnet schools as a key desegregation tool for public education (Wells, 1993b). Because magnet schools "are purposely intended to be more popular than non-magnet schools .... school districts spend an enormous amount of money promoting magnets and advertising their offerings" (Wells, 1993b, p. 81). Magnet school programs grew and increased parental choice of schools beyond that of their neighborhood school or assigned desegregated school choice options. With the many special offerings that magnet schools provided, the stronghold of neighborhood location lost some of its grip on school choice (Rossell, 1985).

School districts' needs to meet desegregation mandates set in place a pattern of capitalizing on parents' desires to secure the best possible education for their children. Maybe the political contexts at the time and the historic inequities that resulted from residential segregation required this type of manipulation of parents, but unfortunately, since most magnet programs were limited in quantity (and still are), these practices led to increased competition among parents.

Magnet schools renewed the opportunity for parents to make their enrollment choices based on cultural capital, social class, and special access to information about schools. Most of the magnet programs that went into place had application processes, and some required satisfaction of certain criteria for admission. For example, gifted magnets required students to qualify with high tests scores or grades. Racial ratios varied among the different district designs, but in urban areas with increasing minority student populations, the ratios tended to continually favor white applicants (Ascher, 1994; Bastian et al., 1986; Lowe and Miner, 1992; Raywid, 1985; Rossell, 1985; Wells, 1993b).

The unquestioned historical precedent of sorting students through tracked curricular programs and the implementation practices of desegregation plans allowed schools to maintain the appearance that they were integrating schools. For magnet parents and those parents who stayed at neighborhood schools, educators were still able to use tracking as a means of differentiating curricula for middle-class and high achieving students (Oakes, 1985). Researchers studying the long-term implementation effects of desegregation continued to see white and/or middle-class students advantaged in some of the districts' plans. While black and Latino students were allowed to attend the same schools as white students, the education they received has often been significantly different. Grouping practices for special education and gifted classes and selective discipline further resegregated schools and reduced the access of black and Latino students to equal quality education (Meier and Stewart, 1991; Meier et al., 1989; Orfield, 2001).

With desegregation constituting an active part of efforts to equalize schooling for black and white children, and corresponding to the civil rights legislation and the subsequent increase in federal funding for disadvantaged students, the educational community attempted reforms to provide equal educational opportunity for all students. Many of the new educational policies were compromised in the legislative process, but even more were compromised in the implementation process (Elmore, 1982; Tyack and Cuban, 1995). As in the case of magnet schools, policies originally intended to improve educational opportunity for minority students became policies that benefited only a select few (Moore and Davenport, 1990). It is an unfortunate outcome that the white or middle-class parents who signed up for participation in integration programs were also unknowingly signing up for criticism of the advantages they received by doing so. Middle-class and white parents gained an advantage in securing better schools for their children in the new choice arrangements. This is a troubling outcome and so is the role played by education institutions in constructing those advantages.

Schooling institutions, which were creating new programs to comply with court mandates, were also finding ways to hold on to at least some of their white students and high achieving students, the same group that had historically been privileged through testing and tracking policies (McNeil, 2000; Oakes, 1985). Regardless of how choice was used as a desegregation tool, educators still had a system in place that could provide an advantage for middle-class families. Even if conscientious and equity-minded educators were offering choices that would improve the educational opportunities and outcomes for some underrepresented poor and minority students, far too many students were left behind in poor performing schools. And perhaps, far too many white and middle-class parents were offered advantages without any demand that they become aware of the effects these practices were having on other parents' children.

School Choice and Accountability

Professional educators' attention centered on egalitarian issues in the 1960s and 1970s, and this would shift as parents and the public began perceiving a decline in the quality of public education. As Republican administrations came to public office in the 1980s, educational excellence became a component of the individualistic, market-economy models they promoted. It was at this time that parents' choice options became more varied. It was also a time when talk about the quality of individual schools grew louder than equity and diversity among *all* schools.

While various developments around school choice as a means for integration took place, the ability of public schools to educate children effectively was being called into question. Presented in the spring of 1983, a report commissioned by the U.S. Secretary of Education, *A Nation At Risk*, stated boldly that the U.S. had in fact engaged in past years of "educational disarmament," allowing its schools to fall into mediocrity, placing the very foundations of a democratic society at risk (National Commission on Excellence in Education, 1983). Criticism of public schooling mounted, and many perceived that America's children were not learning enough of the right things to ensure the nation's future global competitiveness.

Probably the most influential book to pick up the argument about a lack of excellence in public schools and connect it to the debate on school choice was *Politics, Markets and America's Schools*, by Chubb and Moe (1990). From the dominance of the state and district administrations, to the unions, to the shallow results of much of the school-based management plans, Chubb and Moe criticized what previous reform had actually accomplished in academic achievement for students. Their proposal for reform was a radical decentralization of public education that undoes the bureaucratic institution completely and puts in place a system of school choice based on market principles answerable to parents and students.

Scholarship critical of large bureaucratic schooling institutions may have done little to change the educational bureaucracy, but the proposed combination of a market-based system of choice with decentralization of control in schooling did bring many responses from the educational community, including renewed efforts to establish voucher programs and the innovation of charter schools (Good and Braden, 2000). Hoping to allay concerns about racial inequities and increase interest in new choice schemes spurred on by the entrepreneurial spirit of the marketplace, choice advocates argued that there need not be a tension between individual choice and school integration (Henig, 1996).

The discussions around increased school choice also led to serious reflection by those often critical of marketization and the neoliberal and neoconservative agendas. Dehli writes,

> "Critics of marketization cannot ignore the depth of rage and frustration about public schools that many people feel. Interpreting all criticisms of schooling as though it arose from a right-wing, market perspective would be insulting to those, including many teachers and parents, who have worked for decades to make schools more democratic, meaningful, fair and equal" (Dehli, 1996 p. 272). Certainly, advocates for equal educational opportunity in large urban districts throughout the nation shared such a frustration. The continuous disparity among the achievement levels of

disadvantaged minority students compared to more advantaged students attending better resourced, higher achieving schools forged much of the recent political compromise between liberals and conservatives that led to the passage of the NCLB act (Ruda-levige, 2003). As in the days of Ronald Reagan's Republican administration, conservative advocates of choice did not insist that NCLB's choice options include private or parochial schools (Henig, 1996), accepting instead transfer rights to charter schools.

Providing poor and minority parents with the option to transfer their children out of the lowest-performing schools to another school is a program requirement of the NCLB. Because the NCLB requires disaggregated achievement data, schools that continue to underserve disadvantaged and minority students can be identified and an opportunity to choose a better school can be extended to their parents. For many, this is seen as an important addition to federal and state education policy. Since the lowest performing schools are often racially isolated and located in high poverty communities, some civil rights leaders see the choice provisions of NCLB as offering possible opportunities for desegregation (Brown et al., 2004). Still, others caution that the effects may harm desegregation efforts (Boger, 2003; Orfield, 2004).

THE PRESENT-DAY CONTEXT OF PUBLIC SCHOOL CHOICE

So we arrive at the context shaping public school choice policies and practices today. The literature on school choice is vast, and this brief overview attempts to show that parents are positioned within the much larger debate on whether educational institutions can provide both excellence and diversity in the schools, and if so, how. Urban public school parents, in some way or another, will have to make sense of how the issues of excellence, diversity, and equity affect their choices. The growth of public school choice options puts parents in a position where they can choose or not choose among schools on behalf of their children. I posit that how parents choose is closely related to how their knowledge of schooling has been produced through institutional discourses, texts, cultures, and practices.

To support my argument I want to describe the institutional context that situates parents' choice decisions in the Deluca USD[1] and I do so for the following reasons. While there is much written about different school choice policies and implementation practices, we seldom get a picture of the many choice options that are organized to work in concert in large urban districts. To understand better how inequalities and inequities happen as a result of school choice, we need to look closely at how the various choice policies overlap and interact with other enrollment policies and school district operations. We need to search for how the institutional discourses of achievement and integration constitute and are constituted by district policies and practices.

This leads me to the second reason for telling the story of school choice in Deluca USD by beginning with the institutional context. When parents walk into an elementary school office to enroll their children in kindergarten or first grade, the institution of schooling with its history, policies, organizational structures, cultures, and practices already exists there — at the school; on the office counter with the enrollment forms, health forms, newsletters; in classrooms with teachers and state-approved textbooks; in the principal's office, with district policy bulletins and school-wide test score results. At the moment of enrolling a child in public school, the broader social relations that help to shape the local school context that parents are likely to encounter is not within the sight of most parents. Whether the school is integrated or not, has space for school choice or not, enrolls high-achieving students or not, is a "good school" or not, is determined institutionally and outside of the control of any one individual family. What I want to present first, then, is the existing institutional context of choice into which a parent choosing among schools in Deluca enters.

SCHOOL CHOICE IN DELUCA UNIFIED SCHOOL DISTRICT

There are four main programs operating in Deluca public schools that provide parents with choice options: magnet schools, open enrollment, permits, and charter programs. Implemented after the completion of my study, the new NCLB choice requirement provides an additional option. The parents in this study reported experiencing choice in all of these programs with the exception of the charter school options. Each of these choice options was controlled by separate departments at the district's administration offices. Each department has its own policy bulletins describing the procedures and guidelines for the programs they oversee, and each choice option has accompanying texts and documents for parents to complete, such as applications, verification materials, and forms.

The most popular choice option and the one in which most parents wanted to participate was the district's magnet schools, a part of the district's voluntary integration program. Magnet school choice invariably comes up in conversation first when choice in the district is discussed, so it is addressed in detail throughout the book. The Transportation for Participating Schools (TPS) program is a permit-type choice option in the voluntary integration program. Parents choose to participate in TPS, but parents do not choose the schools for their children. The district selects the schools for the students, and this is coordinated to pre-established transportation routes.

Though not actually part of official school choice policy, the oldest method of choice in use by parents is the permit option, which allows students to attend schools other than their residence school for reasons such as child care, parents' work location, or medical needs. Another option for parents is open enrollment within and between school districts allowing parents to transfer their children to schools with available space.

Figure 1 illustrates the district's various school choice options and guidelines. In the diagram, the complexity of organizing and operating choice programs in a large urban district becomes evident, as does the institutional context in which parents' participation in school choice is situated.

In order to offer more choice to parents, space must be available. It was not a surprise to learn that creating enrollment spots for choice in a large, centralized district like Deluca is not easy, especially for a district also burdened with an ever increasing student population. As administrators were interviewed about school choice options, the district's method of allocating classroom space was regularly mentioned.

The Space Walk

Determining how much space is available for open enrollment for each coming school year is done through a process the district calls the Space Walk. This was explained to me by a couple of different administrators, and it is important to understand that this process is one of the many ways to see the extended social relations in the school district's operations that help shape the school choice context for parents.

Before the annual Space Walk takes place, there has been a tremendous amount of data gathered about student populations and school community growth projections at the district offices. Principals and assistant principals come to the Space Walk to determine how much classroom space the school will have available for student enrollment in the subsequent year. Principals may have already met with their regional administrators to lobby for new or existing programs that require classroom space (e.g., a computer lab). Consequently when the

Each year schools must determine how much classroom space they have for

Resident Enrollment Special Education Placement Continuing Permits (including TPS)
Magnet Enrollment (if magnet program on site) Open Enrollment (including Adv Studies)
NCLB Transfers New Permits

Charter Schools

- Application required
- No transportation provided
- Very limited space given size of district

Magnet Schools

- Court-ordered voluntary integration program
- Racial-ethnic formulas required by court
- Application process and lottery
- Verification of high ability or achievement for gifted magnets
- Matriculation rights for next level of schooling granted to students enrolled in magnets
- Limited number of schools and spots
- Thousands of applicants denied each year

Open Enrollment

- California school choice legislation
- Application process and lottery
- Admission practices should follow integration guidelines
- Once enrolled, reapplication not necessary each year
- Used for Advanced Studies Program
- Continuous decline in available space each year due to increasing student population

Permits

- TPS students – part of voluntary integration program (application required)
- Childcare, Employment-related, & other permits (application and verification of need required each year)
- Permit availability limited
- Inter-district permits (application and screening process at receiving district)

NCLB Transfers

- Resident Title I school designated as needing improvement for 2 years
- Priority to lowest achieving students
- Choices may include charter schools
- Not enough space at higher performing schools
- Transportation until resident school improves

The magnet school program is usually parents' first choice

These are the options for district parents who wish to choose a public school other than their regularly assigned school. Different choice options are subject to qualifications, verification, application processes and available space.

Figure 1. School Choice Options in Deluca USD

principals meet with the district personnel at the Space Walk, they can each have very different interests and needs.

Meeting at a room in a regional office, they go through a series of stations in a particular order. Principals know their own school context and lobby at the different stations for higher or lower allocations. A drastic increase in the number of students a school has to accommodate could result in unpopular decisions at the school, for example, high school teachers having to rotate to different classrooms.

The first station at which principals stop is with the district demographers, and here they determine (1) what their resident population is and (2) their permit/transfer population that is fixed, that is not expected to change. They leave the demographers with an enrollment number which is their basic nonnegotiable number. The second station is for special education enrollment, where things such as the number of special day classrooms that schools have set aside and the lower student/teacher ratios in those classrooms are considered. It also means that in many of these schools, where there are strong needs for special education programs, there is less room at the school for other programs.

The third station is where principals meet with the people who deal with school capacity. For example, El Rancho is one of the schools in this study and is allowed to have 450 magnet spots; that magnet number is also a nonnegotiable number. Principals then have to take the magnet spots out of the total number of spaces. After accounting for the nonnegotiable spaces, the school capacity station determines how many seats the school has available at that point. Principals go to the fourth station where their school is considered for the TPS program, a part of the district's integration program, and the Overcrowded Schools Student Placement program (OSSP). The school is looked at in terms of how many spaces it can lend to alleviate overcrowding and or support TPS.

It is at the fifth station where district staff finally identify how many open enrollment spaces schools have. Having taken care of the resident students, continuing permits, OSSP students, TPS, magnet programs, all special education needs at this station a new number of available classroom space is assigned to the school. The principal is then advised of how many spaces the school has for open enrollment, if any. And throughout this process, principals and district staff must be thinking also about the need to provide seats for integration.

Choice programs are often based on a limited number of spaces. The Space Walk exemplifies how choice options for parents are contingent upon allocation of the scarce resources available in large urban districts. The Space Walk process and the enrollment requirements of various choice options (including those now added by NCLB) are parts of the organization and coordination of choice that parents do not see.

Open Enrollment

The open enrollment process allows one to make another school, a school different from your resident school, your new resident school. Once enrolled, students can remain there up to the last grade offered at that school. State law makes it a parent's right to participate in this transfer program. One of the community advisors interviewed for the study explained it this way:

> Now, for open enrollment, if the student is granted an open enrollment permit, that school becomes the student's home school just as if the parent lived right across the street from that school. That permit cannot be revoked. If the student has behavior problems, attendance problems, whatever, the school deals with it as if it were happening at the home school. A student cannot be sent back to the home school, nor can a principal cancel an open enrollment permit.

An administrator from the district department overseeing open enrollment made it clear that the department does not want the open enrollment program to create segregation, whether it be segregated white schools or segregated minority schools. Because the open enrollment program was designed to both provide choice and follow the district's court-ordered integration guidelines, parents are asked to indicate the child's race/ethnicity on the application.

After passage of the California initiative, Proposition 209, in 1996 which eliminated affirmative action programs in the state, the district consulted legal counsel regarding the use of racial identity for school choice placements. The administrator told me that they were advised that Prop. 209 required that any court orders or consent decrees that were in effect on election day would not be retroactively repealed. Because the court issuing the order for the voluntary integration program has released all jurisdiction over the district's case, the order will remain in effect indefinitely. With the court order in effect, neither policies nor administrative practices that in any way would resegregate schools are permissible. Under this interpretation, the district can ask about race on open enrollment applications and expect principals to take integration ratios into consideration when assigning open enrollment spaces.

Another issue that arose during the study was matriculation rights to the next level of school following feeder patterns or magnet programs. By state law, the selection for open enrollment is supposed to be random and unbiased. The same department administrator told me that the way open enrollment exists now, "You get the good, and you get the bad, and you get the in between in regards to students. And that's the way it should be …. and you'll get a little of everything." When asked about how the district handles matriculation concerns of parents he said, "Well, matriculation is kind of a controversial issue." He added that the Board of Education acknowledged that students and parents would want to stay within the feeder patterns of the school and should be given a priority in open enrollment at the next level of schooling.

Speaking again about open enrollment, the community advisor pointed out how the two criteria, integration guidelines and matriculation priority, could change the intent of the state law.

And, you know, if they're drawing randomly, I don't know how that would work. Because if they're drawing, you know, ten of these students, and they say, "Oh, no. We have enough of these." Will the eleventh one get put aside until you get more of these [other] type of students? …. So that kind of takes the randomness out.

This suggests that allowing some kind of priority sets up the possibility that there would be no space for parents new to open enrollment. They could find themselves not able to get in because the space is already protected for continuing families. The limiting of choice for parents who enter programs midway will be shown happening with the magnet program too, in Chapter 4.

One of the parents whose choice work will be profiled in the next chapters signed her daughter up for a new program in the district called Advanced Community-Articulated Studies (ACAS). The new program came up in discussion with the administrator in the department that handles open enrollment. I asked him if these advanced studies were going to be part of open enrollment and he said, "If it's up to me, no." He said the ACAS programs focus on particular qualifications, often gifted or high achieving status, and since they are based on qualifications, it would not be random and unbiased.

This same administrator told me that when the open enrollment program was first implemented they had thousands of applicants and now they are down to almost half of what they had in their peak year,

1997. The statewide class size reduction program for grades K–3, the increase in the student population, and the limited construction (in his opinion, the district "has been just horrible about new construction") mean that more schools are at capacity. When there is little space, this will cut down the number of open enrollment spaces that can be allocated during a Space Walk, because they have to be used for housing students from overcrowded schools. "It effectively is squeezing out choice," said the administrator. When districts squeeze out choice, they often squeeze out choice for everyone else but the most knowledgeable parents.

An achievement discourse is driving part of the change that programs like ACAS and class size reduction make in the district's instructional programs. Those parents who want to participate in school choice can easily get caught between the overlapping, and sometimes conflicting, choice policies, the discourses of achievement and integration that underlie these policies, and the very real issue of lack of classroom space.

Permits as a Choice Option

As already mentioned, permits to attend a school other than one's regular neighborhood school have been available for many years. It was also indicated that unlike open enrollment, permits of various types often require verification and renewal. Deluca has several permit options for parents that cover a wide range of student and parental needs. An administrator in the office that reviews and approves permit applications explained that permits are not really part of school choice but are based on need. The most common need is child care, therefore, that is the most common permit in the district. He stated that child care permits are meant to assist parents who have to work during school hours and cannot be there to pick up their children from school and meet the hours of the school day. Parents in school or training programs full time can qualify for child care permits as well. Although some are granted more often than others, the administrator said that besides child care, the permit options in the district include work-related, medical, residence, sibling, and interdistrict permits. In addition to using the permit option legitimately for child care or other needs, permits also become an option for parents when other means of choice fall through.

Like open enrollment, which must take into consideration the court-ordered integration guidelines, certain permits require the same. During the interview with the administrator from the permit office, he quoted a sentence from the district bulletin that reflects what "this is really all about: 'No district employee should engage in any activity that would segregate a school.'" He added, "The flip side of that would be to make every effort to desegregate the schools."

The administrator gave the following example:

> Let's say a school is 75% white and a white child and a minority child apply at the same time for a permit, a child care permit in this case. Well, it's written in the bulletin as to what they should do if they had to choose. In order to maintain integration, the minority child would have preference.
>
> He added that principals know to do this. But he also stated that within the policy guidelines is a parent's right to appeal, and parents will win in almost every appeal.
>
> That could present a problem for if a parent were to plead hardship and say 'I have no other source for child care. I have to have this permit. This is my only choice." When parents do that, because it's based on need .... then the school would also have to find a place for the child.

Continuing with the example, the administrator added: "So if the white parent made that appeal, what would happen is that they'd have to make room for both children, the white child and the minority child."

These situations that arise from parents seeking choices can become problems as schools become crowded and still need to take as many resident students as possible. According to the district administrator, the state forbids schools from enrolling students on permits over resident children, so schools in that context should no longer be accepting permits.

Child care permits as well as most of the other permits are only good one year at a time and need to be renewed each year. The school district policy states that they are not supposed to be canceled because of poor grades or behavior: they should not be canceled for any reason other than loss of eligibility. Interdistrict permits between districts can have guidelines stipulated with the permit, such as that students must maintain certain kinds of grades and certain kinds of behavior and permits can be canceled for various reasons. The district that grants a student permission to attend one of its schools on an interdistrict permit can put these stipulations as to what would cause cancellation of the permit. One of the parents in the study has a child on an interdistrict permit and was contacted by another district to apply to do the same there.

The community advisors answer questions about permits regularly. One added this information:

If the condition under which the permit was granted has changed, then the permit can be canceled. So if you get a child care permit because your child care is right across the street, and you no longer have the child care, your permit can be canceled. Or if you get a work permit and you no longer work close to that school, your permit can be canceled.

This community advisor pointed out the potential problems for parents:

As far as working, if you can't supply proof that you work at this job, then you cannot apply for a work permit. So if you're in the process of getting your job, or looking for a job in that neighborhood but don't have anything yet, then you cannot apply for that permit. If someone has promised you that in January you're gonna get this job, and you want to send your kid there in September so you won't have to move from school to school. No. Won't get it. Now, a principal can decide, "'Well, okay. I believe you. I'm going to let your kid in." They can make that decision. But if you mess up in any way, or you question the authority, or complain, they can just as fast say go back to your home school. …. If the principal doesn't like you for any reason, you can go to whoever you want, and if that person cannot convince the principal, too bad. The principal has all hundred percent authority on who gets the permit or doesn't.

This could put parents who need child care or work-related permits in a difficult position to advocate for their children, as the advisor goes on to say,

So if your child is not learning a thing there and you want to say something about it, or you happen to get a teacher that's awful and you want another teacher, you want anything, then at any moment the principal can say, "Well, if you don't like it, we're gonna send you back," at the drop of a hat. I've known parents who have called me in tears saying, you know, "The principal called, told me to come get my child. He's no longer going to this school."

The administrator I spoke with at the permit office was very clear when he said: "Well, open enrollment is the better option. Period." He believes it is better because it is strictly the parent's choice, and once the child is transferred into that school through open enrollment, that school becomes the school of residence. Unlike permits, with open enrollment the child's right to attend the school cannot be revoked or canceled because of behavior or other kinds of problems. These two options for school choice are commonly used by parents and they do supply many, many parents with alternative ways to attend a school other than the neighborhood school.

Finding appropriate, affordable and licensed child care has been an ongoing issue for working parents, working mothers. Parents in this study use or have used child care. This district's need to consider space availability and racial integration guidelines before granting child care permits, like a principal's authority to deny or cancel permits, demonstrates how vulnerable parents are to local school and district policies and practices.

Each of these options poses its own potential problems for giving all parents equal opportunity to participate fully in these programs. The accounts of the administrators and community advisors confirm that there is a larger social organization for each of the choice options beyond the procedural guidelines written in a district bulletin. Figure 1 only begins to illuminate what is, in fact, a broad intersection of social and institutional relations underlying choice in the district. How principals negotiate for the number of choice options they can offer at their schools, be they child care permits or open enrollment spaces, could determine the kinds of students they enroll and the kinds of control they have over students and their parents. It can impact the racial/ethnic balance at the school and the school's achievement data. The social relations organizing what happens at the bureaucratic level may be located beyond parents' everyday worlds, yet are still present in the organization and coordination of parents' experiences as they choose schools. Similarly, the history and politics that underlie the bureaucratic organization of school choice is seldom fully known to parents in the present-day context of choosing schools.

DESEGREGATION IN DELUCA USD

After the landmark rulings stemming from *Brown v. Board of Education* in the 1950s, Deluca, like many other school districts around the state and country, came under attack for providing segregated educational experiences for its students. By the late 1960s, the courts started mandating that desegregation efforts begin, particularly for districts like Deluca that had been resisting full compliance with the law. A district administrator recalled:

Well, when the lawsuit was originally brought we had, you know, a lot of white kids in the district, and you could have done it, but you most certainly couldn't have done it at that [later] period of time …. You have to understand that the district had been under a court order and the district fought it for almost twenty years, and so you can't say that the district willingly went into a desegregation program. But when the final court order came, it was plain that the district had to follow the law, and because of that, great attempts were made to establish an integration program. And then the formulas that came out for how to do it, in retrospect, were really unrealistic. At that time [in the late 1970s], you did not have a white critical mass in Deluca that could effectively desegregate all of the schools. So that was a very large problem, you couldn't do it [desegrate all schools].

The administrator said that people inside and outside the school district were designing and submitting desegregation plans.

And we had people running all kinds of models, that's all we were doing was doing models …. And there was nothing that effectively on a physical basis could desegregate the schools, so we were kind of stymied at that …. The things that we were getting from the demographers at the time said, mandatory or not, you're going to wind up in the 80s and 90s with less than fifteen percent of white kids in the district. You know, you might run them out now or they'll go later, but sooner or later you have this white population [that] is diminishing, and the Hispanic population is growing. And they said, too, and no one believed them at that time, that the Black population was going to diminish greatly, and in fact it did. Percentage-wise it did. And of course, with the tremendous growth of the Latino population, you know, no matter what the black population would have done it would have been a smaller percentage of the whole.

This administrator went on to say that many of the different schools' desegregation programs that had been established voluntarily were not well designed. School pairings were formed putting different implementation plans in place. One example of such a plan involved busing students to one school one year, then allowing students back at the neighborhood school the next year, followed by busing again in the third year and so on. Still, he said, the burden of desegregation was carried more by the minority students. Another district administrator commented:

The whole integration program was [from] the NAACP and those theorists behind what we call the White Hostage Theory, that if we hook up schools mandatorily and say they [white students] have to come here — and we don't care if they come or not — but if they improve the schools, that was the bottom line. And that didn't take place.

One of the administrators told me that when the district and the court realized the difficulty in trying to desegregate schools in Deluca, the groups involved in the development of an integration plan began to think differently. "Rather than looking at the physical isolation of schools, rather than looking at something where you're going to actually move kids in and out, which didn't make sense, it didn't add up numerically," he said, a new way to approach the problem was worked out by the court.

The court wanted the district to take reasonable and feasible measures to alleviate the harms of segregation whatever their causes. The court stated that low academic achievement, low self-esteem, lack of access to postsecondary opportunities, and interracial hostility and intolerance were four identified harms that result from racial isolation. As one administrator recalled, he felt the lawyers working with the court had saved the day by coming up with the harms of racial isolation. The lawyers' plan focused attention on how the district could address those harms with resources and programs even if the district could not completely desegregate all the schools. "[And] you could address those harms theoretically by not moving kids," he said, "So the civil rights groups accommodated the plan by not having kids mandatorily moved, they gave that one up, but they got barrels of money into schools. The more formidable opposition got what they wanted; kids weren't mandatorily moved."

During the years that the district, the civil rights groups, and other intervening parties were in and out of state courts in the effort to desegregate Deluca's schools, various voluntary integration plans were in development that included magnet schools, the TPS program, and "all kinds of permutations of moving kids around." The administrator added:

And also, as it evolved, it worked out as a savior for the district too, because in the meantime one of the characteristics of these racially isolated minority schools was they were getting crowded as all hell, and it served the purpose of the district to move kids out, so these programs were in effect relieving overcrowding.

In fact, the district added overcrowded schools as the fifth harm of racial isolation it would address in its voluntary integration plan.

Given the length of time it took to move the lawsuit through the courts, more than one judge had jurisdiction of the case. One administrator recalled how the judges would finally realize that because of the size of the district and the location of many of the racially isolated schools, some school communities might never be integrated, often just because of the traveling distances. Also, he added, a characteristic of those schools on which the courts were focused, was that the schools had student populations that were identified almost totally with Latino, African American, Asian, and other nonwhite racial or ethnic groups. The designation that the court established for these schools was to call them Predominantly Minority Population (PMP) schools. The district level administrator further explained:

> They established this new class of schools …. and schools received moneys in that category, and smaller class size, and there were a lot of other goodies in there, and there was a lot of bucks that came with it. And it was totally voluntary, so you had a little for everybody in there, and you know, that's what most compromises are.

Eventually the groups involved in the lawsuit stipulated to the voluntary integration plan that later became the court order. What also came with the ruling was a formula the court would use to determine whether a school was integrated. The formula was called the 60:40 to 40:60 rule. A school would be considered integrated if there were between 60% white and 40% PMP students and 60% PMP and 40% white students. As the white student population continued to decline and schools struggled to maintain a 40% white population, a subsequent court decision allowed a second formula to be used, 70:30 to 30:70, to designate an integrated school, and a school was considered PMP if it had 29% or fewer white students.

Residential segregation, demographic changes, racial politics, all had a role in the resulting court-ordered voluntary integration program that Deluca USD operates under today. The geography and housing patterns of the city made it impossible fully to desegregate the district's schools, short of adopting a county-wide metropolitan plan, and there was no political or community support for such recommendations. The demographic predictions would come true, and the numbers of white students in the district would decline, as the minority student population, Latino students in particular, would increase. Many people had a hand in designing what has become one of the more stable voluntary integration plans operating in large urban school districts. A member of a community committee monitoring the implementation of the court order reflected on how the judge's decision seemed to be based more on what was maximally feasible for white children than the necessary relief required for racially isolated minority children. And although records show[2] that the groups supporting the desegregation of Deluca's schools, as well as some judges overseeing the court cases, understood that overwhelming white schools were also segregated and wanted white families' participation in the racial integration of schools, the resulting voluntary plan let most white families in the district escape the burdens of desegregation.

I believe that looking at the historical context of the district's voluntary integration program with today's newer theoretical tools helps us see problems with the court ruling that might not have been visible then. However committed proponents were to the equal participation of white families in desegregation, as the voluntary integration plan worked its way through compromises, the language and the discourses that could have oriented actions toward equal participation never made it into the texts that would define the integration plan. Intended or not, the court played a major role in supporting privilege for white students in two ways. First, while it recognized harms for minority students who were racially isolated, it did not address how living in racial isolation (and with racial privilege) poses different "harms" for white students. Second, via the formulas and designations it put in place, the court fixed the subsequent enrollment and program advantages that came with being a white student in a predominantly minority district.

Community Involvement in Implementing a Voluntary Integration Program

In the late 1970s and early 1980s the district was busy trying to implement the court order and accommodate the voluntary integration plan. An administrator who remembers that time told me that at first the district and the people working in the integration office "were just happy anyone signed up for the integration program." He continued,

> So they weren't looking at whether a magnet was a theme magnet, or if it was really anything more than a regular school that was part of the integration program. Monitoring the goals of desegregation was not the issue. The concern was compliance with the law.

Another administrator pointed out that Deluca's desegregation plan resulted from a California court case based on the state's constitution, which she felt was a lot more liberal than the federal courts at the time. The state's court-approved plan allowed the district to continue implementation of some of the programs already developed by the district's integration department.

Prior to the implementation of the voluntary integration program, schools had paired up or formed what were called triads. While these early pairings were between communities of different racial/ethnic backgrounds, they were often between communities of similar social class backgrounds. One administrator stressed that it is important to understand that the history of the district's desegregation efforts were not only about race. As an example, he told of parents whose children attended Roy Sands elementary school in an affluent African American community:

> We know there's racism. Let's put that over here. Okay. But along with that parents want the best for their children .... So they [Sands Elementary School parents] said "Let's hook up voluntarily." They didn't go out to Brenning or Elsgrove to poor white kids to hook up with them. They went out to Sunrise [an affluent white community] in the northern part of the city, which is a distance, to kids they felt were on the same [socioeconomic] level. And the parents out there said, "Yeah, you guys are basically on the same level as us." They hooked up on that basis. So there is of course, you know, racism, but beyond that, you have to think about what else were the players going on?

Some of those school pairings that began around the city at that time became predecessors to the district's TPS program. Since the district already had the voluntary TPS pairings, the court required them to keep the TPS in place as a continuing permit program as well as create the new magnet schools for the mandated voluntary integration plan.

One of the community advisors also tells how African American parents whose children attended Del Mar elementary school, located in another upper middle class community, were initially involved in the different desegregation efforts:

> We realized that during the forced busing that the schools were assigning where you go. And the parents felt then, why should you [the district] assign? Why shouldn't we be able to choose? And that's where we went out, and we as a community went and

looked at other schools ourselves. And that's when we had Edlens Elementary School come to Del Mar to be part of that pairing. "Let's get together. Let's not wait for the district to assign us. If we feel we're matched, let's go with it."

As the magnet programs were planned, she said, "A lot of our community in the Del Mar area, which is African American and Jewish and Asian also felt that, 'I don't want to have my kid being bused, period. We have enough resources and teachers in our own community. Why don't we start up our own school?'"

The community advisor told me that these parents were actively involved in helping start the Cabrillo magnet, a K–12 school, and the Carnegie magnet, a 6–12 school:

When they came with the magnet schools, [it] was for us to be able to make a choice of where and how far we wanted our children to travel. And be aware of who was going to be teaching our children and what is the curriculum going to be. But we wanted structure, because as minorities, we realized that our children were always going to have to struggle and always have to be twice as better than the other person. So we needed to have that structure to make sure we got all the academics that we needed, then after that, we can get the enrichment.

We can see how race relations *and* class relations constituted some of these early efforts to organize and coordinate the participation of white families and families of color in the district's voluntary integration program. Yet the decisions made at the time were not addressing families' class-based preferences and advantages. While his work focuses on whites' racial advantage, Wellman's analysis is helpful in understanding how race and class relations operate to limit the perspectives of economically privileged groups:

As a result, middle-class sentiments about such issues as busing conflict with their tolerant world view. They do not become "prejudiced" when they resolve the contradiction between their ideals and their realities, however. Instead, they develop ways of explaining their opposition to change that do not explicitly contradict egalitarian ideals. Some people say, for example, "I'm not opposed to busing; I'm opposed to the time it involves." Other people don't object much to blacks like themselves living "next door." By asserting egalitarianism with respect to race, they endorse inegalitarianism with respect to class and class cultures (Wellman, 1993, pp. 52–53).

Learning about the school pairings that were acceptable to the minority and white middle-class parents during the late 1970s when the district was initiating a voluntary integration program, helps us understand how access to magnet school choice could be reorganized to class relations in subsequent years.

Locating Magnet Schools

As already mentioned, enrollment in parts of Deluca public schools, the white enrollment in particular, was decreasing at the time the district began implementing the court order and establishing the magnet schools. The interests of the wealthier African American parents worked in concert with the white parents' interests and the district's needs to get a voluntary program under way. As the African American communities described above were seeking programs that met their needs and did not impose the burden of travel on their children, other parents, a large percentage of whom were white, were supporting gifted magnets.

One of the administrators from El Rancho Middle School, a school discussed throughout this book, provided additional information about how some of the magnet schools were started.

> Once they were facing the court order, they were looking for places to site the magnet schools. El Rancho, at that time, had a very low enrollment. When the magnet program at [El Rancho] opened up, it had about seventy-eight kids in its first year. And over the years the enrollment has grown. The projection, obviously, was to grow some, but what's happened with the magnet schools, as you're probably well aware, is that they are the most popular programs in the school district .... And what's happened, of course, is that at this school, because of the fact that there is a gifted high IQ magnet here, it has had a tendency to draw other people here as well.

He also told me how other magnet school sites were determined. Lawrence Webb middle school, which was located in a diverse middle-class community, was in consideration of closure because enrollment had declined. Carnegie, a 6–12 college preparatory magnet, was one of the first magnet schools established in the district. As its reputation grew, it outgrew its various temporary sites. Given Webb's low enrollment and location in a community with a large percentage of African

American families, Carnegie was given Webb's school site. Once Carnegie moved to the new location, the students who would have attended the now closed Webb middle school were reassigned to middle schools that had space available. The El Rancho administrator tells how this was done:

> They divided the area up for three schools, Madison, El Rancho, and Wilson .... And, ultimately, the kids sent to Wilson, that's another story, were then moved to Foster. So the kids in that old area go to Foster, Madison, and probably the smallest number go to El Rancho. But at the time our magnet was established, there was another middle school [Webb] on this side of town.

In my fieldwork, I noticed that, as with the voluntary pairings for the desegregation programs discussed above, the decisions about which schools the Webb community students would be assigned to also seemed sensitive to community socioeconomic status. For example, the students from the old Webb attendance area who lived in an area with single-family homes were assigned to El Rancho and Madison middle schools, located in middle-class communities. The students living in areas with mostly apartments, some of which were Section 8 housing, went to Foster, a school community with smaller homes and many apartments.

There are parents in this study living in the old Webb area whose children, because there no longer is a nonmagnet middle school in their community, are automatically matriculated from their elementary schools into one of these middle schools, or zone schools. It is actually possible for white or wealthier students to get on a bus in the morning and go to the Carnegie magnet as their school of choice, and on the way to school pass the bus with the poorer and minority students who are forced to attend an assigned zone school, the very school the white and/or wealthier parents did not want their children to attend. In such a situation, white students participating in voluntary integration may be sharing the burden of travel, but what they receive at the end of the bus route proves to be very different.

DISCUSSION

Wellman (1993) has stated that there are numerous sources of disadvantage and advantage for Americans related specifically to race. He says that a key feature of race relations in the U.S. is the minimization of the structural impact of racism on American life, downplaying racism or overemphasizing class so that the organization of advantage is ignored. Wellman proposes that analysis should look for privilege and advantage manifested in the ways white people talk about race (Wellman, 1993, p. 26). He notes that the racial consciousness of whites and the many difficulties faced by African Americans can be interpreted as struggles over scarce resources. He suggests that studies of racism should analyze culturally acceptable beliefs that defend social advantage based on race:

> The analysis recognizes the structural or stratified nature of racial advantage without reducing race to class; *and* it takes racial consciousness seriously without analyzing it independently of social structure. It sees racism as a system of exclusion and privilege, *and* as a set of culturally acceptable linguistic or ideological constructions that defend one's location in that system (Wellman, 1993, p. 25, italics his).

Listening to people from the district tell the history of these schools and doing field observations and interviews in these school communities, I was struck by how seldom I heard people speak of segregation, the reason for desegregation. Instead, when the court-ordered voluntary integration plan was discussed, an integration discourse was taken up. It began to appear to me that it is the district's policies and institutional practices for school integration that are helping to shape the race relations in school choice in the district, not the desegregation discourse of years past. As some of the administrators' comments suggest, the district's inability to desegregate its schools was caused by many social, political, and economic constraints. Those were powerful forces that may have had the effect of reconstructing desegregation goals and implementation practices to a more acceptable discourse of voluntary integration.

Civil rights scholars have pointed out that integration is not the same as desegregation (powell, 2001; Steinhorn, 2001). However, it is sometimes the case that different discourse formations can appear to be saying the same thing, when in fact the semantic relationships between discourses can be very different (Lemke, 1995). Mandating that no child shall attend a school that is racially segregated, the goal of desegregation, suggests action very different from the goal of integration, that children of diverse racial and ethnic identities will attend school together. Taking up an integration discourse could make it easier to no longer orient actions to a desegregation discourse and make it easier to sustain systems of privilege and exclusion. Unfortunately, if we consider the increasing dominance of an achievement discourse, like that embedded in NCLB and like what I described in the introduction, we can predict that future actions oriented toward desegregation will continue to decrease while the meaning of integration evolves.

The historical perspectives and experiences shared in these sections seem to indicate that along with race relations, class relations were also part of the construction of the district's voluntary integration programs. Many of the different district level and local administrators who oversee school choice options available for parents have worked for the district long enough to have personally experienced the many changes in school enrollment that were brought about by court-ordered desegregation. Many of the administrators and community advisors either raised issues of social class directly or seemed to imply class issues as they spoke about the implementation practices of the different school choice policies. One of the administrators I talked with said he has a sense sometimes that they have a system of haves and have nots.

> There is the magnet school, and then there is the not, and there is the open enrollment, and then there is the not, so that what happens is that you have these programs that become haves and have nots.

Class relations create systems of haves and have nots, be it by material resources, education, or cultural capital. These administrators seem to want to support equitable outcomes for all students in this large, urban district, and in many cases are just as stuck in the social relations organizing and shaping their everyday worlds as the parents in the district.

The addition of NCLB's public school choice requirements to Deluca's existing choice programs further complicates an already complex bureaucratic process of allocating seats in classrooms in the increasingly overcrowded district. NCLB requires that the worst performing students in the lowest performing schools be given priority should their parents exercise their right to request a transfer to a higher performing school. With the exception of annual permits such as child care permits, other choice options offered in the district allow students to remain at the school of choice for the duration of that level of schooling (i.e., magnet programs and open enrollment). Since parents who participate in school choice options other than the district's magnet programs are already choosing the better nonmagnet schools, schools with good reputations, there is not much room left to accommodate the transfer requirements of NCLB. Charter schools — the other transfer option included in the NCLB public school requirements — make up a very small percentage of schools in the district, have application processes of their own, usually have waiting lists, and have raised concerns that they may contribute to social stratification (Wells et al., 1999).

Moreover, the school choice transfer options of NCLB can conflict with existing desegregation and voluntary integration plans. The NCLB act states that school choice transfers must be offered even if it means that districts need to seek court approval for possible amendments to the judicial orders (U.S. Department of Education, 2004). For a district like Deluca, this presents a problem because the court order under which the district operates its voluntary integration plan states that there should not be an undue burden of travel for minority students. The only available space for NCLB transfers may be in schools a great distance from students' neighborhood schools establishing the very lengthy trips the court disallows.

Piecing together some of the history of school choice and its current grounding in neoliberalism with the district's history with voluntary integration and its organization of school choice, this chapter portrays the messiness and complexity of public school choice in Deluca USD. Lack of adequate funding and space has inhibited the district from expanding its voluntary integration program and creating more magnet schools. It can be expected that similar conditions will impede the full implementation of NCLB school choice requirements. While NCLB may intend to provide choice for the have nots, those families that the act purports to help in reality have limited options. Neoliberal and neoconservative promises that higher achievement results when parents can choose among schools means nothing when there is no place for the lowest-performing students to go. Thus it is important to recognize not just the strengths and real consequences of neoliberal and neoconservative policies but the regional and local struggles and renegotiations taking place around policy technologies and practices (Gandin and Apple, 2003) during the implementation process.

2

BUREAUCRATIC STRUCTURES, PRIVILEGE, AND DISCRIMINATION: PARENTS NAVIGATE THE APPLICATION PROCESS

Whereas I discussed the historical development of choice options in Deluca USD in the last chapter, there is another level of institutional organization constructing parents' participation in school choice in the district — one not often explored. The bureaucratic organization of text-based communication with parents about school choice is where we can better see how race and class relations make their way into the school choice processes and practices constructing (and constructed by) parents' participation in the district's choice options. The perspectives and experiences shared during interviews suggested that along with race relations, class relations privileging those with more material, social, and linguistic resources were also part of the construction of the district's voluntary integration programs. In this chapter I bring forth an analysis of a particularly key document, the magnet school brochure and accompanying application form that parents in Deluca USD must make sense of and complete to apply successfully for a magnet school choice program. By looking closely at the magnet school application form (its production, organization, distribution, and content), it is possible to see that the document assumes much of its readers: an advanced facility in reading and comprehension skills; an understanding of schools' curriculum, instruction, and assessment practices; the broader goals of voluntary integration programs; and class-based resources, such as transportation, easy and accessible communication, and flexible time schedules. In a diverse urban context, the implications of these kinds of assumptions have the effect of privileging parents who are white, middle-class, English-speaking, and more educated over parents who may be less educated, not native English speakers, poor, and unfamiliar with formal documents. Consequently, the application text itself becomes active in constructing and maintaining class and racial disparities in Deluca's magnet school program and among families.

THE MAGNET SCHOOL BROCHURE

Deluca USD needed to implement its voluntary integration program in ways that would provide access for students from Predominately Minority Population (PMP) school communities to these new magnet schools, while offering programs that would attract enough white families to help the district meet the integration guidelines established by the court. Deluca began its efforts in 1978 with a small number of magnet schools and over the years has added many more, requiring the district to refine how it promotes the voluntary integration programs and application processes. The magnet school brochure advertising the voluntary integration program that the district provides for parents has taken on different styles and forms over the years. In the next sections I take a detailed look at some of the recent formatting changes along with situating the brochure and application form in parents' school choice decision-making.

Cable Television Programming

For five weeks each year, the district airs a video on local cable television that highlights the magnet program and explains the application process that parents should follow to choose magnet schools for their children. These televised promotions for magnet school programs are not available on regular network television channels, making the video information only accessible for the families that can afford cable television. The three videos viewed for this study varied as different schools were featured year to year, but the basic information about the district's program did not vary significantly across the three different years analyzed. One video shows how the district describes the magnet program and illustrates the information the video provides viewers:

> Host #1: It's easy to get involved in the district's magnet school program and the educational choice offered there. The only requirement is an interest in the specialty field offered at the

magnet center and the willingness to work hard for academic success. There are two types of magnet schools in the district's program. One concentrates on a particular curriculum, such as math, science, or language arts. The other uses a special teaching method, such as fundamental or alternative. And curiously, there are two purposes to the magnet program. First, this is a way for district students to participate in a voluntary integrated educational study, and second, the magnet program gives parents and students the chance to learn more about the fields [in] which they are interested. And once you choose which school you want your child to attend, you get an application booklet and you fill it out. Now this year all students at the district's schools will have the brochure mailed to their homes. Brochures will also be available at every local school, too, and it's simply that easy.

Within this short statement are key messages to parents. First, the host states that students must have "the willingness to work hard," implying that students not willing to work hard will not meet the requirements, and that students are working for *academic* success. Notions of discipline and ability, traditionally associated with academic achievement, underlie the statement and help define the magnet school program. The video also sidesteps the actual purpose of the magnet school program by using the more ambiguous phrase "voluntary integrated educational study" versus stating that the intent is to promote racial integration of the student population. The video indicates that the brochures are being mailed home to students, which was in fact a new policy in the district that year. Additionally, the video states that once a parent makes a choice, getting the brochure and filling it out is an easy process. As the parents' stories will show, "simply that easy" it is not.

Change in the Application Brochure

The videos mention the district's application brochure. Both old and new brochures were written by the Department of School Integration (DSI), which is in charge of Deluca USD's voluntary integration program. In 1996, the department made major changes in the design and distribution of the Deluca's magnet school brochure.

The original brochure. For years, elementary and middle school students brought home the *Opportunities for Success* brochure. They were available for parents in English and Spanish at all K–12 schools and would be translated into other languages as needed. The brochure promotes magnet schools as "special environments for learning" (see Figure 2). Not only is this consistent with the historical representation of magnet

---

Introduction

The District has been at the forefront of offering exciting educational choices to its residents. Two of these choices are the Magnet and Transportation to Participating Schools (TSP) Programs. From kindergarten to twelfth grade, your child may participate in a voluntary integration program while pursuing his or her academic interests in a special environment for learning. All participating students take the required coursework necessary for promotion and graduation, and have the opportunity to meet all requirements for entrance to the state's universities.

All integration programs, including Magnet and TPS, were established by court order to address the five harms of racial isolation:
• Low Academic Achievement
• Low Self-esteem
• Lack of Access to Post-Secondary Opportunities
• Interracial Hostility and Intolerance
• Overcrowded Conditions

Take time to review the following pages and decide whether any of the programs fit your child's individual needs. We think you will agree that these programs are choices that work - for students, parents, the community and the nation.

Sample from district application brochure with pseudonyms.

Figure 2. Sample of Introduction from the *Opportunities for Success* Brochure

programs discussed earlier, it implies that because magnet schools are special, they are likely better, thereby helping the district attract families' participation in the court-ordered voluntary integration program.

The original brochure was a 27-page booklet and included pictures and graphics to break up the text space. There were a few pages that provided information about the various magnet programs (such as International Studies, Science and Technology, Performing Arts, and Gifted Magnets), the nonmagnet integration program, transportation, and how to apply, all in a "most frequently asked questions" format. A map was included that provided approximate locations of magnet schools throughout the district. Addresses and phone numbers were provided for *all* magnet schools.

The redesigned brochure. Having heard that not everyone was receiving the old brochure through the original distribution plan, the DSI recognized that the district would be out of compliance with the court order if access to the magnet program was found to be inequitable. The department decided that brochures would be mailed to each student's home.

The state pays for 80% of the district's integration costs, and Deluca USD pays the remaining 20%. The amount of money available for mailing the brochures was limited, and because there were over 600,000 students, postage would be costly. To save on this expense, the brochure was redesigned to be smaller in size and have fewer pages. The descriptions of the various magnet school themes were removed and put into a separate booklet, available only as a counter copy at local schools. In place of descriptions, all the magnet schools were listed by theme in a four-page table with school name, nearest high school, phone number, grade levels, the number of openings, magnet capacity, and the number of applications received the previous year.

The new brochure's introduction contained a statement about the five harms of racial isolation. An administrator told me that it was added by the DSI so that "parents would have to read it and know that this was an integration program." Supporting the same statement made in the video excerpt, the administrator said there were two purposes for magnet schools. One was to have special learning centers with special themes and special approaches, because, "the court wanted magnets that would attract all the various ethnicities, racial groups, into the program. That's why it allowed these different kinds of programs." The other purpose was to provide an opportunity for a voluntary integrated education. The administrator said that including the information about the harms of racial isolation was "to really try to reinforce to parents what this was about." Figure 2 shows how the information is presented to the parents in the brochure.

The new introduction states that students can take courses that meet requirements for graduation and college entrance. In the latest year's video analyzed for the study, magnet schools are mentioned in connection to higher education. An administrator from the DSI is featured saying:

> Our magnet schools are designed to meet the needs of all students who attend and wish to go on to higher education. Our magnet schools are not comprehensive high schools, therefore, do not have all the extracurricular activities, but the students will receive types of programs and classes that they need to continue on into higher education.

If the message in the introduction and on the video is to encourage parents and students affected by the harms of racial isolation to apply for magnet programs to increase their opportunities for college access, those statements could be misleading. The integration formulas established in the court order reserved 30% or 40% of the spaces in magnet schools for white applicants. With white students making up less than 11% of the student population in Deluca USD during the study, they are proportionately favored in the district's magnet school selection process. While it is admirable that Deluca might want to promote magnet schools as a means for college access to its 89% minority student population, because there are so few magnet schools in proportion to the total number of schools in the district, this path to higher education remains quite limited.

Wanting to include as much information as possible about the application process, the new brochure was designed using bullets, with some text boldface, underlined, or boxed, and the character size was reduced to 10 point (and in some places even smaller). The district also needed to advertise its new charter schools and the dates and times the district video would air, and to supply information for special education students who wished to apply for magnet schools; such additional information was added to the back cover of the brochure. (A current version of the brochure now lists the schools designated Program Improvement schools by the No Child Left Behind Act and information about requesting transfers out of those schools.)

For the new brochures, the department contracted outside the district with a private business forms printing company. The business forms company is able to take all the individual information from student records provided by the district's Information Systems Department and coordinate the student data to print on the brochure, print individual letters to parents about the outcomes of their application, and print out individual transportation route assignments. Because of budgetary restrictions over the years, the district had been slow to upgrade its technological support. With the huge numbers of applicants and the complexity of allocating students to various magnet schools, it was evident from one of the administrators I spoke with that the DSI truly welcomed the new technologies provided by the private business forms company.

The new brochure, then, that arrived at the homes of families was addressed to parents by name, with each student's name, address, sex, birth date, grade, and resident school preprinted inside the application brochure. There were no longer graphics or descriptions of the schools, and the text was crowded with small type. Making the changes to the brochure may have gotten more application brochures into the hands of more parents, thereby making distribution more equitable, but clarity of and access to the information in the brochure suffered.

New Application Deadline

One of the major changes that came about with the new brochure was moving up the application deadline. The old brochure had a deadline date in the middle of March, whereas the new application procedure set the date for the third week in January. A community advisor explained the timeline the following way:

> Well, our schools are on winter break from December. And then by the time they come back from winter break, there's about a week left before the deadline for the magnet application. So when you get the application, you have a week before Christmas, [before] the winter break, and then I guess you could mull it over during the break. You have no opportunity to go visit schools, because they're all closed. And then when the schools come back in session, you have about a week I guess, if you have time to take off your job that week and go on a visit, you know, that's the only opportunity you have.

Two different administrators said that the application date was moved up in response to parent requests. One said that parents wanted to be notified sooner whether they got into the magnets, because if they were going to do open enrollment or other kinds of options, they wanted to know about the magnets first. Moving the application date up allowed the DSI to get everything done so they could notify parents sooner. The other administrator was more specific about which parents had made the requests:

> Those dates were in response to outcry from private school parents who wanted to be notified before they had to pay the tuition. So now you can have your cake and eat it. The same parents who pushed to be notified early enough so that they wouldn't have to make a down payment on [tuition], are now the same parents who are complaining about the narrow window of opportunity.

While those parents are not likely all the same parents, parents who are active choosers have found it too short a time period from when the brochures arrive in the mail to when the applications are due. An administrator in the DSI said that getting the brochures mailed out in

December is about the soonest they can do it because that is when schools settle down in their schedules and programs, have their records updated, and would be ready to start tours, and so on. But those are reasons that support the needs of the schools and the DSI, not increased access for families.

As the application brochure makes clear, there are various things parents should do before sending in their application, such as call the magnet school coordinator and get information on meetings, tours, and uniform requirements, check transportation routes to see if the bus pick up and drop off locations are a reasonable distance for their children to get to each day, and if considering a gifted magnet, confirm with the school principal that their child qualifies. These are examples of how the application brochure is actually organizing and coordinating a specific work process for parents, but it is a work process that must be done within a very certain time frame.

COORDINATING THE SELECTION PROCESS

Selecting students for the voluntary integration program is done by lottery and is based on the integration formulas established by the court. The explanation provided in the brochure about how the integration formulas work in conjunction with Deluca's complicated school selection process is not clear and can exclude some families from magnet school assignment. For example, Figure 3 shows how the district explains its priority points system in the brochure.

What is *not explained* is that the more points an applicant is assigned, the better his or her chances are of getting accepted to a magnet school. An applicant who qualifies in all categories (either by matriculation or by three years of being on a wait listing) can be assigned up to 23 priority points. Throughout the study, both parents and community advisors commented on the confusion generated by the "magnet points" (priority points) and the district's system for allocating those points.

When students do not get accepted into a magnet school, parents sometimes contact the school and ask for an explanation. Therefore the application process must be well understood by those working in magnet schools. A school administrator explained how the magnet selection process would work for parents interested in his school, El Rancho Middle School, which includes a middle school gifted magnet program:

> Well, the magnet school [selection process] is all done through central offices. Any parent who lives within the district is eligible

---

Magnet Selection - Priority Point System

The priority point system for magnets is based on the court-ordered reduction of the harms of racial isolation. Once information on the application is verified, the District's Information Systems Department, through a computer process, automatically assigns priority points to each applicant.

Points	Rationale

12   **Matriculation**
Applicants who have completed one magnet program and apply to continue in a program at the next level, receive 12 matriculation points. These points are assigned for one year only at the time of matriculation.

4-12   **Waiting List**
Applicants who have been on a valid magnet waiting list and are not already enrolled in a magnet program, receive 4 points for the school year. They may also receive 4 points for each of the two consecutive previous years, up to a maximum of 12 points, four points per year. There is no credit given for submitting an application, or for applying to a program for which the applicant is ineligible or for which the application is late. Applicants currently enrolled in a magnet program are not eligible to receive waiting list points when applying for a new magnet program.

4   **Predominately Minority Population (PMP) Schools**
Applicants whose resident District school is designated PMP by the District, receive 4 points.

4   **Overcrowded**
Applicants whose resident school is designated overcrowded by District criteria, receive 4 points.

3   **Sibling**
If an applicant is applying to the same magnet in which a brother or sister will be continuing, he/she receives 3 points.

Note:
Each magnet's openings are determined by the need to maintain a racially balanced enrollment and by available space.

Sample from district application brochure with pseudonyms.

Figure 3.   Sample section from District Magnet School Application Brochure

to apply for the magnet school. The only difference from our school and most other magnet schools is that because it's a gifted and high ability magnet, the child must either be tested as, identified as a gifted student by a school district psychologist, or have scored in the seventh, eighth, or ninth stanines[1] in overall reading and math. So there isn't any other way. And then you're assigned points based upon a number of criteria. You get points if you got a sibling already in the school. You get points if you've applied in the past and not been accepted. You get points if you come from an overcrowded school. You get points if you come from what's considered to be a predominantly nonwhite school. Which, the last category almost covers every school in the district now. And then there's a random selection made by computer. And then everybody's name is pulled, essentially, and what you do is you end up with a waiting list to get into the school. The only other thing is that we must be no more than 40% white, no more than 70% minority.[2] We happen to be what they call a 60:40 school. There are other schools that are 70:30. But since the school population of the district falls about 11% white, other schools have fallen into that category [70:30] as well. At this school, we've always been able to maintain at least a 40% white. It's not been difficult.

The enrollment data for El Rancho Middle School shows how the magnet school application process results in different racial/ethnic ratios for the gifted magnet as compared to the non-magnet part of the school (see Table 1).

White and Asian students comprise 71.1% of the students in the gifted magnet program, which illustrates how the integration formulas (along with gifted identification) determine who will be accepted into the school's magnet program.

In order to achieve the integration ratios required of the magnet schools, the DSI requires that students' racial/ethnic identity be indicated. The district provided a multiracial category on the new brochure but emphasized in the application form instructions that parents must

TABLE 1. El Rancho Middle School: Racial/ethnic enrollment percentages in 1998

	Asian Students	Black Students	Latino Students	White Students	Other Minority Students	Magnet Applications Received	Expected Openings
El Rancho Non-Magnet	8.5	34.8	35.0	19.1	1.9	—	—
El Rancho Gifted Magnet	29.9	19.3	7.3	41.2	2.3	521	156

also check off one of the federally identified categories. A DSI administrator told me that it does not help the district comply with the court order "if everyone's checking multiracial." The administrator said that the district must keep the racial/ethnic categories in order to compare the number of white students to that of nonwhite students, adding that with the declining white population and the court-established racial integration formula, the DSI had to include the immigrant Russian, Armenian, and Iranian students with the white student population in order to maintain the 10.5 percent white population that they have.

The integration formulas help construct the magnet choice context so that every applicant will be considered for selection based on race/ethnicity. This was reinforced in each of the three years' videos with statements such as the following:

> Host: But remember, your chances of being accepted to your first choice school depend on the following: the number of grade openings at the magnet, the number of applicants, and the race, ethnicity categories for that grade. If you should have any questions you may want to call the magnet of your choice and ask about the expected number of openings upcoming for your child's specific grade and ethnicity category.

Community advisors have reported back to the DSI that people in the school communities are figuring out that is easier to get into the magnet schools if you are white and that they have heard some Latino parents say that they think about checking off the box on the application that would identify their children as white or multiracial. In fact, in Chapter 4, a Latino mother states this herself. A DSI administrator told me that the department is concerned that some Latino parents consider listing their racial identity as white but added that Latino parents are not applying in their representative numbers. During an interview, a Latino community advisor talked about parents' confusion with the brochure and the points system. The advisor commented that "it's not enough" to get the brochure to every parent because immigrant parents who do not understand the language in which the brochure is written would not know how to use the application even if it does include a wide variety of information about school choice programs.

Gifted Verification

Many of the parents in my study have children who had been identified as gifted. There is literature on gifted education (Sapon-Shevin, 1994) and tracking (Oakes, 1985) that shows how gifted education programs can be a source of inequities. Staiger's powerful study of a partial-site gifted high school magnet captured how the magnet "ended up a tool for preserving white privilege rather than for attaining racial equality" (Staiger, 2004, p. 180). What this book can help us understand is that past policies that established some magnet school themes based on gift-edness or high ability and high achievement partly determined how parents, some of whom have children identified as gifted, participate in such inequitable practices.

The requirements for qualifying for gifted magnets have not changed from the old to the new brochure; only the organization of the informa-tion in the brochure has changed. What is required for verification is, nonetheless, an important issue for parents wanting to take advantage of that particular type of magnet school option. The information neces-sary to verify that a child qualifies for a gifted magnet program is shown in Figure 4.

Obtaining this kind of information for gifted verification takes time for parents and local school personnel and is further complicated if most of the district schools are closed for winter vacation for three weeks during the period from when parents receive the brochure and when the application is due. The administrator in the DSI believes that the vacation is "an upside not a downside for parents" because their children will be home from school making it easier to figure out what they might want to do for school choice. This administrator believed that if they get the brochure to parents early enough, parents "can make the calls that they need to make, and when they come back from vaca-tion, they can do what they need to do." The administrator also said that their office is only closed for one week during the winter vacation and that there are people in the office to answer questions for parents.

So while the administrator in the integration department seemed convinced that the vacation coming in the middle of the application period was a good thing for parents, an administrator in another dis-trict office responsible for verifying gifted status, disagreed:

> Well, see, we have no control over their dates. We don't support those dates. We were never even informed about them. Yes, the window is too narrow. It really is. And that's why there are so many different ways to qualify for [gifted] magnet. It has to be that way. And if you study magnet programs across the states, you will not see this kind of verification for the most part at all. Because it's simply too much …

There are problems with different administrative departments over-seeing different parts of the application process. The community advisor

---

Gifted/High Ability Magnet Criteria

Applicants to gifted/high ability centers must be verified as meeting one of the following criteria prior to the second week in January:

A. Be identified as gifted by a Deluca USD school psychologist in the intellectual, high achievement, specific academic or creative ability categories.

OR

B. Have national stanine scores of 7, 8, or 9 on standardized tests in both total reading or total mathematics.

OR

C. Demonstrate the ability to meet ALL FOUR of these critical thinking and problem solving skills in their primary language:
  • Explain meanings or relationships among facts, information or concepts that demonstrate depth and complexity.
  • Formulate new ideas or solutions and elaborate on the information.
  • Use alternative methods in approaching new or unfamiliar mathematical problems.
  • Use extensive vocabulary easily and accurately to express creative ideas or demonstrate creative ideas non-verbally.

Verification that the applicant meets these four characteristics will be determined by the principal of the school your child is currently attending.

Applicants currently enrolled in an DUSD school: No parent request for verification is necessary. Upon receipt of the application, the District will automatically check the applicant's eligibility through school records.

Sample from district application brochure with pseudonyms.

Figure 4. Gifted/High Ability Magnet Criteria

elaborated on the problems parents encounter if they want to have their child evaluated in order to qualify for a gifted magnet:

> That's a big issue. You know, gifted testing is done by the school psychologist. Testing of special education students or students with special needs, the school psychologist must test, assess, and evaluate those students. And that testing is mandated. So if you want your child tested for gifted or highly gifted, you can wait a year, you can wait two years, you can wait five years. There's no law saying that the district must test in a specific time period. So in light of that, the gifted testing has kind of been pushed off to the side. And when the school psychologist comes to your school once

a week, then they're going to do that special ed testing, which is mandated, and put your gifted kids to the side.

The advisor goes on to explain that if applications for gifted magnets are due in January, and if a student has not been tested by January, that could be another year of missed opportunity for that student. This advisor told me that many parents complained to the district after they had been asking for testing for months and months and nothing was done:

> And what they did last May, they did a gifted roundup where they had ten psychologists come into school on Saturday and test these thousands of kids — well, maybe not thousands. Hundreds of kids in a kind of a gifted marathon roundup with students all in one fell swoop …. And I question how accurate was that testing when you're doing a revolving door type of testing. Because you really have to take your time. And I'm wondering, were twenty kids sat down in a room and said, "Okay, here's the paper. Okay. Pass this out." Or were they actually done one-on-one? And I think the former is more likely than the latter.

The comments on gifted verification demonstrate how discourses can operate within broader social relations and institutional structures and practices — in this case, testing for gifted programs — to shape and determine how parents get access to the different schools of choice for their children. The achievement discourse discussed in the introduction is embedded within the tests that district students take as well as within gifted instructional programs. The procedures for meeting the needs of gifted students compete with the legal mandates the district must address to serve students with special educational needs. School psychologists are in short supply in the district and do not have the time to respond to schools' and parents' requests for testing both gifted students and students in consideration for special education services. Ensuring equity and access for students with special needs is complicated by district staffing shortages and budgeting problems.

The verification process is a requirement for advancing in the selection process for a gifted magnet school. Even if the verification is obtained, gifted students are often placed on waiting lists. These are existing conditions of the district's voluntary integration plan. The district has since added three more gifted magnets, I assume in part due to pressure brought by the more politically active gifted parents.

I could add allocation of classroom space, racial/ethnic integration formulas, and so on, but the point is to see what is happening in the "doings" of different people working with the different textual representations of students and schools (for example, high vs. low test scores) that shape how some parents will have access to choice, and not others.

The textually-mediated choice process can have other effects as well. Instead of thinking critically about public school choice, some parents reading the brochure and application may be lead to understand that their participation in the integration program — one increasingly focused on academic achievement — is a choice that, as Figure 2 states, "works for students, parents, the community, and the nation." Many parents in this study might see some of this social organization. But I suggest that for most parents, all this is located beyond their everyday lives with their children and is known only partially, if known at all. What the district tells parents is that magnet schools are special environments for learning and that they must complete an application and mail it in by the deadline if they wish to be considered for selection to a magnet school of their choice. The district needs parents, particularly white parents, to do this, so it can stay in compliance with the court order.

ACCESS TO THE VOLUNTARY INTEGRATION PROGRAM

Each year Deluca receives approximately 70,000 applications, and of those, only about 18% will actually be accepted at a magnet school. The rest end up on wait lists and have to reapply year after year. One of the administrators in the DSI explained that there are actually several waiting lists: a First Choice On-Time Wait List, an Other Interested List, and a Late Wait List. The first is for the applications received on time and for which that school was the parent's first choice. Students earn waiting list points only from this list. While many of the white parents in the study understood the intricacies of the selection process, such as waiting list points only being assigned for a first choice school application, the poorer minority parents in the study did not. There are thousands of students on all these lists, but only those on the top of the First Choice On-Time Wait List would likely be selected for an opening.

At the start of Deluca's voluntary integration program in 1978, only 2% of the district's students were enrolled in magnet programs. At the completion of this study, there were over 150 magnet schools enrolling over 45,000 students in a district of more than 600,000 students. Of the total student population in the district, 6.6% currently attend magnet schools — the very schools Deluca USD promotes as its most successful schools. Table 2 compares the differences among racial/ethnic groups' acceptance into the magnet program from 1978, when the district first began reporting enrollment data for schools of choice, to the enrollment data through 1998 (the children of the parents in this study are included in the 1998 enrollment data). While there is improvement in the percentage of students participating in magnet programs over 20 years, it is still a small offering of "good" schools to parents who wish to participate in the program.

It is evident that certain racial groups have been privileged in the selection process since the inception of the magnet programs. The district did find money, however limited, to mail the *Opportunities for Success* application brochure to over 600,000 students' homes in the hope of making the process more equitable. Regardless, given the 70,000 applications received each year, thousands of families will apply for their children and never get selected. Table 2 makes clear that a vast majority of those students not selected for participation in the voluntary integration program will be from Latino and African American families.

It is a powerful statement when the school choice brochure is sent to every student's home and says to parents that the magnet schools are excellent schools and address the harms of racial isolation. Just as powerful is the lack of a statement about the remaining 75% of Deluca USD's schools not a part of the magnet school program. What is left unsaid in the text also shapes how parents understand the meaning of integration.

PARENTS' READINGS OF THE MAGNET BROCHURE AND APPLICATION

Once parents receive the application, they are left alone with the form to make sense of it. Many parents experience "ordinary problems" like confusing format, deadlines, and so on and yet are able to navigate the process and successfully accomplish school choice. The parents in the study each had unique experiences with the magnet application, from forgetting to sign it and having it "kicked back," to driving the application to the district office so it would not get lost in the mail. But if the application engages parents of different racial groups and parents with children of different achievement levels in dialogue with the text differently, the text can position some parents to go forward in the magnet school choice process but not others. As parents discussed the application, it became clear how the application brochure and the selection process it describes contribute to the privileging of some families while excluding others.

TABLE 2. Racial/Ethnic Enrollment in Deluca USD and at Schools of Choice

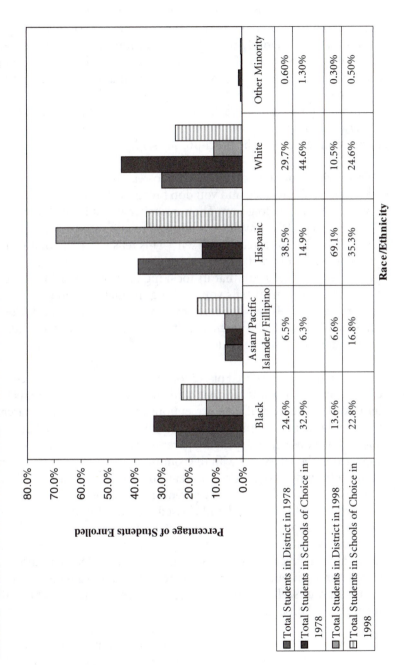

	Black	Asian/Pacific Islander/Fillipino	Hispanic	White	Other Minority
Total Students in District in 1978	24.6%	6.5%	38.5%	29.7%	0.60%
Total Students in Schools of Choice in 1978	32.9%	6.3%	14.9%	44.6%	1.30%
Total Students in District in 1998	13.6%	6.6%	69.1%	10.5%	0.30%
Total Students in Schools of Choice in 1998	22.8%	16.8%	35.3%	24.6%	0.50%

Race/Ethnicity

Percentage of Students Enrolled

Two white college-educated mothers expressed their frustrations with the text of the application brochure. They were sensitive that the process could be even more difficult for noneducated parents. One parent, Karen, works closely with the city's minority communities. She said, "I don't think it is a parent-friendly booklet .... [With] an average of a sixth-grade education, how are they gonna be able to read this? They can't read this. They get very turned off by it."

Bonnie, a parent and a teacher in the district, was a strong advocate for her own Latino students to participate in the magnet school program. Commenting on the brochure she said,

> This is dependent all on being able to read. I mean, so if you're not very well-educated and you don't read the language, you have nothing by which to go on. They may or may not be able to read it in Spanish. It's complicated enough reading it in English .... This is saying "research it yourself." This tells you that what you have to figure out is if you're interested in .... Haggerty Elementary School, it tells you that its local high school is Karlin. What does that tell you? It tells you nothing. It doesn't even give you addresses here. It says, "Before making your selection, call the magnet school." These parents can't even call the school their kids are at in some cases. They don't know what questions to ask.

Karen and Bonnie secured places for their children in magnet schools because the new brochure format made it more likely that parents like them would be successful. The perceptions they shared of those parents who would have more problems with the text were directed at less-educated or non-English speaking parents. Although this was partially supported in the interviews with the community advisor from the Latino community, and in some ways by a Latino parent in the study, the critiques by these middle-class white parents reinforce how the department is contributing to racialized and classed readings by the very parents positioned to be privileged in the application process.

Manuel is a non-English speaking immigrant parent who saves the many papers he receives from his children's schools. During our interviews he brought out weekly progress reports, Stanford Nine test score reports, and miscellaneous school-related papers. He said about the magnet school brochure:

> *Pero yá me llego, sí, pero no venía en español. Oh, ya lo tiré esa cosa. Sí, sí yá me acordé no más que creí que era del bus, porque como allí dice Transportation y no sé qué. Ajá, si no aquí mire aquí dice*

"Transportacion." .... *Creí que era del, pero sí yá me llegó eso, si yá nos llegó eso, pero creí que era del bus. Es que, o sea, si ustedes ahorita no me dicen, como viene puro en inglés, yo cuando viene en inglés, o sea, por más que trato de quebrarme la cabeza y no [lo puedo leer].*

I got it, but it wasn't in Spanish. Oh, I threw it away. Yes, it's just that I thought it was about the bus because I read that it said "Transportation" and I don't know what. Yes, look at this. It says "Transportation." .... I got that, yes I did, just that I thought it was for the bus. I mean, if you hadn't told me right now, since it's all in English, when it comes in English, I mean as much as I rack my brain, I can't [read it.]

Manuel's children do not use district transportation to get to school, so he might not have read any further or applied for a magnet school even if the brochure were in Spanish. Still, it raises the issue that although the Department of School Integration prints and distributes the *Opportunities for Success* brochure in Spanish, apparently there still are problems identifying which families need it in English and which in Spanish.

Parents who do need to consider transportation told me that there are problems with the information and directions about transportation services provided with the integration programs. One of the community advisors told me that parents have many difficulties with transportation routes and believes the problem is in the application brochure:

Well, in little teeny, tiny print it says on the *Opportunities for Success* application "Please check the bus route. Because we establish routes. We won't change it." Well, you really have to search and read every single word on that page. Ninety-nine percent of parents skip that part. Unless they've had past experience, they don't know to call transportation and investigate the bus route. The bus routes for magnet schools are set .... and they are not flexible.

In past years, the DSI did have to bring transportation costs down due to budget cuts and during that time it implemented the "pre-established stops" policy. Unfortunately, inadequate transportation funding contributes to the existing social inequities and further reduces the school choice opportunities for many children. A side note here: the NCLB act requires districts to provide transportation for the low-performing students seeking to transfer to higher-performing schools, but only while the resident school remains a program improvement school.[3]

Race and Class in the Application Text

Parents interact with the application text, bringing their own experiences, understandings, and racial, ethnic, gender, class, identities to their understanding of the text. Comments about the harms of racial isolation statement were cogent examples of how the application text is read and responded to differently by parents of different racial and social class backgrounds and interests.

Robin is an African American single parent on welfare who recently completed her associate's degree. When she spoke about the application brochure, she pointed to the harms of racial isolation statement and questioned why the district would associate low academic achievement and low self-esteem with the people in her community. She does not believe the magnet program addresses the harms identified.

> It doesn't address low academic achievement, low self-esteem, lack of access to post-secondary opportunity, interracial hostility, intolerance, overcrowded schools — you figure you send your baby to this school where she's getting a better curriculum and everything, and maybe. I can't say if her self-esteem is any better. Low academic achievement: but some kids still go to better schools and still get D's. So we're looking at something more here, um, interracial hostility and intolerance, overcrowded conditions. Well, that's still in some of the schools that these kids are being transported to.

Mary is white, married, and college educated. She lives in a racially diverse part of the city where there are few white families. Her comment below about the harms statement captures what I think may be an often unspoken yet honest interpretation that white parents could make when reading the brochure. Discussing the court's use of the harms of isolation in establishing the voluntary integration program and, subsequently, the district's inclusion of the statement in the application brochure, Mary said:

> It certainly makes racial isolation sound pretty bad, doesn't it? And if I were black and my kid's in an all black school, I'd say I'd better get out of there fast. Well, you know, I probably would read this and I'd probably not think too much about it because to me, I would think that this applied to black parents and, you know, all

black schools, and I wouldn't think that it necessarily applied to white schools, particularly. Now, it might lead to racial hostility and intolerance to go to an all white school. But you know, I don't think white parents at white schools worry so much about low academic achievement and low self-esteem and lack of access, because that's something that as white people you've never really had to face. So I'd probably read this and go, well, okay, that's nice for the black parents. That's not really my concern. My concern is that my child go to the absolute best school, and I don't care who else is there. I mean, to some extent, but certainly if it's ethnically diverse I'd consider that a plus and not a minus. I think I always thought that the fact that it was established for integration reasons was nice. It benefits me, but I'm not really the reason it was established. I'm just profiting by it, you know, by being able to live here and send my child to the magnet school.

As a single white mother, Suzanne's bottom line is similar to Mary's:

I don't sit and read this whole thing anymore. My understanding is that the whole magnet program was conceived to help with integration. I mean, that was the whole point of it. So they're trying to, they're selling the purpose of the magnet program. I don't care. I want the magnet program for my own purposes. So, fine. Terrific. And, let's get to the meat of it for my concern. So, you know, you don't have to sell me on integration.

DSI administrators' concerns about complying with the court order were not lost on some in the parent community. Comments by mothers Bonnie and Meryl, both of whom are white and middle-class, were clear that they thought the inclusion of the harms statement was meant for another audience.

Bonnie: I think it was to cover their butts with the federal Department of Education and Equal Opportunity [sic]. Because people probably were saying "Well, magnets are not equal opportunity," and so they're addressing it right here. Magnet schools were to address integration issues. Why do you think they were called magnets? They weren't low self-esteem. Hello. And just 'cause you're a member of a majority does not automatically exclude you from low self-esteem or low academic achievement.

Meryl: It means nothing much to you. It's their way of covering their butt. It's saying that it's basically done for integration and harmony, you know, racial harmony. But it really doesn't mean anything to you except for, what they're saying is, that this is why they have to ask, you know, to choose what background your child is.

If the district administrators hoped that by including the harms statement in the brochure's introduction they would encourage parents to reflect on segregation and racial isolation, I doubt these are the kinds of interpretations that they anticipated.

Priority Points and Equity

Another important feature associated with the application process is the priority points system shown in Figure 3. Meryl's work as a parent volunteer has provided her with opportunities to learn a great deal about her local schools as well as the district's many programs. Meryl commented about the application:

And then it says about charter schools. I don't think most parents really understand the difference. I'm a parent who goes to meetings and I make it my business to know the difference between these, but even so I don't feel that I know exactly what all the charter school offers that makes it different than a non-charter school. And the thing that's confusing about that, too, some of the charter schools, a few of them you have to apply for points, I think, but the majority of them say you have to apply separately, do not use this application. How confusing is that?

Parents' comments provide further evidence of how the application continues to differentiate parent readers. The community advisor from the Latino community is aware of the difficulty of deciphering the application brochure and tries to help Latino parents understand the priority points system:

Most of the Latino parents don't know about the points. They feel that they made the application, they sent it, and they never get anything. [I tell them] "You should get a letter saying yes or no. And then you can apply the following year. And you have to understand that by being on the waiting list you accumulate points." [Parents say] "No, I didn't know that. And I didn't know that I had to apply again." [I say] You have to apply again and again. And they give you certain points. The limit is three years, then you got four, four, four points, you got twelve points for that. So submit them to be on the waiting list. You just have to wait for three years.

The Predominantly Minority Population (PMP) schools actually generate priority points for resident students who wish to leave a PMP school and apply to a magnet program. It is possible that, at the time the court determined the PMP designation for those schools, there was a reason to assign points to applicants wishing to leave minority schools for more integrated schools. One administrator already noted that the context today has changed. But much like the harms statement, the priority points system and the racial/ethnic formulas printed in the text lead to different interpretations by parents of different racial backgrounds:

Meryl: Okay, then this other, the PMP, Predominantly Minority Population schools. Okay, that's assigned by the district, and you get four points supposedly if you're at a school that isn't predominantly Caucasian, but now what school is nowadays? …. So you get four points for that, but if everybody else gets the four points, it's not really a plus or a minus — it just is.

Karen: And I was surprised where you get points for, you know, being in a school that was mostly minority. And I thought, well, in a way it sounds kind of racist to say, "Okay, well, this is a black school. So we give points so your kid doesn't have to go to this black school." But I guess it's because of the interracial hostility and intolerance, I assume.

Some school integration plans assign points only to students whose transfer from a school would improve the racial balance. That is not the case in Deluca. Any student attending a PMP school gets points for transferring out of that school whether they are white or a student of color. White parents like Meryl and Karen understood the inconsistency of such an allocation.

Parents of color also discussed the allocation formulas and points system. African American, college educated, married, and successful in a family business, Natalie felt that the racial balance formula was not fair for minority students:

There's something wrong with this lottery thing …. I haven't figured out how can you justify having a system that's supposed to be integrated when the [formula] is set up for it not to be balanced? I mean, magnet schools have a predesigned ratio of 40% white and 60% "other." I'm sorry. We're not all the same. "Other" does not classify us all, you know. Why isn't there 20% white, 20% African American, 20% Asian, 20% Hispanic, or 20% whatever else is goin' on in the city at the time, you know? And this "You're not white" [while] the white kid is special because he's in this whole other spot that's just for him, and you guys have to share this small piece of the pie over here. You know. Kids see that. I mean, I see that as a parent.

Among the minority groups enrolling in magnet schools, and in gifted magnet schools in particular, Asian students enjoyed a larger proportional representation in the magnet program. Mimi is Korean, a college-educated single parent, and shares a different view of whether the system is fair:

And so I don't think there is a fairness issue about anything because people who get into magnets are active parents. And active parents, majority of times, they are going to be more of the educated parents. So, therefore, you have more Jewish parents, more white parents, and more Asian parents that's going to be in there. Because they're educated, and they're more informed, therefore, it's fair. But if you're trying to say, "Okay. It's unfair because demographically the kids are not in there." Well, I think, that's just, you know, not interpreting the information correctly. Because the system is fair. Everybody can get in if you apply, and we all went through the same procedure. So most of the parents in there, they seek out, you know, they tried for many years, and they got in there because they're informed. Just because the Latino parents are not in there, does that mean the system is not fair? No. System is fair but they are not informed.

In discussing the magnet school brochure and application process, the mothers quoted above raise issues often discussed in the desegregation literature. Their comments question if integrated magnet schools do in fact address the harms of racial isolation, or impact white parents' understanding of racial inequality. They ask how integration formulas that are centered on whiteness can accomplish equity and equality for people of color, and whether magnet school programs that tend to enroll the children of more educated and involved parents are organized for fair and equal access by all parents.

DISCUSSION

The *Opportunities for Success* brochure is an example of how the discourses of achievement and integration will overlap in the textually-mediated choice process to structure parents' relations with their neighborhood schools and schools of choice. As stated in the previous section, the magnet application brings parents' choice of school into the bureaucracy and what Smith calls the relations of ruling by tying it into students' school records, gifted verification, federally identified racial categories, transportation routes, and compliance to a court-ordered voluntary integration plan. While various other departments in the district add information and language to the application brochure, the district has written the brochure so that the information in the text is accessible in the same way to all readers. In this sense the knowledge available in the text and the language and meanings in the application brochure are intended to be fixed. Newer theoretical understandings about how people "take up" discourses, and how discourses help to shape and are shaped by institutional practices, would suggest otherwise (Bowe et al., 1994; Lopez, 2003).

What the district may see as a simple application procedure is read and responded to differently by parents of different racial and social class backgrounds. Parents, as readers, interact with and enter into these social practices, social relations, as part of the process of choosing schools. The application organizes the "choice work" parents must do as well. The application document, then, becomes an active text in the construction of the school choice process for parents. While I have tried to be careful about identifying numerous discourses, certainly other discourses are part of the application brochure besides an achievement discourse and an integration discourse. The application, when analyzed discursively as a text, can be seen as manipulating and differentiating parent readers; orienting parents' choice work in ways that support the dominant discourses in education.

Desegregation and voluntary integration programs have had a profound impact on the family-school relationship in urban communities, changing how districts and schools view families — by race, by class, by where they live, and often by whether their children are "good" students. The magnet school programs and the texts associated with getting into these programs have also affected how families view one another. Recall how readily the white, middle-class mothers, Bonnie and Karen, interpreted the application brochure through the eyes of minority or immigrant parents.

Texts are a main way that educational institutions communicate with parents and get information to and from parents about their children's schooling. Educational policies and practices incorporating concepts such as *ability, discipline,* and *involvement* regularly find their way into texts written for parents, from report cards to the *Opportunities for Success* brochure. Griffith (1992) states that the surfaces of textual discourse, the texts themselves, shape but do not determine our knowledge and action:

> By locating the text in its production as a set of actual activities, we can bring into view the links between policy and the everyday actions that reaffirm, often without intending to do so, the normative structuring of the relation between families and schools (p. 418).

In the district's efforts to let parents know what the voluntary integration program was about, to make sure the information they were providing parents fitted into the brochure, and to get the application brochure into every parent's hands, the district failed to understand how the choices they made reinforced privileges for those parents who can access and manage dominant discourses and textual practices. None of the information shared with me gave any indication that the district administration overseeing the magnet school program consciously designed the magnet school application text to generate such divergent readings and unintended consequences. Nonetheless, the bureaucratic organization and managerial decisions aimed at compliance with the court-ordered voluntary integration program guidelines created a new set of problems for realizing the program's goals.

It could be argued that the problems of access to the integrated and excellent educational opportunities that magnet schools offer might be solved with increased funding. School integration programs were intended to be educational programs, not transportation programs. However, in large urban districts like Deluca, where transportation costs for integration programs are a heavy burden, just a rise in gasoline prices (as is happening now because of the U.S. war in Iraq) can severely impact voluntary integration program budgets. The added promise of free transportation for students granted public school transfers as a result of NCLB can compound the costs of transportation. So, clearly, for some problems more money would help. But other issues still need to be addressed. The magnet school program brochure is loaded with the discourses of integration, excellence, and achievement and of competing understandings of fairness and access, as well as the inherent relations of race and class. The magnet application text and the polices and practices that put it in place, which were intended to increase access, ostensibly *limited* access for many parents. The district failed to recognize how the magnet program brochure would work for (or against) the families in racially, economically, and subordinated communities.[4]

Moreover, this chapter uncovers how the district's efforts to alleviate segregated schooling were mediated by many managerial and technical processes and practices. Certainly there is need to pay close attention to the new technological practices that districts are employing to manage their voluntary integration programs and magnet school programs. As districts begin to rely on new technologically-based practices to support their communication with parents, as in Deluca's case with a private business form company, or on the internet, as other districts do, these new means of communication will require a sophisticated parent reader, thus further privileging the social, cultural, and linguistic capital of some families over others.

The information learned about the magnet school application brochure reveals the broader racial and class relations, as well as the institutional patterns of privilege and exclusion, found in the production, distribution, and interpretation of a document intended to support the integration of students of different racial and ethnic backgrounds. The textual analysis of the magnet school brochure and application opened a new window, so to speak, from which to view the bureaucratic organization and implementation of the district's voluntary integration program. Yet, there should be a cautionary note here. The analysis also identifies a window of opportunity in which neoliberal choice advocates can shift the discourse from school choice in support of integration to improved academic achievement through school choice. I discuss how this happens in Chapter 5.

3

CHOICE WORK: GETTING ACCESS TO
MAGNET SCHOOLS

A parent choosing a school for his or her child today may not think about the many changes that resulted from the Supreme Court's *Brown v. Board of Education* decision fifty years ago. Yet, central to many of those changes were magnet schools and the notion that schools designed around a special theme could entice parents to choose integrated schools for their children. However, many years have passed and the enticement of magnet schools may now be more about the perceived quality of the schools than the racial and ethnic identities of magnet school students, or even the particular magnet school theme. On the other hand, parents choosing a school for their children today may very well be thinking about the changes resulting from the implementation of the No Child Left Behind Act. Schools, and teachers especially, have been put on notice that the standardized test scores of their students will be available for all to see and for all to judge how well the educators responsible to those students and their school communities are performing their professional duties. NCLB gives parents in low-performing Title I schools the right to transfer their child to another school with higher test scores; it is required that a letter be sent home advising them of such. In this way, NCLB makes the perceived quality of a public school, its teachers, and the performance of its students public. And because the public school choice requirements of NCLB give priority to the lowest-performing students at the lowest-performing schools, the implementation of the new policy could also make public the various ways that existing school choice processes and practices are organized and coordinated by districts. The next chapters should help raise the issue of whether NCLB's new public school choice option, when implemented alongside current choice plans, particularly those developed as voluntary integration programs, will accomplish more access to equal educational opportunity for poor minority and underachieving students in low-performing urban schools.

The stories that unfold in this chapter are centered on magnet school choice because in Deluca USD this is the most popular form of school choice and what the parents talked about most when discussing their school choice experiences. The previous chapters captured the institutional and text-based organization of school choice. To explore further how the parents, mostly mothers, understood and negotiated the socially and textually organized magnet school choice process, this chapter looks at what was happening in parents' everyday worlds (Smith, 1987) as they actually went about making their school choice decisions. While Chapter 2 discussed how parents' interpretations of the magnet application brochure varied, this chapter shows how the work that the application organizes and coordinates for parents results in different choices for and by the different parents. Consequently, this chapter focuses on parents' experiences with the processes and practices of school choice for the district's elementary and secondary magnet schools.

The parents whose stories are shared in this book are only a small number of the many parents the district needs to attract to participate in its voluntary integration program. Most of these parents have a partial understanding of how choice differs for different parents. We know from Chapter 2 that the application is not parent friendly; it lacks specific information about the many magnet schools and forces parents to research schools on their own. Some parents also understood the privileged status that being white brings to magnet school applications. All of these factors set the context for how parents experienced choosing schools in the district.

GETTING INFORMATION ABOUT SCHOOLS

Whether it is the district's videos, or local newspaper articles, or state-developed pamphlets,[1] materials are produced that suggest questions that parents should ask and the things they should look for when choosing a school for their child. The research and information-seeking that these suggestions and questions entail is extensive and time-consuming and requires considerable knowledge of schooling institutions. Parents who were successful in the school choice process depended, in part, upon social networks as an important source of information and support. Parent networks can help parents manage such an information gathering process. Yet, this kind of networking is complicated by the fact that these are primarily networks used by mothers — who work full-time at jobs outside the home, who work in the home, and who work as volunteers in schools — networks that have developed from the social world that they share with their children.

It is no secret among school district personnel that parents use networks to get information about schools and school choice. One administrator in the Department of School Integration (DSI) said some "ethnicities" probably network more carefully than others. The administrator said, "The ethnic groups make it their business to help instruct members in their group via their churches or other programs" and added that the district cannot do anything about the fact that some groups share information better than others. A local administrator at El Rancho Middle School, who has been involved in helping parents learn about the school, commented on the kind of networking parents are doing to find out about El Rancho:[2]

> I'm seeing conversations in offices at the workplace being very influential. Very often an African American parent will call me and say I've been speaking to the people at my work or on my job, number one, or I have a relative who works in a school, and my relative, my auntie told me that this is the best school. They may have, you know, a relative who's a clerk. They may have a relative who's a teacher. They may have a relative who's a principal, but somebody who has, you know, hooked into the education system in Deluca has become the family advisor. So I think, a lot of it has to do with mentor advisement from the community at large. It could be from the family community, from the church community, from the work force community, but it's someone whose opinion they respect. Now, as far as the Hispanic community, it's very interesting. In a much reduced way that same thing is true. Something that I am observing from this area is that the older children are advising the parents regarding the younger children. The older children, you know, who may be in high school are advising the parents that this is the good school for their younger siblings which I think is really a healthy trend.

Getting Information: Parent to Parent

Parents did talk with other parents. Robin, one of the African American mothers, said she asked other parents, "How is this school? What do you think? Does it work for your kid? How is the curriculum? Is their work displayed? Is the school clean? How do the teachers work with you?" Mimi told me that she did not go to family members for information about schools but instead asked other Korean parents she admired. "I didn't go to just any source but to those parents, I thought, really did a good job [getting their children through school]." Manuel and his wife divorced, leaving him to raise their four children alone. He would talk with other parents when he picked up his children from school, and his questions for other parents focused on safety and quality teaching.

> *Es muy tranquilo. No he visto ningún problema. Y los padres que yo les digo, platicamos así. Dicen si la maestra de mi hijo también es muy bien. Porque tengo un pariente que tiene su hija en Hughes. Yo les digo, '¿Cómo está tu hija en la escuela?'*
>
> It's very peaceful. I haven't seen any trouble either. We also talk about the teachers. This father told me that his child's teacher is very good as well. I have a relative who has his daughter at Hughes. I ask them, "How's your daughter [doing] at school?"

Linda, who is white and college educated, lives with her husband and their two children on the middle-class edge of an upper-class community in Deluca. Her neighborhood school is one of the more popular schools among Korean parents, and at the school's PTA meetings she learned that:

> There was a lot of infighting in the school and it probably took me most of the year to realize that. I still felt, "O.K., that's not a problem, we'll still go there," but everybody said to me that I should at least apply to a magnet school so that my child had points, if and when it became an issue that I wanted to change.

Mary has two sons, and she and her husband own an old restored home in a predominately Latino and African American neighborhood. They are among the few white families in the community. The information Mary received from other parents about her neighborhood school was negative:

> And see, most of the neighbors, particularly the white neighbors, they don't send them to the schools in this area. So they ended up sending their children to Del Mar Gifted magnet. And so I'd heard a lot about Del Mar from neighbors.

Suzanne has a professional degree and works in her own business. She makes it a point to find out about schools whenever and wherever she can. She believes that parents can get a much clearer picture of what is going on at schools by asking other involved parents.

> Everywhere I go I ask people, because I want to know, do they know about any programs that are good or better, do they know some that are bad that I should stay away from, what should I look for? So then I knew that, you know, watch out for the English and History teachers at El Rancho gifted in 7th grade.

Suzanne said that she would never consider putting her daughters in a school where she had not spoken to the very involved parents first.

> I find that other parents [whose] kids that are in gifted programs and magnet programs are also very, very involved and they're all asking too. I don't think I'm unusual .... I mean I'm just thinking about every school that I've looked at. I always have found parents that, you know, I either know somebody or know someone who knows somebody. And the parents that are involved know this process. So you know, if someone said to me, "Well, do you know something about X program?" I say, "I don't, but I have a friend who ...." and put them in touch with each other.

She goes on to share how she networks with people she knows to connect with other people in schools.

> When you're sitting there at the play or the concert or whatever and they're saying, "Oh, gosh, how are you going to do this?" And you go, "Well, O.K. let me tell you. This is what you do." And so some of the tricks are — first of all you get to know the people ahead of time so that they know when you're on the wait list. I call up and say, "Hi! I work with so and so and my daughter is on your waiting list. What can we do about that?" You know, you do anything you can. "So, I know we're on the waiting list, but I just want you to know that it's there and that we're really serious about getting in, so whatever you can do to help us, you know."

It is easy to look at the many studies of parents and cultural capital and see Suzanne as another example of a parent getting more for her own child than others may be able to get for theirs. But this is not just occurring in the Davis high school complex where the study took place, or only among white parents. One of the district's community advisors said that this kind of networking takes place all around the district with parents of all racial and ethnic groups:

> They're choosing [schools] by word of mouth. In the grocery after school, and they'll say, "Where is your child?" And by you bragging on it, "That's where I want to go." And you're bragging about this teacher, "That's where I want to go." And this is district-wide, "Get into this particular school and get here."

Considering the little information provided in the *Opportunities for Success* brochure, the complicated application process, and the time it takes to get information about schools, it is hard to blame parents for establishing and relying on these kinds of networks. As Bonnie pointed out in Chapter 2, the district is relying on parents to research it themselves. When choice and involvement in schools is part of women's work, mothers' unpaid work (Griffith and Smith, 2004), why would these mothers not take advantage of shared knowledge? I have no doubt that some kind of networking would still happen among parents whether the district provided more information or not, whether the application was more parent friendly or not. And some networks may always be more helpful than others. However, making more visible the complexities and intricacies of parents' choice work — work that is constructed around the district's policies and practices — helps us avoid the blaming that usually accompanies parents' participation in their children's education.

Many parents in the study were also aware that other parents do not always have access to the information they need. Meryl has been an active parent at her children's schools for many years and has learned much about the school choice process. She told me about a friend at her local neighborhood school and how she helped her with the "ins and outs all during fifth grade" so her child would be able to get into the magnet at El Rancho. "And I know for a fact if it wasn't for me like telling her, her child would not have gotten into the magnet from Ridgecrest into El Rancho, because only six children from the whole school got into the magnet and, of course, mine was one and hers was one." Meryl talked about the problem of other parents not having this information.

> It's sort of a closed thing. It's like a lot of parents don't know about it or they don't know who to ask .... They really just don't know the system .... But then, if there's parents that are in the

school now who have fifth graders, you know, if they ask me, I will honestly tell them. I want people to be able to get in, especially the ones that have worked hard in the school, I mean, they should know what to do.

Brenda has four children, and her husband, who is a day laborer, works on and off between Mexico and the U.S., so she is primarily responsible for raising her children. At the time of our interviews, Brenda was participating in a state-sponsored workfare program and lived in an apartment on a subsidized housing voucher. Brenda saw that parents in her community were unaware of other options for school choice. Because of her concern about her fifth grade daughter's low reading level, she asked her daughter's teacher for advice about middle schools. After her conversation with the teacher, she talked with other parents and suggested they look closer at the schools to which the district had assigned their children. The teacher was upset she was talking to other parents about schools:

> But then, I think when I start talking to the other parents, she thought I was saying to them what she was telling me. And she was telling me like, "Oh, you know, well, just like between me and you." Not to share with anybody else. But I wasn't telling them to take their kids to Kingston. I was just saying, you know, "Have you started to look at Foster? Do you know what you're getting into or why, why are you sending your kid to that school?" [Parents were thinking] Because they're bused, you know, that's the way it is. So she thought, I guess, I was sharing the information that she had shared with me, but I wasn't. I just wanted to know why [other parents] were just letting it go without them speaking up or saying something.

As a group, the parents I spoke with may be more information-seeking than other parents. Regardless, because of the lack of information from the district, parents have been placed in a position to share their secrets and strategies about school choice with other parents. Some of the most useful information parents obtained through networking came from parents who were very involved donating their time and resources to the local school. Coming from the same not-so-good neighborhood school, Robin and Brenda had to go outside their neighborhoods to get the same information the more privileged parents had access to, if they obtained the information at all.

Information from Teachers and Schools

Local schools and teachers should be a good source of information about school choice. However, while some parents received information from teachers and schools about choice, others did not receive any. I found that far more information about middle school choice was provided to elementary parents at magnet schools than parents at regular elementary schools.

Because of what she has learned about choice as a parent and as a teacher, Bonnie takes a very active role in encouraging her students to enroll in a better middle school than their assigned school. She informs her students when the magnet application brochure should arrive in the mail and tells them to bring it right to her at school once they receive it. She says to them:

> I'll circle the school that I recommend and if your parents have questions, they can call me. And they all had my home phone number and everything. Those who had siblings I said, "Bring your siblings' [applications] too." And, you know, I just circled the ones and gave them back to the kids and then it was up to the parents to hand them in. I said, "You do not want to be in this middle school; it's really very disorganized." And they know that, they got older siblings in some cases, who are there. They know that it's crazy and out of control.

She also reminds her students when it is time to apply for open enrollment and encourages them to have their parents fill out an application for other middle schools:

> I said, "Make sure your parents go there and fill out an application to see if you can get in there, because that's a real middle school and they got all the supplies and everything that you need in a campus and you'll get a better education there." .... I said to the parents, "Apply to a magnet and keep applying until you get in. Your child deserves something better." If I stress the fact that they'll get a better education somewhere else, these parents perk up.

The kind of information Bonnie shared with her students' families would have been welcomed by Robin or Manuel. Manuel could only recall one teacher who encouraged him to look for a better school for his son. His family was his primary source of information about school choice:

Eso sería bueno, esa cosa, para que cuando uno va a una conferencia
ellos motiven a un padre para que a uno también lelevante elánimo.
Sí, porque motiva al padre para que uno les inyecte más ánimo al
hijo, o que diga uno, se ilusione uno.

That would be good so that when we parents meet at the [parent]
conference, the teachers encourage the parents so that we may feel
motivated. Yes, because that encourages the parent, so that we
encourage our children as well, we get dreams.

Robin was frustrated that teachers did not provide information
about good schools for her daughter:

Some teachers ain't up front with you; they need to be frank.
They should be saying, "You know, Mrs. Jackson, you got a good
kid, you got your child in this and that." The fifth grade teacher
should say, "Your kid's got it, she's got what's going on. I recommend a mirage of schools, I recommend ta, da, ta, da, ta, da."
That's what I should be hearing. I don't hear nothing.

These parents indicated that many teachers did not inform them
about choice. This too can be connected with how knowledge about
school choice gets organized by the district. Unless a teacher is also a
parent in the district, as Bonnie is, information is not provided to them
about schools of choice. Furthermore, with the magnet school brochure mailed home, classroom teachers no longer have the opportunity
to review the brochure's content as they once could when the brochures
were distributed through local schools. As part of the justification for
listing only schools' phone numbers in the application brochure, an
administrator from the DSI said, "You know, my philosophy is that if
you want to find out something specifically about a school, why would
you want to call centrally?" The administrator thought that parents
could just call and find out the information from the people who have
the information. This not only delegates responsibility for obtaining
information to parents, it assumes that local school personnel will have
access to the kinds of information that parents seek, which may in fact
not be the case.

Some parents locate the information they need, but as Robin talked
about the school choice process in general, it was clear that not all parents can sort through the complicated information network the
administrator envisions. For example, according to Robin:

There's something, I can't pinpoint it, but, the more you ask for
help the more they send you in different directions. It's just silly.

You shouldn't have to go in all these different directions when you're looking for one answer. They should direct you appropriately to where you need to go to get the right information and to get the things done and go on to the next step. If you limit me to the resources and the information I'm trying to get then you're holding my child back really.

The parents whose children attended Spring Street Elementary Magnet school (Suzanne, Karen, and Linda) told me that the fifth grade teachers discussed middle school choice at conference time. The parents at the elementary magnet schools all reported receiving notices about meetings for middle school choice. Suzanne describes how these meetings were planned and coordinated with those schools the magnet students might want to attend:

When we have parent/teacher conference, I assume they do this with everyone, they say, "So where are you thinking about sending your child?" .... I mean even before, when they used to send the stuff home, Spring Street made sure every kid got one of the *Opportunities for Success* books. They will send flyers home saying, "O.K., El Rancho, Carnegie, certain schools are having their open houses, even private schools. They're all having their open houses. These are the dates. Please sign up."

Now that Suzanne's children are no longer at the elementary level, she finds the same kinds of meetings offered through El Rancho Middle School Gifted Magnet:

El Rancho has the same thing, they have a high school open house and they send notices home saying "We're going to have these schools, please come. I went a year ahead of time. But they were open to anybody. They're very, very involved with it, and some of the teachers who know [my daughter] well would ask me at back-to-school night, "So what do you think about sending her to high school?" Her science teacher said, "You know, I want you to consider Columbia because they have a very strong science program."

This difference in information about school choice coming from regular elementary schools located in the poorer communities of the Davis complex vs. that available at magnet schools means that parents from nonmagnet schools who wish to participate in school choice must find ways to learn what they do not know about choosing schools in the district. Meryl, whose children attended their neighborhood elementary school, expresses the importance and benefits of staying connected to the school choice process at all times:

> I mean, basically it's you have to just be totally aware and not miss some important dates and meetings. And just hanging around the schools, not be afraid to find out any information that you need to find out. The parents that are active, that go to the board meetings, who know the principals, you know, who do things for the school, it does help your children, because if you have a problem then you have a little bit of clout.

In one way or another, these mothers have all worked as volunteers in the schools to support their children's continued achievement. Clout or not, the parents in this study could not walk into a public school that was not their assigned school, but that they thought would be best for their child, and successfully enroll the child at the new school, not without some additional choice work. This includes those parents, like Meryl, who benefit from the privileges that accompany a college education, a good family income, and the means to own a home. There is literature from the U.K. that addresses the influence of class relations in parents' school choice processes.[3]

Reay's (1996) work in England about how mothers' social class backgrounds affect their choice processes and practices is evident in the stories of the parents, mothers primarily, presented here. Class relations, when they take the form of cultural capital, are important in understanding parents' participation in school choice, as Ball explains:

> The role of cultural capital in relation to choice is both general and specific. General, in the sense that certain types and amounts of cultural capital are required in order to be an active and strategic chooser. For example, knowledge of local schools, access to and the ability to read and decipher significant information, ability to engage with and decipher the "promotional" activities of schools (like open evenings, brochures and videos), the ability to maximize choice by "working the system" (making multiple applications), and the ability to engage in activities involving positive presentation of self (e.g. when meeting key gatekeepers). Specific, in the sense that the making of "successful" choices, getting your first choice, can depend upon direct engagement and advocacy and pursuit of your choice. There are *key points of articulation* in the choice process when certain kinds of cultural capital are crucial (Ball, 1993, p. 13, italics his).

Parents using their cultural capital surfaced throughout the study. I use the following stories to provide evidence of how public school choice in Deluca USD is organized institutionally so that parents need to use their cultural capital at key points of articulation. It is assumed by the district that they have it to use, or that they can get the crucial cultural and social capital on their own. While I could see how class relations and cultural capital did indeed help some parents be more successful in the choice process than others, the way schooling is structured and organized by large school district bureaucracies still positions parents (even those successfully choosing schools) in subordinate roles where the work they do on behalf of their children's education is coordinated to the needs of the district and the local schools.

MAGNET SCHOOLS: THE FIRST CHOICE

I have been describing how the work parents did was socially organized by the district's voluntary integration program; the implementation practices of different choice options; and the various application processes. In the magnet school choice process it is possible to see how parents of different racial identities and social class backgrounds engage in choice work that is at times the same (visiting the schools, talking with other parents) and at times very different (reading and understanding the magnet brochure and application). As I mentioned in the introduction, the institutional ethnographic method I use begins with parents' choice work, "exploring with [parents] the character of that work process, how it is put together, what it involves for them: its problems and its rewards" (Griffith, 1990).

When talking with parents, I noticed that there was a difference between how they approached elementary school choice versus secondary school choice. Parents' knowledge about education and experiences with their children's schooling took a bigger role in choosing secondary schools as they expressed interest in more academically oriented choices. In this regard, parents' work processes for choice seemed rooted in their concern for their children's future academic success and postsecondary opportunities. From the district video to the statement in the introduction of the magnet school brochure, the message sent to parents that magnet schools provide excellent academic programs that meet university entrance requirements increased their desire to secure a place for their children at a middle school magnet.

The Draw of the Magnet School Program

I have already made clear that the magnet school choice process requires that a great deal of choice work take place if parents want to submit an application that will be successful. Parents do this choice work because they want to find a school (or at least consider another option) that suits their child and their family's circumstances and is better (or maybe different) from their regularly assigned neighborhood school. Gifted magnet programs are popular choices for the parents because they are perceived as meeting the needs of high achieving students. Magnet schools and gifted education were fused together in the district's gifted magnets almost from the start of the voluntary integration program. An administrator explained:

> In reality, you understand, the magnets were implemented for integration. They were not to be the delivery instrument for gifted programs. We didn't need that. They came to gifted and wanted to offer gifted centers, which in effect hurt us, because the gifted programs were in the regular schools. Now human nature that it is, adults then took it upon themselves to move gifted options into magnet schools.

I think it is a reasonable assumption that there were historical and political factors constructing the development of the gifted magnet program option. White students have consistently been overrepresented in the percentage of gifted students in the district and were so at the time Deluca began implementing the court-ordered voluntary integration program, which may have suggested to those planning the magnet programs that gifted magnets would be acceptable to more white parents (Ladson-Billings and Tate, 1995; Staiger, 2004). But the blending of gifted education with the magnet school has offered other benefits for parents. For instance, a district-level administrator shared how some parents are using the gifted magnets to address multiple considerations:

> There's a whole big construct of parents who may not necessarily be gifted but are interested in safe environments for their kids and consciously chose gifted programs because the children who participate in that, who are motivated to succeed, more often also are parts of safer environments. And we have large groups of parents who are escaping neighborhood school environments that are not supportive for the child doing well or experiencing his or her potential. And they consciously choose to go to schools that are further from the neighborhood. I have talked with a lot of parents who choose, because we have more parents who are now both working or either single parents, and they need the child to be,

conversely enough, far away. So that's a kind of a child care. So that when the children get back to the home neighborhood, the parent is also off work. Those are very, very conscious choices. They make conscious choices now that we publicize the scores and so on. They make conscious choices about what those scores mean in terms of environment. I've heard parents say to me, "Gifted is the only game in town. I don't necessarily support gifted education, but if my kid wants to go into advanced classes, that's the only game in town."

Parents do have concerns when thinking about where they will send their children to school, and a safe learning environment is going to be near the top of any urban parent's priority list. Working parents bring the added concerns of finding appropriate child care for their children. That some parents might use magnet school choice as a way to address their concerns about safety, child care, and a quality instructional program is not surprising when viewed from the everyday lives of urban, working parents.

El Rancho Middle School Gifted Magnet is one of those schools to which parents of high-achieving students regularly apply. Parents in this study described trying to get into El Rancho, and they often mentioned the points they would try to accumulate to improve their child's chances of being selected in the magnet school lottery. One local administrator at El Rancho Middle School discussed how, aside from moving into the neighborhood, parents could have their children attend El Rancho. The administrator clearly articulated the process parents must go through:

If [parents] really wanted to get into the magnet school, for example, which is the desire of many people, even those who live in the community, they would have to start to apply for the magnet school at least three years before the child's ready to enter. [Parents] know they can't get in, so they get the waiting list points. That way they would have a greater assurance of being able to get into the program. And I always run into parents every year who are unhappy. They say, "Well, I just moved into the community. I didn't know about this. I don't think this is a fair system." I don't argue with them, because there's no system that's gonna be perfectly fair. And it's true. If you're aware and knowledgeable and you've been around for a while, you know that's what you have to do [accumulate points]. On the other hand, obviously, if their child's not gifted, [parents] have to find other ways. But, again, they would have to face either child care permits or work-related permits. Or, I mean, it may be some time in the future, that we'll have [space for] open enrollment again.

El Rancho's popularity has the school operating over what the administration at the school believes is an optimum enrollment for a middle school. The administrator also told me that it will be easier to keep El Rancho's size under control as neighboring schools improve their programs. The administrator considers a school's academic program most important for parents:

> I think in most people's minds, that's the most important thing. You know, the quality of instruction and all those things that are related. And then I think probably a pretty close second for most parents is a question of safety. Although, I don't think if the school was safe, but the academic program was poor, they would want to make that choice.

The comment from another administrator at El Rancho also suggests school quality is an issue for parents:

> In all of my years at this side of the desk and even in all of my years in the classroom, I think I could count on my fingers the number of parents who really were motivated by something that was unrealistic or unfair. What most parents want, in my eyes, is something that's reasonable .... From an administrative point of view, I think that it's the quality in the school district that probably needs more work.

The comments of the two local administrators at El Rancho reinforce the perception that parents are looking for "good" schools and that the good schools are most often fully enrolled.

The responsibility for the successful implementation of the magnet program goes to the local school site. The complementary role of the local school in attracting parents' participation in the magnet program is important for the district's compliance to the court-ordered voluntary integration plan. Both El Rancho administrators discussed how they promote the school through visits to elementary schools, tours, and talking with parents about El Rancho. One of the administrators described what the school does:

> When we open up our school, you know, for visits, we don't ask people where they came from. We send out notices to the local

schools. Where it's possible, we have a notice in the local newspaper. We'll try to do that .... The theory of the school visit is designed so that you can see what the school is all about, so that if you're going to make a choice for this school as a magnet school, in particular, but also in general, you know what you're choosing. You see it yourself as opposed to listening to what your neighbors may say or your friends may say. Because sometimes our perceptions are different .... We provide tours that are led by students because students have a different perception than the adults. My job is to sell my school. My job is not to disparage it. And we tell the parents, "Ask them anything you want. You'll get a straight scoop from these kids." And that's worked, actually, to our benefit. Because most of the kids are very happy, and they're happy to tell the parents that they're very happy. So it doesn't seem like I'm just a show-off here. You know, there's a great deal of truth.

I went on a tour at El Rancho and the students leading the tours were students from the leadership class. One student gave me the classroom visitation schedule. The principal had said to the audience that the tour would include the whole school, magnet and regular classes. Looking at the schedule, I and the other parents were taken to almost all gifted magnet classes, or honors classes in the regular school (we toured an art class and a P.E. class also). While we did see both programs, the regular and the magnet, the academic classes we visited were those serving the higher-achieving and better-behaved students. Good student behavior is an important part of El Rancho's reputation, and another administrator discusses how this is communicated to parents interested in choosing the school:

One, I always tell parents that all of the staff members at this school when they have children of middle-school age send their children to El Rancho, and to me that is probably the strongest endorsement of the school that I can say. Right now we have ten children who are the children of staff members, teacher, secretaries, cafeteria workers, and I think that that's a very important thing to tell the public .... and one of the best consequences [for misbehaving] in this school is you don't get to come here, and that's the strongest threat that you can ever infer to children because they want to be at this school. And so it shapes the behavior when children want — when their place in the school is coveted, it helps to shape their behavior .... I mean, it's out there on the street. It's very cool to be at this school. It's very hip to be at this school. And, yes, it is a coveted school. Most definitely.

The administrators' promotional talk illustrates that within the notion of the good school is the well-behaved student, the good student. These institutional practices and the underlying achievement discourse help maintain the school's reputation in the community, further shaping the school choice context.

The racial formulas determined by the court-ordered voluntary integration plan must also be interpreted by local school sites. In chapter 2 an administrator stated that historically, the El Rancho magnet program has not had problems maintaining a 40% white student population. The school administration does monitor the racial balance at the school. As one administrator said:

We need the white population, quite frankly. I just looked at the statistics. We are holding our own in our white population. Our Hispanic population has dropped this year because our feeder school pattern has changed somewhat, and our Asian population has jumped. We are a school with 14% Asian enrollment. That is very high. And our African American population has increased slightly, and our Filipino population has increased somewhat slightly.

Because of the court-ordered racial formulas, magnet schools are very aware of which students, white or nonwhite, are needed to maintain their school's racial balance. The stories that follow highlight how El Rancho's need for white students could be an important piece of information for parents trying to enroll their children in the school.

SCHOOL CHOICE AS WORK

According to Smith, work in people's everyday worlds is also organized by various relations operating in concert in multiple sites (Smith, 1987). This concept is explored in the following sections by looking more closely at parents' work choosing elementary and secondary magnet schools. The choice work described by parents was a process that included such things as a school tour, talking to people about the school, visiting the school with their child, researching information about the school (e.g., test scores, crime rates), gathering together spouses' and children's thoughts and opinions about the school, and keeping track of the application deadline. This is the work for one school alone, so these tasks may be repeated a number of times depending on how many schools a parent is considering.

Doing Choice Work — Elementary Magnet Schools

Here I focus on the mothers whose children attended one particular school, Christopher Street Elementary Magnet, and on what their stories reveal about elementary magnet school choice. The importance of the racial formulas, priority points, and the computer lottery in the organization of parents' school choice experiences will surface in their stories. These are racially diverse, educated women. Their stories illustrate how their individual race and class identities, and their experiences and knowledge, come to bear on the work they do choosing schools for their children. This choice work is framed for them by the district's choice policies and organized and coordinated by the application text.

Previous sections have explained how the application process is constructed to privilege parents who can research schools themselves, who can make sense of the *Opportunities for Success* brochure, and who are white. Moreover, the magnet school priority points system benefits those families already participating in the magnet programs at the elementary level. Because they will receive matriculation points for secondary school choice, they gain an advantage over families trying to enter the magnet program for the first time at the secondary level. For those parents who understand the points system, entering the magnet school program during the elementary school years is a smart strategy. Several parents in this study had children enrolled in elementary magnet schools.

Mimi is one of the mothers whose children attended the elementary magnet, Christopher Street School. When her daughter reached school age and Mimi started looking into schools, she explored the possibility of sending her daughter to the local school. She had also heard about magnet programs from several sources. Mimi describes how she prepared for sending her daughter to school:

> So before she went to school, so a year before is when I started doing all the research. And I had first plan, second plan, and third plan, all drawn out. So if she wasn't going to get into magnet, because I applied for magnet the year before. And, you know, there were dates, and I sort of made a time line for myself. And I applied to all different schools. And I had all kinds of schools lined up so if there was a choice of magnet schools, if she got in, that's where she would go. If that didn't work out, there was

private schools that I was considering. If that didn't work out, there was open enrollment where I would commute the child myself, but not in the area. And that was the choice that I had for my child.

Mimi was pleased when her daughter was accepted into Christopher Street School because it meant her work had paid off. Mimi was happy at the school because there were other Korean parents there and she welcomed the opportunity to volunteer to represent the Korean community:

Christopher Street is a very nurturing place. The population is very dynamic and diverse, ethnically diverse. And they get along very well. The education of multiculturalism is done very well and in a fashion that's very equally represented .... So I thought, you know, I'll work very hard to represent our culture there and that our culture is very well respected. So any Korean parent that gets to Christopher Street gets to automatically assume that you are good.

Natalie wanted an environment that would be supportive for African American children. She also chose Christopher Street School after considering other schools for the first of her four children. She talked about her choice process:

I remember calling my mom, and I said, "Mom, I have done more research for my child to go to kindergarten than I did when I went to college." I researched. I talked to parents. I talked to kids. I went and visited schools. I drug my husband .... I chose the magnet system first because everyone chooses to be there, doesn't have to be there. I figure if you choose to be someplace, you come with much more dedication and passion about making things work. I chose Christopher Street because it was known as a Noah's Ark place. It not only had a diverse student body population, but it had diverse staff population. That's important to me as a mother of an African American male that he looks up in the classroom and sees the person of authority who looks something like him, who has some understanding of what it is to be that kind of person in this kind of society. It also had an academic kindergarten, and my child had been in preschool for three years, and I did not want him to start over with "This is the letter A." .... I even talked to the janitor at Christopher Street because I thought the janitor you can trust. And he said, "You know, this is a great school. Kids are great." I mean, he was just really excited. When you hear that the janitor's excited about a school, there's something going on there, you know.

Both Mimi and Natalie were happy with the integration program they experienced at Christopher Street. Clearly, how they talk about the school shows that in some ways the district's voluntary integration program is accomplishing some of the goals of desegregation — children with different racial and ethnic identities are learning together at this school.

Karen, who is white and remarried, chose Christopher Street for her daughter, who is African American and white, for many of the same reasons as Natalie and Mimi. Karen's stepchildren, both white, went to Spring Street School:

> Well, because Neema is black and white, when I first tried to get her into Christopher Street, I put her down as black. Well, thinking like an idiot, you know, like a white, liberal, nice, well-meaning lady, "Well, you get all these extra services if you're black, right?" Hello. Had I put her as white, she would have been in like Flynn. Now had I probably tried to get her into Spring Street to begin with as black, they might have been ready to take her. But Christopher Street had all the black kids. They were looking for white kids …. and if you go on the Spring Street campus it looks very white. Oh, the demographics reflect da, da, da, da, da. I don't care what they say. It looks very white, and I think that it's just the reputation of Spring Street School, the parent network that is tied into it. I think they have very few Hispanics there really, relatively few blacks. Although blacks make up a pretty small percentage of the city, but certainly the Latino kids do not reflect the demographics in the city. No way in hell. And El Rancho, I don't really think that that magnet program does either. It seems to be, you know, WASP and Jewish.

It is important to remember that the introduction in the application brochure, the integration formulas, the magnet priority point system, the computer lottery, and the various other messages that come to parents from the district through texts and discourses construct how white families compared to families of color will be able to participate in the magnet program. Karen's reference to the parent network at Spring Street School relates to the race and class relations that help coordinate being white, being wealthier, with getting into a magnet school, whether it is Christopher Street School where her daughter attends, or Spring

Street School where her stepchildren attend. Spring Street School is demographically diverse, but Karen's critique points out how a school with well-resourced and actively involved white parents can take on the appearance that it is a white school.

Like the other mothers, when Bonnie was ready to send her oldest daughter to school she visited her neighborhood elementary school. She observed the kindergarten classroom and she felt it was not the place for her child:

> Did I see a piano? No. Did I see art work? No. Did I see blocks? No. I had done all of my Master's level training in nursery school and kindergarten, plus summers I have spent also working in pre-schools and kindergartens and I said, "No, this is not the experience I want my daughter to be having and certainly not with this teacher," so I said, "This is not it!"

At the same time, Bonnie was learning from other parents about magnet schools, the racial formulas, and the priority points system. She continued to look around for a school she thought was more like what she wanted for her child:

> I wasn't a teacher in Deluca Unified yet, but I understood from other parents that you choose a school that's on the edge of an acceptable community for you, and that's why I chose Christopher Street. I knew that they would want white children because it was on the edge of what has always been a very mixed community. But in the books, demographically, it says it's a middle-class black community. So I mean, that was definitely part of my manipulation and my machinations …. I applied to Christopher Street and Jessica got in and that was it.

These mothers' comments bring forth some of the ways that parents have learned to understand how race enters the magnet school choice process. They were able to read and interpret the magnet brochure so that their children would benefit from the racial formula used in the voluntary integration program. Those mothers whose children attended elementary magnets used demographic and geographic knowledge in skillful and sophisticated ways.

Mary already knew when she began looking for schools that her neighborhood school was not the school to which she wanted to send her child. She also wanted an academic kindergarten for her son:

> There were not very many magnet schools that have kindergartens. Cabrillo magnet, and that is a kindergarten to 12th grade

school, and then there was Christopher Street magnet which is kindergarten to fifth. And so I went to Cabrillo and it was sort of like part black and part Hispanic .... There were more examples of the children's work on the wall and everything so it was more impressive than Mountain View [her neighborhood school]. It was very close, but the only thing that bothered me was this thing about him being the only white kid. And I thought, okay, is that what I want for my son, for him to be the only white child in the class? .... In fact, I asked up at Cabrillo, I was in the school office at the end of my tour, I said, "Well, how hard do you think it would be to get in here?" and all the teachers start laughing, "You're in! We need racial balance here, you're in. No question."

Mary realized quickly that where she lived gave her advantages in applying for magnet schools:

We've never had any problem because if you're in this neighborhood, Mountain View is overcrowded, it's primarily minority, they're on all the different tracks. I think, too, if you apply to a school that has a lot of minority, like, even though it's west of here, Christopher Street and Carnegie, they're still pretty much in a black neighborhood. And, you know, they get a lot of minorities apply so then you need the white kids to balance it out. So anyway, I went over to Christopher Street. That's about a 15 minute drive from here. And it was, the moment I walked in I knew this was it, this was it. It was like a little United Nations there. It's about one-third black, one-third white, and one-third everybody else, Hispanics, a lot of Koreans go there. I went to the kindergarten, just you know, stuff all over the walls.

How Bonnie and Mary perceive the classroom practices at the different schools they looked at, such as artwork on the walls and children playing with blocks, brings meaning to parents' notions of the good school. Mary's comment about Christopher Street being like a little United Nations and Natalie's comment that the school is known as a Noah's Ark place, show the kinds of metaphors parents use to describe the integration at the school.

In commenting on race and education, the critical race theorist john a. powell distinguishes between integration, which he defines as similar to assimilation, and "real integration," which transforms racial hierarchies.

Segregation is not just the exclusion of people, but also the limitation of their opportunities and economic resources. It creates and maintains a culture of racial hierarchy and subjugation …. Traditionally, desegregation in education has meant either removing formal barriers or simply placing students in physical proximity to one another. These remedies are limited …. Real integration involves fundamental change among whites and people of color, as people and communities …. Integration, as a solution to segregation, has broader meaning: it refers to community-wide efforts to create a more inclusive society (2001, pp. 143–145).

In many instances, when discussing her views on education in the district and choosing schools, Natalie's comments showed a keen understanding of racial issues as well as how these issues are evident in the magnet schools her children attend. Spring Street magnet is the elementary school to which some of the other parents (Suzanne and Linda) sent their children, and it is not far from Christopher Street School. Natalie visited the school when she was deciding on a school for her children. Natalie's comparison of the two schools raises the issue of the extent to which a magnet school could be desegregated (Spring Street School is) but not integrated (Steinhorn, 2001):

There's no African American teachers at Spring Street School. There are no male teachers at Spring Street School. There's only two Asian teachers at Spring Street School, and one of them is new. There's no integration going on in Spring Street School. It is predominantly white. Their concepts, their view of themselves is not integrated, you know. If you integrate your views, then you are creating integration. At least at Christopher Street the view of ourselves is an integrated view. That is what integration is about, change your views, not change people you see on the bus or you're exposed to during the day. Exposure is nothing, you know …. Exposure is not integration.

As I listened to the parents speak about the diversity in magnet schools, it seemed that the integration discourse in which they were participating was, in some ways, a euphemism for partially successful desegregation. Still missing in the integration discourse is any language that speaks to the segregation and exclusion of over 90% of the district's students who do not attend schools like Christopher Street.

For the most part, Karen, Mary, Bonnie, Mimi, and Natalie did the same amount of choice work and networking. The racial formulas and priority points system clearly worked to the benefit of white families wanting to get into Christopher Street School and Spring Street School. The work the mothers did, the knowledge they acquired, rewarded these mothers with an integrated educational experience for their children at these magnet schools.

What the mothers are less aware of is the social class privilege that they bring to the process, how it allows them to do the work of choosing, negotiate the application, visit schools, and so on. This is the unseen part of how class relations operating in and through institutional practices are reorganizing the integration program to one of haves and have-nots. These class relations and institutional practices are even more prevalent at the secondary level, where academics are much more the concern of parents making choice decisions. So while these magnet schools may be racially diverse, the racial diversity masks the class relations among the student populations at these schools. A comment by one of the El Rancho administrators provides an example of this:

> In our school we did something very radical recently. We got two buses and we took our whole staff to all of the neighborhoods from which our children come. And for some of our staff members, for them to see the neighborhoods in Laurel Grove, Roy Sands, and Del Mar where our African American families come from, for many of them, it was a really enlightening experience. Because they actually had a chance to see that for every Davis Park, and Starrett Hill, and El Rancho neighborhood that is lovely, there are other neighborhoods that are in primarily African American areas, that are just as lovely if not more lovely. And so it dispelled a lot of notions.

The community in which El Rancho is located currently maintains a majority white population, as does the Davis High School complex, but there is a rich diversity of people from many racial, ethnic, and cultural backgrounds living in this part of the City of Deluca. Similarly, there is much socioeconomic diversity in the community. There is value in the staff of El Rancho taking a bus tour of the neighborhoods in which their students live, but unfortunately if the focus of the bus tour was to show that some of their African American students live in just as affluent neighborhoods as some of the white students, it could lead to the unintended effect of the school staff thinking that most of their students' families have the same economic resources. This certainly would not be true; Manuel lives with his four children in a small apartment above a garage on a street zoned for both residential and business use that also lies within El Rancho's school boundaries.

Doing Choice Work — Secondary Magnet Schools

The students matriculating from the elementary schools in the Davis High School complex arrive at middle school after experiencing diverse school environments. The administrator at El Rancho recognizes this:

> Well, many of the kids who come here, actually come from schools that have a great deal of diversity. I mean, there aren't many schools in Deluca anymore, on this side town at any rate, where there isn't a great deal of diversity. So a lot of the kids and parents have had experiences with [diversity] in the past .... And I think, you know, particularly on this side of town, which is the more liberal part of the city, that I think it's a goal for most parents. I don't think it's a goal that one should sacrifice everything else that goes on in the school for, but I think that the parents are generally very pleased with the attitudes and values that their children come out with.

And as one of the El Rancho administrators noted previously, there are some parents at the school who have sophisticated understandings of quality instructional programs. Most parents, however, have only a basic understanding of classroom curricula and how schools work. By not providing more information about schools and thereby creating the "research it yourself" context, the district compels many parents to investigate school communities through the use of their own networks and to gather information about schools, teachers, and academic programs however they can.

Suzanne's skill in networking and the information she is able to obtain from schools has been discussed previously. Here she continues to share more of the work she does when choosing schools for her children:

> So I go to everything they offer. I do go on all the tours and I go do the evening programs. All the schools that I have talked about and considered I've been to. I've been through the tours that they have given during the day where you get to see classes in action. I've often gone independently and spoken with the magnet coordinators, the principals, or the vice-principals or whoever. I've gone around and seen the classes, too, and I've taken my kids. Each of my daughters has been to the classrooms of any school that we have applied to.

Suzanne initially focuses on the educational program a school provides for its students. She gathers information from the meetings and tours she attends and uses it as the basis for further research about schools:

> I use it as a place to start. So I figure this is what they intend; this is what the policies are; what the party line is and all of that. I believe them that this is what they intend to have happen and this is the direction that they intend to go. Then I start talking to the teachers and ask questions about, you know, what do you actually teach and what are the materials and how does this work, and that sort of thing. And so it feels like this is their blueprint and then this is how they put it into action and then, what is the actual result. And I talk to other parents and kids that are there and get their opinion — the principal says, da-da-da-da-da does that really happen? or what is that like? or whatever.

El Rancho is Suzanne's neighborhood school. Because her daughter is identified as gifted, her daughter would automatically be placed in the Honors program of regular El Rancho. Suzanne's reason for continuing in the magnet program is one I often heard from other middle school parents.

> It was important to me they stay in the magnet because they get those points, and because I know we're going to need them for high school. Because our local high school is Davis and the regular program for Davis would have been completely inappropriate for both of them. If you look at the scores, I read the text scores in the newspapers and all that, Davis' regular program scores are very low, but the Davis Liberal Arts magnet is extremely high.

And it was not just the white and wealthier parents who worked hard choosing schools. The application process puts demands on the time of all parents who take seriously the search for a quality school for their children. And as already mentioned, the children of more actively involved and more knowledgeable parents from the poorer and predominantly minority communities will often be moved by their parents into better schools. Brenda spent a lot of time deciding on schools for her four children, especially her oldest daughter:

> I started looking at the magnet schools wondering what is magnet, because where I come from there is no magnet; there is no magnet

school or such a program; so I wondered what was it? What's the difference? Regular school; magnet? Magnet school seemed like it is held more accountable and I wanted Sandra to go to school where I thought she'd get the best education. I started applying to magnet three years ago. Yeah, I went out to the schools. It's like a full time job. I looked at the *Opportunities for Success* booklet and I called the different schools and I asked permission to evaluate them. [I've] been doing it over a long period, the last two years.

In addition to visiting schools, Brenda also gathered information through networks and teachers. She learned that Carnegie had been the middle school for her neighborhood before it became a magnet. "Now I don't know how a school can do that, just turn all magnet. I can understand if they turn half of it magnet, but leave some for the neighborhood area. Foster was the only one who would take our kids, which means our kids have to be bused all the way to Foster." Brenda also told me, "I've looked into Foster; I've been there; I've done that. I've asked permission to walk on their campus and so I wasn't happy. It was like, I'm not sending my daughter here, you know." She said one of the first things she does is to talk with teachers at a school. She asks them if they are happy at the school and if they have problems with the administration:

If you have problems with the administration, they bring it to the classroom even though they say that has nothing to do with my child. And that was something I looked at as I asked the teachers, "What do you think of Foster? If you had to rate Foster, what would you say? What would be the number from one to five?" I had really a lot of two's. I got like one three, you know.

She said the teachers also told her that "the kids who have homes in the area come down on kids who are being bused in, and so the teachers say that they've seen, you know, this kind of thing going on." Brenda's position as a poor woman of color allows her to see the social order of schools differently, and she is critically aware of the social relations that could have oppressive effects in ways that many white or wealthier parents may not be able to see. She knows that there is more at stake for her children if they attend a not-so-good school and knows how this could impact her children's educational success.

At El Rancho, Brenda did get a chance to talk to the administration. She was also able to "wander into the teachers' lunch area pretending like I was just eavesdropping." Brenda thought the teachers' view of the administration at El Rancho was much better than what she heard at Foster. Recalling her visit, she said:

> I asked them what they thought of El Rancho. A few of them said their children actually go to El Rancho. Now you don't know how many are at magnet, but they actually have their kids in that school. And I'm not saying that I want my kid to go where all educators' kids go, I just want to give her every fat chance. Because I know how I am a minority, and she is a minority, so at least give her a half a chance.

After doing research on the different schools, Brenda was facing the application deadline for the magnet school programs and needed to make a decision on which school she would apply to for her daughter. She said:

> This was the year that I had to finally say, "O.K., make up your mind and how do you get there? O.K., this is it. I mean, you don't have any more options." You have to say, "O.K., you're going to take her to Kingston, plan to drive there every morning. You're going to have to take her to wherever. We can't go to the east side of town, it's too far." But plan this, because this is it. Next year's 6th grade, you don't have any more time to just say, "Well, I'm going to look at this school; I'm going to look at that school." This is it, this is what you get and so that's when I said, "Boy, now what do I do for a start?"

Brenda's dilemma about which middle school her daughter would attend is, in part, a result of the district's implementation of the voluntary integration program. The school that was once the neighborhood middle school for Brenda's community is now Carnegie College Preparatory, a magnet school. There are two middle schools in the Davis High School complex, El Rancho and Carnegie. Carnegie is one of the magnet schools many parents in the study considered for secondary school choice. Carnegie goes from 6th grade through 12th. It was a featured school in one of the district's cable television promotions. The video transcript shows how the principal, a teacher, and a parent describe the school:

> Principal: Sending students to Carnegie offers any parent, any student, a consistent seven year education, quality education, that is monitored, that is carefully planned by the counselors, and that

leads to a college education. Our graduation rate is about 99%, so it pays off in the end. Our focus has pretty much been unwavering. It is to prepare our youngsters for college.

Parent: We chose Carnegie for our children primarily because it's a fantastic environment for them to learn in. It's very much academic oriented and behavior is kept in check very well.

Teacher: I'm teaching at Carnegie because of the opportunity to deal with high-caliber students who are college bound and very interested in their education. I enjoy the interchange of ideas with bright kids, kids that are interested in education. I'm also very interested in the parent's interest in their child's education, and at this school we have a great deal of parent interest, which is terrific because that way we all work together to educate that child.

Elements of the achievement discourse I presented in the introduction run through the description of Carnegie — "bright kids," "academic orientated," "college bound" students. Through the words of those speaking in the video, it is possible to form an image of Carnegie as a "good school": such a school offers a quality education and has "good students." Parents in the study recognized that Carnegie was considered a good school. Still, they had different reactions to Carnegie. For example, Natalie commented:

I've been on a tour at Carnegie before. I remember getting the feeling that, yes, it's easy to do good when you're taking the best of the best, you know. And that [the principal] was basically very discouraging to parents to apply there. "Lot of kids apply. Not everyone gets in. We have very rigid academics. Not everyone can succeed here." And that was what stuck in my head.

When I took the Carnegie tour, I listened to statements made by one of the school's administrators to a packed parent audience. The administrator was describing the kind of student they are looking for: "A student who is more mature; has self-initiative; doesn't need remedial work; can sit for long periods of time; can handle a college prep program. If a student doesn't fit these parameters, he may not be successful at Carnegie." The administrator said that they test all students before admitting them to the school. She reminded parents to "Be aware of the academic level of your child. Children must be at grade level. If not at grade level, they won't have a pleasant experience at Carnegie."

Adding that the school expects students to maintain 90% attendance, the administrator said, "If you have a child with health problems or one who doesn't attend regularly, Carnegie might not be a good place for your child." These indications of the kind of student a child should be if he or she is going to attend Carnegie send a powerful message to parents. The administrator's reference to children with health problems is a good example of how a school can be engaged in ruling relations (Smith, 1987) through the activities it expects from parents, and mothers mostly. Caring for sick children and keeping them healthy for school is consistent with the mothering discourse Griffith and Smith (2004) describe in the introduction. In Manicom's (1995) institutional ethnography, she found that teachers' time spent on caring for students' health needs reinforced social class differences among students and influenced how well teachers were able to meet the academic needs of all students in the class. In this sense, the Carnegie administrator's statement could be interpreted to mean that they want healthy students and that they are not willing to devote school time for meeting the needs of children with health problems or to risk having those children detract from meeting the academic goals of the school. In essence, the comment puts parents on notice that they should not apply to the school if they have sickly or needy children.

Linda was another parent who did a great deal of research on schools before choosing middle schools for her children. She considered El Rancho for her older daughter but did not like it. She liked Carnegie more. Here she compares the two schools:

> I felt like the [El Rancho] gifted program was not particularly creative. I spent a long time looking at the nonmagnet classes and I was really kind of alarmed what a low track they were on, and I didn't like the idea of my daughter being in a small group of kids who were going somewhere amongst a sea of kids who were jerks. And for that reason, I really liked Carnegie. Because even though that isn't a gifted program, I felt like the goal was that everybody can achieve at least getting into college. And oh, the other thing I didn't like about El Rancho was most of the kids were Caucasian in the gifted programs; most of the kids in the general population were Latino or black. I felt, you know, I don't like this. Interestingly, at Carnegie the white kids are actually the minority. At Carnegie it was so wonderful to see really smart African American and Asian kids — well, Asian kids are generally in the gifted programs. But you see Latino and Asian kids who weren't sitting there asleep at their desk, who were going somewhere.

But Linda, too, heard comments during a Carnegie tour, similar to what Natalie and I heard, in which the principal discourages parents from applying:

When I went to the presentation, you know, she sort of does this thing because the auditorium is filled and it's obviously more people than are going to ever get in. She starts out by trying to dissuade people. She says, you know, "As parents, if you're not completely committed to making this work, then there are other schools. Don't come here."

Student and parent behaviors that Carnegie welcomes are related to class-based issues: parents have the time and ability to ensure that their children are healthy; students do not need remediation and are college bound. One of the community advisors commented to me that Carnegie is the school of choice for wealthier African American families. While Carnegie is a very diverse campus, the message disseminated from Carnegie, that it is a "good academic school," focuses attention on only one of the positive outcomes of the district's integration program; it has, as Linda says, "really smart African American and Asian kids." The culture, practices, and discourses found at Carnegie illustrate how the district's integration program can be seen reorganizing to class relations.

The comparison of the different racial groups' participation in the magnet school program in Table 2 indicates that magnet schools have fewer Latino students in proportion to the overall Latino student population in the district. The Carnegie and El Rancho magnet schools have very few students identified as English language learners, which in a district like Deluca, with a large immigrant student population, could mean that language has become a discriminating factor for getting into these schools as well. At both the Carnegie and El Rancho magnets, it may be possible to see racial integration, but the resegregation taking place within and between schools based on other forms of difference — such as language, immigrant status, health, special education needs — seems to continue to go unaddressed by the district.

Perhaps because she is financially able to work as a volunteer at her children's school and be very involved on a day-to-day basis, Meryl seemed more in tune to the reforms at the school. Comparing Carnegie and El Rancho, she noted:

It's like Carnegie is really more geared towards the small high school. And they're into more testing. Which I personally didn't like the fact, that they test them, and then they say they're in by ability .... But I wasn't quite convinced that sixth-graders should be in with all these older kids when I was watching on the yard. I felt that at El Rancho when they reconfigured they grouped the sixth-graders all together. They have like an area of bungalows on the side of the school. Almost all the sixth grade classes are in there and they team teach the sixth grade, even the magnet. So they basically, except for their electives, they're not in with the bigger kids. So I just like the way El Rancho was geared. They're very caring about the whole total middle school child.

Commenting on El Rancho's racial balance, Meryl added,

And the thing about El Rancho, it's really like equally mixed. It's almost like the perfect mixture, like one-third white, one-third Latino, and the rest is like Asian and African American. It's like no one group dominates. And so that diversity I think works really well there.

There are numerous contradictions in these parents' comments about the schools, the students at the schools, and the racial and ethnic balance in these schools. For example, Linda's refers to the kids in regular classes as "jerks" while she worries about segregating her daughter from other students; Meryl feels uncomfortable that Carnegie tests students to place them in tracked classes. Carnegie's testing is not really any different from testing students for giftedness; Meryl's children were tested to determine whether they were gifted, and once identified as such they gained access to better programs. The inconsistencies in Linda's and Meryl's statements lend support to critiques about privileged white and middle-class parents (Brantlinger, 2003). Contradictions such as these can come about partly because of how parents' participation in schools and choice processes has been constructed through multiple discourses, in particular the achievement discourse, and partly because of existing inequitable institutional structures like ability grouping and tracking that are present in the schools their children attend.

Parents must make sense of schooling as they know it and experience it in the everyday lived world they share with their children. Parents' choice work, then, includes taking into account how their choice of schools will affect their personal lives. Karen and her husband tried to make decisions that worked for their new blended family, including taking into consideration the wishes of Karen's stepdaughters' mother and the girls themselves. As both her daughter and her husband's daughter were ready to attend middle school, Karen describes how they negotiated school choice with the mother of her step daughters:

And Tom and I agreed that we wanted Jayne and Neema to go to the same school [Carnegie] because with the dual custody on the one hand and the one child in the one house, you're trying to create a family. So we said that that was really important. So I collected test scores, crime statistics, talked to people who'd gone there, you know, just collected all the information that I could and to make our case that, indeed, Carnegie was a better placement than El Rancho, and [Jayne's mother] just never bought it. To her it wasn't a rational, quote, unquote, decision based on facts or based on data; it was an emotional decision .... And actually, in retrospect El Rancho would have been the better choice. In hindsight.

Previously, Suzanne commented on the difference between the non-magnet and the magnet programs at Davis High School; she did not believe that Davis' regular program was appropriate for her daughters. The opportunity to attend a magnet high school is one of the reasons parents try so hard to get their children enrolled in middle school magnets. They want the magnet school matriculation points for the lottery. Davis High School, the neighborhood high school for many of the parents, has two magnet programs on its campus. The parents who talked about high school choice were very concerned about the quality of the instructional program in the nonmagnet part of Davis High School. Meryl discussed the differences between the various school programs operating at Davis:

And unfortunately, parents hear rumors, and some of it is things that are not true. And some parents don't want, unfortunately, their children to go to a racially integrated school. I hate to say that, but you know, I've heard parents say things like, "I've driven by Davis High School and I see the wrong mix of children standing out there." And I say to them, "You're not seeing the right representation. That school is integrated, but what you're seeing is the continuation school on the corner." And also, a lot of the kids, they're like looking at the kids that are getting out at 3:00 o'clock; when what they don't know is that part of the school gets out at 3:00 o'clock, and then the part that they'd be most happy with probably gets out at 4:15. They never even know that. So they don't even know who goes there. It isn't what they think at all.

The students who attend Davis' Fine Arts magnet and the Liberal Arts magnet have the longer school day, and these students are the ones Meryl wishes other parents would see — students more likely to be middle-class or white.

Parents' Participation in the Inequities of Magnet School Choice

Meryl's comment illustrates how the district's policies and practices that promote and maintain the notion of the magnet school as a good school help construct for parents (and some administrators, too) the idea that these are the schools to attend. But the same policies and practices can help shape a contrary notion that there are not-so-good schools that students should avoid attending. And I think this is going to become even more problematic with the NCLB requirement that school districts publish the names of the schools that have been designated "in need of improvement."

However, magnet school choice is socially organized around the notion of the good school: through information networks, through the ways that administrators promote their schools, and through school cultures centered on the college-bound student. In such an environment, parents' choice work in Deluca USD becomes an instantiation of both the achievement discourse and the integration discourse. Parents use what knowledge they have about the effectiveness and quality of the district's schools (achievement discourse) and what they learn about a school's need for racial balance (integration discourse) to make the school choice decision they think is best for their children and their family. In this way we can see *how it happens* that parents, and mothers in particular, are set up for participation in Deluca USD's inequitable structures and practices. The gender relations underlying much of the choice work that I observed was not visible to parents, to mothers, in my study. The overwhelming number of references to women friends, sisters, and other moms seemed to go unnoticed by parents. They did not seem to see, as I did, that this was almost exclusively work done by women, particularly mothers. But regardless of the gender relations operating, the work these women did, located within the existing class relations and race relations that privileged many of them over other mothers, privileged their children over other mothers' children. Bonnie's story captures the difficulty that this context creates for policy research.

Bonnie's younger daughter was still attending Christopher Street School when she was considering middle schools for her eldest daughter. She was separated from her husband and she applied for Carnegie so the girls would be close by each other:

I didn't shop around. I did the Carnegie stuff. My attitude when I went there, having been raised in a track system in the public schools, was that I didn't have a problem with the fact that she was going to go to school with kids who supposedly were in the top spectrum of performance and intelligence. And I thought, hey, that's fine with me. I don't care if there's no room in the resource program and if in sixth grade you're still not reading on a sixth grade level, then you need to rethink whether you need to be in a college-bound program or not. I was very elitist in that point of view.

Bonnie's views of the school changed, and after a couple of years, she wanted to move her daughter out of Carnegie:

I was extremely disappointed. The Carnegie program sucks. There is no enrichment for the identified gifted children, and when you ask them, "Well, what do you do for my kid, because I know you're getting X amount of dollars extra a year. Where is that money going and how is it benefiting my child?" And they would say, "Oh, well, you know, she's in the ninth grade, or she's in an eighth grade English class, or seventh grade English class when she was in sixth grade" and I would say, "Excuse me, what does that do for Jessica? All that tells me is that the kids who are older than she is weren't successful the first time around. That's not enriching Jessica's experience any."

During the interviews, Bonnie was always very direct and honest in her views that bright children's needs should be met. Her comments often had an insensitive bias against students who were not on the academic level that she perceived herself to have been as a student or not on the academic level on which she perceived her daughters to be. But she explained her strong sentiments this way:

It's just that I felt strong enough about Jessica's high school education that I did not want her to continue in that same environment in the hopes that maybe the high school part of the Carnegie experience would be better than the middle school. I can't mess with, you know, this is Jessica's life. What she does in high school is going to reverberate throughout her life, both academically and socially. She'll be going to Davis in September, to the Liberal Arts Magnet where she'll see the same kids all day and it's a separate education .... So I'm thinking, Jessica will survive and thrive. And I think the other thing for me is, when I tell my kids that I was being a bigot, they were really very upset that I wanted them to be in that kind of environment. I said I want you to be with kids who are like you and they said, "Well, what do you mean?" And I said, "White, Jewish, middle-class and interested in education, because you've not been in that atmosphere and that's where I want you to be now." I think they were shocked that I was so biased, that I would say so blatantly, I want you in this kind of environment, because obviously their experience [at Christopher Street School] has been so completely different. But I sincerely believe that I am doing what's best for them.

Bonnie's comments, as well as the many other comments parents have made about their choice work and decision making, bring to light another side of parents' participation in the district's voluntary integration program. Studying parents' choice work exposes the underside of public school choice and can make visible to policy makers, educators, and (as Bonnie's statement attests) even some parents the very real, everyday implications of parental choice of schools for equal and equitable educational opportunity.

DISCUSSION

Prior research on parents and their involvement in their children's education suggests that that many white and middle-class parents are operating from ideological positions to maintain their power and privilege, using their cultural capital to secure intergenerational privilege for their children (Wells and Serna, 1996; Lareau, 2003). But the school choice processes of the parents whose stories are shared in this book can offer up another interpretation. As Smith's work (1987) reminds us, parents are also located in an actual "everyday/everynight world" that they experience with their children. Their children are very real to them and their futures of great concern. The structure of K–12 education still does not provide for a coordination of quality *and* equitable schooling over the full education career path of an individual student (Mehan, 1978). So coordinating 13 years of schooling becomes the work of parents, and mostly the work of mothers. As a result, urban public school parents may have no choice but to become entangled in the existing inequitable schooling structures and practices that are historically related to racial and social class issues. This can place parents, and more often white and middle-class parents, in the untenable position of making what appears to be the best decision for their children and family without realizing how they may participate in inequitable outcomes for other parents' children.

Educators have passed on powerful ideologies about what constitutes "good" schools; those schools have served middle-class families well. Principals, teachers, and the schools' policies and practices can all be seen influencing what parents know about their children's education. We must remember also that parents', teachers', and administrators' understanding of education and their roles have been constructed by large centralized bureaucracies over many years and in conjunction with well-intentioned liberal policies (Apple, 2001; Tyack and Cuban, 1995).

All of the parents whose stories are shared in this book believed strongly that they have a responsibility to ensure the best opportunities for their children (Graue and Kroeger, 2001). Still, the advantages available for white and wealthier mothers end up limiting the opportunity to achieve greater equity and equality for other mothers' sons and daughters. Efforts at reform designed to help schools become better at educating children are continuous, though not always successful (Oakes et al., 2000; Sarason, 1990). Privileged white and middle-class parents as well as poor and minority parents get caught up in trying to understand these reforms and what they mean for their children's educations. As the workings of schools become more transparent and school outcomes become more public, poor parents and parents of color will increasingly come to understand how institutional structures, cultures, and practices can further their oppression. But so must the educational community. As Weis states:

> The very structures of our institutions reflect classed, racial, and gendered practices .... We must keep this in mind and examine both the ways in which historical injustices are encoded within culture as well as helped [by culture] to shape social identities. Indeed, one of the reasons why social identities take the shape and form they do is undoubtedly due to the form that school knowledge and culture take to begin with (Weis, 1995, p. 164).

Educational institutions have been instrumental in shaping parents' identities in relation to their children's schooling (Griffith and Smith, 2004). The home-school relationship has been shaped around the values and practices of those who are white and middle-class and the normative orientations of the "good parent" and a "good education." (Graue and Kroeger, 2001, p. 476).

We must continue to deconstruct the tensions developing between the options provided to parents in choosing "good" schools for their children and the inequitable outcomes that result from their participation in school choice. Furthermore, it would be unfair to assume that parents' own ideas about good schools and a good education are based on only issues of privilege. Parents' sense of responsibility to plan for their children's future success, however they define success, cannot be discounted. Parents often have thoughtful, reasoned ideas about the kind of schools they envision choosing for their children, as Mimi's comment makes clear:

> I think the parents must have a big blueprint of what kind of building they're building. Whether it's first story, five story, then, if you're building a twenty-first story high rise, you must have a foundation that goes that deep underground in order to build something that high. And I don't think that really says anything about what kind of career you want them to have or how much money you want them to have, but the kind of quality that would take them to the success they're gonna have later in life. And selecting school is part of that big picture. You know. And, I think, selecting school is almost like picking a material. Like you have this great blueprint, but what kind of material are you going to use? Whether you're gonna use the prime material or, you know, just any kind of material and, I think, the school is that material.

As policy makers, as educators, and as citizens, we have yet to provide a good school for every child living in the urban areas across the nation. We have struggled with this for some time. Before we blame parents — and this is mostly placing the blame on mothers — for choosing good schools over not-so-good schools, we need to consider that the programs and processes they are encouraged to participate in are of our own creation as educators, and that the information they receive about schools, teaching, and learning is primarily communicated by the people in the schools themselves. And as for how parents define "success" — well, educators have played a role there, too.

These issues will become more of a problem as the accountability reforms of NCLB, which stress standardization and high-stakes testing, force more schools and their teachers to be labeled as "bad" or "good." Mothers (and many other women working for educational institutions) will be caught in the conflicts and contradictions that are generated as a result of educational policies — policies that count on mothers' work and good mothering to accomplish reform (Griffith and Smith, 2004). It is important that we push for a better understanding of parents' everyday lives, as mothers and fathers, and look more critically and carefully at the way educational institutions have constructed the very roles parents may have no choice but to assume.

4

PLAYING THE "POINTS GAME": UNFAIR ADVANTAGE IN SCHOOL CHOICE

The previous chapters have uncovered the social relations and district organizational structures, cultures, and practices that were operating in the school choice context at the time of my study. The chapters illustrated how local schools, district level departments, and administrators are all active participants in helping to shape the discourses that construct (and are constructed by) parents' choice work. Picture the four pages of magnet schools listed in the *Opportunities for Success* brochure that I described in Chapter 2, grouped by theme and containing only a phone number to call for more information. Think about how parents negotiated the application process, about the constraints established by textually-mediated processes and practices so evident in the brochure; think of all the work that needs to be done before an application should be filled out and sent in by parents. Now picture the work parents actually did and the new knowledge they had (or did not have) as a result. The application sent in to the district, then, had various social relations shaping and constructing how the choice that was made *happened*.

Because the district is only 10.5% white, and yet requires wherever possible, a 30% white student population in the magnets, white applicants have an advantage over nonwhite applicants. Administrative practices that are focused on compliance to the court-ordered voluntary integration program (e.g., maintaining racial/ethnic ratios for schools) and rooted in the achievement discourse (e.g., student grades, test scores, and gifted identification) have shaped and constructed parents' work for choice in ways that reinforce historical advantages for some groups over others (Staiger, 2004). The combination of formulas favoring white families, and a magnet program that is really an allocation and distribution of limited spaces in what are advertised as high-quality integrated schools, demonstrate how institutional structures and practices generate privilege and racial advantage (Wellman, 1993).

The integration formulas and priority points system, while allocating classroom seats by race, ironically support the reorganization of the magnet program to class relations. Gifted programs for high achieving students, which historically enroll students from more economically secure and educated families, contribute to the class-based reorganization as well. The district, whether intentionally or not, is organizing the magnet school program to privilege white, wealthier, and more knowledgeable parents. Clearly those parents with more knowledge and more resources were *gifted* with access to the good schools. These practices further implicate the parents in this study, who were predominately mothers, as participants in the inequitable opportunities that result from their choice work. This is made powerfully evident through more detailed accounts of the parents' choice work.

The stories shared in this chapter continue to present inequitable opportunities for accomplishing choice and how those opportunities are constructed and organized. This chapter looks at not only the work process for choice but also the coordination and intersections of the different levels of policy implementation within the district that bring race and class into the choice process. It makes visible how the choice process, while still powerfully linked to race, reorganizes access to good schools or magnet schools to class relations.

Ethical dilemmas emerge in these stories as parents use knowledge from their everyday, practical understandings about how to get into schools and use the various application procedures and choice options in ways that stretch the truth so that they accomplish their choice. In previous chapters, parents talked about the importance of accumulating magnet points, and in this chapter a mother describes how parents play the "points game" to aid their children's chances for placement in a magnet school. Help, for some parents, also comes from local school or district level people and takes place within written and unwritten local school policies, and reflects multiple institutional cultures, practices, and interests.

This chapter looks closely at how individual parents negotiated the social organization of the district's school choice options on behalf of their children. Past chapters looked at the social relations operating to help coordinate and determine parents', mothers', choice work. The outcomes of their choice work are presented in this chapter. Some of the parents were able to get their children into the schools they wanted by using other choice options or other means, such as political favors or "playing the points game" and their stories will be shared first. The stories that follow will be those of the parents who did not initially get their children into the school they wanted and then needed to try other means for getting into the schools they wanted their children to attend.

GETTING INTO THE SCHOOL OF CHOICE

As a result of the work they did, Mary, Bonnie, Karen, and Natalie were successful in getting a school allocation for their children to the magnet school of their choice through the computer lottery. They did not need to do anything more than research the different magnet schools, learn from others how to take advantage of the district's priority points system and racial formulas, make a choice, and master the application process.

Both of Mary's children were accepted at Carnegie. Bonnie had one child accepted at El Rancho Gifted Magnet and one at the Davis Liberal Arts Magnet. Karen had one child at El Rancho Gifted Magnet and two children accepted at Carnegie. Natalie's child was accepted at Carnegie. All four of them had their children enrolled at Christopher Street Elementary Magnet and were enjoying the privileges of matriculation that comes with participation in the district's magnet program. With the exception of Natalie, unless there were some major changes in their circumstances, their K–12 choice work was a success. Natalie, unsure if Carnegie was the environment for her oldest son, chose to send him to a private school instead.

For the rest of the parents in the study, their choice work would continue into other choice options or other ways of getting into the magnet schools. As the administrator from El Rancho explained about getting into that school, if a child did not get into the magnet, the parent would have to know how to get into the school through other ways. Chapter 1 discussed the two most popular options, open enrollment and permits, which provided parents alternative ways to get into the good schools. These other choice options require more choice work — parents may have to interact with additional texts — and some of the same organizing criteria will still impact the choice process. As Chapter 1 explained, most of the permit options as well as open enrollment must follow integration guidelines, and openings will still be determined by available classroom space. Because Carnegie is a full magnet school, these two options are not accepted for enrollment into that school.

El Rancho has an Honors program in the nonmagnet part of the school, so for some parents, enrolling your child at regular El Rancho is considered the next best choice. Some parents also negotiated the other available options in order to get their children into the schools they thought were good schools, not all of which were magnet schools. Their stories about how they got into those good schools follow in the next sections.

Favored Status

In this section of the chapter, Natalie, Mimi, Meryl, Manuel, and Paul and Jenny are presented individually to show how they drew on different social locations within the district and its schools to accomplish choice through the magnet program or through other enrollment options. The parents successfully negotiating choice are the parents with particular kinds of social or cultural capital. In discussing with me access to schools of choice in the district, one of the community advisors said that since there are more white parents with higher socioeconomic levels than minority parents, it would stand to reason that more white parents would know how to work the system. But the advisor also pointed out "the upper-class African Americans and Latinos and other parents are able to work the system just as well as the upper-class white parents." The advisor said that if one were to look at the *Opportunities for Success* brochure and at the schools like Carnegie and other popular magnet schools with a high volume of applications, the majority of parents applying to those schools are from higher economic levels:

> They feel that those are better schools. And in a lot of cases, they're right. I mean, if you look at the teaching, you look at the quality of teachers at these schools, they far exceed regular schools. I mean, especially at Carnegie. Those teachers were hand-picked, each one of them. There's no must-hires there. I doubt that there are any emergency credentialed teachers there. Probably aren't. You know. And that's why parents are fighting to get in those schools. Their programs, their innovativeness, what the teachers are doing, the initiative they're taking, the motivation of the staff. It's far superior. The graduation rate, the amount of students that graduate from these schools that go on and graduate from college are higher than the other schools. I mean, who wouldn't want their kid to go there?

Multiple discourses are embedded in how Carnegie gets constructed as a good school, as having good teachers, innovative programs, high graduation rates, and future college attendance. The last chapter indicated that in addition to the selective teaching staff at Carnegie, there is a select student population.

Natalie

Natalie's son was accepted at Carnegie, but she chose not to send him there. Natalie disagrees with the singular academic focus at Carnegie, saying,

> They're educating the child one way, too rigid in their academic focus. I think of a child as being a whole person, and when he's eighteen, I want to send him out into the world a complete individual, you know. I didn't get the impression, it may go on, but no one gave me that impression that that's what they were concerned about.

Yet the special privileges that come with the magnet school programs and Carnegie in particular were difficult to leave behind for private school. Natalie was very aware that not going to Carnegie and leaving the magnet system meant giving up her magnet points. "Tough choice. Big choice. I lose twelve points for matriculation, and I also lose potential sibling points if I decide to send my next child there. So, yeah, fifteen points in all. Lost forever." And then she added, "Of course, forever is a dubious term when you happen to know Mr. Hartman and a few other people in the office, you know. Nothing is really lost forever."

Knowing administrators in the district and still having younger children at Christopher Street School seemed to ease some of Natalie's concerns about jeopardizing her magnet school matriculation privileges. But Natalie's second concern was that her son would not benefit from the racially sensitive program at Carnegie.

> I mean, African American parents look at Carnegie where it's predominantly African American and is run on an African American slant, you know. Those are the privileged people at Carnegie, which is kind of nice. Sorry I'm gonna miss out on that.

She also knows that for many parents who don't get into the school it is terribly disappointing:

> But when you don't get in, you know, that is like the only place for you. You know, that's your place in the district. That's where you shine. That's frightening because you can't go somewhere else

like, I mean, if your kid goes to Paul Smith [middle school]. He's gonna be okay, you know. As long as he doesn't get into any violent situations, he's gonna be fine. You're gonna see to it. You know. My kid goes to Paul Smith. That's not exactly the same thing. You know. I have a whole other set of issues goin' on there that I can't exactly get in there and fix right away, you know. That's scary. Carnegie is the only real option for an African American kid. And people are on the waiting list ages down, you know. They don't get to go. They have to go to their neighborhood school .... They just take it and try to get in honors classes.

Much of what Natalie says is supported by district demographic information. The school is 43% black, which is considerable for a district that is only 13.6% black. The school has historically served the African American community, offering it an academically focused program. As a magnet school, though, it still must take in white students, and whites make up 32% of the student population, keeping Carnegie in compliance with the integration formulas. Given the reorganization to class relations taking place in the district's magnet schools, it could be expected that the majority of these African American and white students are from wealthier or more highly educated families.

Mimi

One of the things Natalie mentioned about Christopher Street School as she was talking about her children's teachers is that the upper grades were poor compared to the primary grades. Mimi, also at Christopher Street, felt the same way. She decided after a lot of thought to pull her children from the school and applied to a highly gifted elementary magnet:

But I love Christopher Street .... And this is a very good place for your child to go to school. So I fought off the desire for a couple years because, you know, I had known many parents from Highland [the highly gifted magnet], and they've been trying to get me over there. But by the time third grade came and gone, I said, "No. I cannot do this any more." Because the disparity between children's ability was becoming very much apparent .... And I felt that my daughter had the ability to be academic, and she enjoyed being academic. And I wanted to put her in a situation where she had to work and not just get good marks whatever she did.

Both of Mimi's children got accepted into the highly gifted magnet, which was unusual. She said that even if children have points for magnet schools it still does not guarantee that your children will get in right away:

> You would never get in there unless you had many, many points of waiting or whatever. But I pulled heavy strings from the administration because I had been active. You know, I know all the administrators and the Board members .... the School Board member and the person who was in charge of Department of Integration. So, you know, I know, they got me in there.

Mimi went on to tell me that it did not go unnoticed by other parents:

> So both kids went at the same time, so there was some ruckus there. Because the Korean parents all knew that I had never applied before, and they had been waiting for many years. And if one got in there, they'd say, "Oh, my God. Fluke." You know. But both of them got in at the same time so there was some, you know, problem.

She did say she felt bad about the other parents who may have been waiting many years and still were not able to get into the school. And she commented that had she not been able to "pull this kind of string" after she had been so active, people would "probably lose faith" in her. She said:

> But I felt that somehow I was justified getting there because I had worked very hard in the school system as far as volunteer and stuff. And then I don't think the Board member would've done it for me unless he knew that. You know. So there were some merits of my own. And, you know, as much as we try to reach fairness in all aspects of our life, I think certain work or certain avenues grant you more perks in life. And, I think, if you volunteer to death and never get any kind of recognition, I don't think there would be enough drive to work, you see what I mean. So, I think, in certain ways, I felt that I was appreciated, and that I was entitled to go there because I had spent many, many hours organizing parents, informing parents, and doing good with other parents. And, you know, I'm sure this wasn't a good method of proving that, I don't think. It looks kind of bad in a way, but there just wasn't enough space, not enough good schools, not enough good schools to go to, to begin with. I mean, just very, very limited selection.

Of the reasons she gives to justify using political favors, her volunteer work was primary. Mimi discussed with me the kinds of things she has done and clearly has had extensive involvement in the school and district. She considers the many volunteer activities *work*, and there should be some return for all the work she has done for the local school and the district. This is not just Mimi constructing her privilege. As a bilingual Korean parent, educators needed Mimi to help reach out to the growing non-English-speaking Korean community. Additionally, while she did a great deal of work for her favors, she is not alone in benefiting from knowing someone who can help her get into magnet schools. I asked one of the community advisors if many parents know how to work the system and the advisor said:

> I think the majority don't know. Maybe a small, select 10% know. And those that know, what they know, is to know somebody. And that's your best bet. 'Cause your child can have the highest of grades, be the most intelligent, and you still won't be able to get your child in the school that you want. But the ones that know, really, will know somebody on the Board, or upper administration, or a staff person, or a principal, or a friend of a friend, that can get you in. And that's what it is they know.

An administrator made comments that support what the community advisor said. He said that for the most part, the magnet lottery is "very legit." But he went on to say,

> And do some people have greater influence than others? Uh-huh, sure they do. Board members call, you know, "I don't know if you can do anything, but …" And of course it's a constituent, maybe it's been a really dear friend or someone who's been a happy contributor to their campaigns or what have you. But I'm not saying that is the problem. There are other influential people, district staff themselves who want their kids, you know. God knows how many district staff people are in [magnet] schools, you know.

The same administrator also talked about parents of gifted children, like Mimi, who grow impatient with schools that they perceive to be not meeting their children's needs:

> But as soon as you identify a kid as gifted — that's what the principals of the minority schools are telling us — soon as you identify a kid as gifted, they want to leave that school and go to a magnet.

So here we're telling the schools, "Seek them out, work with them, identify them, and start doing some gifted programs." Parents don't want to wait for that, and you can't blame them. "My kid's been ID'd as gifted and I want a gifted magnet, get me out of here." So then you've got to tell somebody to go against their better nature and say, "Well, I'm willing to wait." Well, there are not too many around that's going to do that.

Mimi's experiences and the comments from the district staff continue to provide opportunities to analyze how the institution constructs the context of school choice. The number of good schools is limited, and not only parents have learned which are the good schools; district staff know them as well. The work you do for the district's schools as a parent volunteer or as an employee are among the ways to get your children into the good schools. Identifying them as gifted is another. As this administrator's comments point out, the district's solution to the low numbers of Latino and African American gifted students has not been to think about, and talk through with parents, what gifted education means and the inequity it has created, but instead to find more minority gifted students, thereby reinforcing giftedness as the identification to have and for which a student should be rewarded.

Maybe one could argue that identity politics are behind the push to have more underrepresented students identified as gifted, but such politics are still part of the extended social relations that are extralocal to parents' everyday worlds with their children and their involvement with schools. As Natalie and Mimi learned from other parents and their own observations, Christopher Street's upper grades are not very strong. As active parents, involved in the school's leadership and well-read in parenting literature, these experiences shaped their interpretations of the school context and their search for other school choice options. Natalie's comments cannot be taken lightly:

I feel that I was suckered into Christopher Street, you know. I had a fabulous kindergarten experience, and I'm still having a fabulous kindergarten experience. I'm sick of kindergarten. I told the teacher the other day I've done this project three times. I can't do it anymore. You know. But it's still a fabulous experience, and my child, my daughter comes home thrilled death to do her homework, thrilled to death that she can do something different. You know. That is wonderful. That's what keeps them going. My fifth grader comes home and just wants to die if he has to go to school another time. I put him in school with the hope that maybe today will be better than yesterday, and they send him home every day with the concept that, oh, mommy, lied to me again. I mean, it gets worse and worse each year ending in this year with, he would rather flunk out than go to school, which is very hard for someone who's tested gifted, scores in the ninety percentile C.T.B.S. and loved school up until the third grade. You know, that's very hard to watch. I got gypped, you know.

Blaming parents who are making decisions for their children based on the knowledge they get through schooling experiences is of no help here. How could we reasonably expect them to do otherwise? A goal of my project is to explicate those relations operating to shape and help determine parents' school choice decisions, to make visible where the possibilities for alternative relations might exist. One obvious place is the magnet school choice application process.

THE GAMES PARENTS MUST PLAY

One of the most powerful stories that emerged during interviews was how parents have learned to play the points game in order to get their children into the middle schools they think are best, usually the gifted or college preparatory magnets. If they were at a neighborhood elementary school, beginning in third grade, they would apply for a place at an elementary magnet school that was oversubscribed with white students and that rarely admitted students other than for incoming kindergarten and first grade. Expecting to be rejected by the computer lottery, they then could accumulate waiting list points over a three-year period and be ready with 12 points for the middle school lottery.

Meryl

In previous chapters, Meryl was introduced as an active parent who bought her home with the local elementary school in mind. The reputation of the local school was very good, and she made no plans to attend an elementary magnet school. She was active at the local elementary school PTA from the start. Although the regular part of El Rancho was her neighborhood middle school, her children had been identified as gifted and she wanted them to be in the gifted magnet there. "And my friends all said it doesn't really matter, because if your child is tested gifted they will get the Honors classes, which are equal to the magnet. But still you have your reservations until you see for yourself." Not having matriculation points to carry over from a magnet elementary school, she explained to me the process she learned for acquiring magnet school points for her children's applications:

Meryl: With my son, well what happened was, being active in the PTA and Friends of Ridgecrest, some of his friends' older siblings whose parents were involved in the school and they sort of mentored me and basically you really need to ask because you don't know what's really going on. Because of the point system to get into the magnet and it being my first time, I was afraid of like applying and getting in too soon so I actually had delayed by one year and he was on the waiting list, the top of the waiting list, but he didn't get in for seventh grade. So he was in Honors for seventh grade and he was in the magnet in eighth grade, so he actually graduated from the magnet. The second time around I knew the ropes more and I knew when to apply for the points. Actually I think the first time I applied for my daughter was I think after second or third grade because if you don't get in you can keep the points for up to three years

Lois: So you have to pick a school that you don't want to go to?

Meryl: It seems to me like a kind of backwards way of doing it because that's the thing, you have to hope that you don't get into the school. For instance, like last year when I was most concerned. She already had 8 points and then there's other ways to get other points besides just the 12. Well, O.K., I knew she had the 8 points and I wanted her to get the 12 points for sure. So when it was time to apply this last time, what I had to do was look at all of the list and then see that Spring Street School doesn't take very many children at fifth grade, if any. So what I did, I called the office at Spring Street School and asked, "How many openings do you have for fifth grade?" And they said, "Oh, none." So I said, "That's the school I'm applying to."

In the previous chapters, parents and administrators referred to the points needed for magnet schools and how important it was to be knowledgeable about how the priority points system worked. This knowledge about the school choice process was critical for parents. Just as parents in the last chapter pointed out the importance of knowing a school's racial/ethnic balance, so is it important to know how many applications the magnet schools receive at the different grade levels. The parents like Meryl who have this kind of critical knowledge about the application brochure are also reading it with more sophistication:

I mean, that's the whole sad thing. Like applying for points to a school just because you want to get on the wait list, then you're really not applying because you want to get in that school. And it makes that school look like, you know, everyone wants to go to Spring Street School, but really not everyone wants to go there, it's just that everyone knows it's a popular school. But the applications are inflated because parents know that they'll have a good chance of being turned away, especially in the upper grades where there are hardly any openings. So they use it as a way to, you know, just save their points.

And this is, again, not just of the parents' own doing. The district has helped to construct this scheme for parents by organizing the application process as "research it yourself," allocating limited spaces by the various racial formulas and priority point systems, and emphasizing the academic qualities of the magnet school program. This was also the message in the video that reminds parents to be sure to check out the race/ethnicity needs of grade level openings at the magnet schools of interest. The application, as an active text, not only coordinates parents' understandings and actions in the choice process but also masks the school district's administrative role in constructing a context where playing points games is necessary. Just under 7% of the district's student population is enrolled in magnet schools. The percentage of elementary students enrolled in elementary magnets is proportionately smaller because parents are more likely to have their children remain at their neighborhood schools during the elementary school years. Therefore the vast majority of elementary school parents begin their experiences with their children's schooling in regular elementary school programs. Through various permits and open enrollment it is also possible to choose among the regular elementary and secondary schools. Some parents exercised school choice in this way as well.

Jenny and Paul

Paul and Jenny live with their two children in a small home in a middle-class neighborhood. Even though they are middle-class parents, Paul and Jenny still did not have access to a parent network when they first enrolled their children in school. Like Meryl, Paul and Jenny did not apply to elementary magnet schools. They both work full time and needed to send their children to an elementary school with an after-school child care program. Even then they were careful to look closely at the schools they would consider:

Paul: [We are] certainly trying to make an effort to visit the schools. But even though that's been important to the both of us, ultimately, you know, their message is very well rehearsed. And so what the reality is, isn't what you hear. They may be two different things.

Jenny: Also, you know, watching the newspaper for things. Looking at the test scores. And I think, location also. I mean, there are probably wonderful schools, but we're not gonna spend an hour truckin' our kids off to some school that they could never participate in the activities and we couldn't really, you know, easily go back for the open house or whatever. It just doesn't make sense to me.

Paul: Our concern was that being both working, I mean, my biggest concern was if the kid's sick, I wanna be able to get to my car and get to them and not have to drive for an hour .... Especially since our daughter had a lot of problems with asthma.

Paul and Jenny were able to get their son, first, and then the younger daughter, into Brookhaven Elementary School on permits. They were told the school had limited space to honor permit requests because Brookhaven needed to save space for students from the Overcrowded Schools Student Placement (OSSP) program.

When their daughter, Cathy, was ready to attend Brookhaven, she was granted preference through a sibling permit. Jenny said, "I wanted to try this year for Cathy on open enrollment. There are no spaces. Siblings is their unofficial policy of how people get in. Like Cathy would not have gotten in on a child care permit if Paul wasn't with the school. Cause that was really just because she was a sibling, and that's, you know, not policy."

Jenny and Paul wanted their son, who was identified as gifted, to attend El Rancho Gifted Magnet. They had decided that if he did not get into the gifted magnet they would try open enrollment. If that did not work, they knew they could do a child care permit for the nonmagnet part of El Rancho. In fact, their son did not get into the magnet at El Rancho. They discussed how they found out about the points game:

Paul: And when we brought Cathy to Brookhaven we had no clue about this point business and we didn't learn about it till pretty late in the game. And nobody told us about it. Nobody, you know, there was no orientation that this is how the system works. So to me there's some kind of failure in educating parents on, okay, here's how the system works. You know, it's like all this hush-hush. We finally, when some of the parents that we started socializing with realized we didn't know what the heck they were talking about, you know, "Oh," and then they explained it. But we didn't know. I mean, the school didn't tell us. City didn't tell us. You know, district didn't tell us. So to me there's something wrong with that .... But who creates the points game? Who creates the points? It sounds like it was a bunch of bureaucrats.

Jenny: Well, they didn't think about the implications, Honey. Not everybody could get into the school of choice. So they figured, well, if you don't get in, they'll give you some points and the next time you'll have a better chance of getting in. What they didn't think about is people who are happy with their elementary school, will start applying for schools that they know they could never get into so they can rack up points to go to the [middle school.] I mean, they didn't think about that.

Paul: But it's a no lose situation. I mean, you look in the brochure and it tells you how many wait-list kids there are. It's like, the odds are better than Las Vegas.

As middle-class white parents, Jenny and Paul were still out of the information loop about the points game. Their position outside of the group of parents who got this information early on shows how naive they were when they entered the public school district. Yet that same position allows them to critique the bureaucracy that they believe is behind the points game. As administrators and community advisors have said in previous chapters, Paul and Jenny didn't have someone who could mentor them in how the system works. Once they got the information, it is their more privileged class and racial positions that allows Paul to see it as a no-lose situation; it can be a sure-lose situation for other parents.

Since their son did not get into the magnet, Paul and Jenny filled out an open enrollment application for El Rancho. They were unable to attend the open enrollment lottery drawing held at the school, but their son's name was selected:

Jenny: We got a letter in the mail — it was like one in four [students got in]. And then you [Paul] took the letter into school and Phyllis Langer said, "It's like, oh, it's better than winning the lotto."

Paul: And I don't understand that process real well either. Because our son who was in the gifted program in elementary school is now in the honors program at El Rancho, which they claim is the same as pretty much the magnet program at El Rancho. So, you know, they say it's very comparable. I don't believe that it is, and I don't understand quite honestly the distinction between it all.

There were other parents whose children did not get into the magnet at El Rancho. All of the children earned waiting list points. Once they are in El Rancho's Honors program, parents keep applying to the magnet:

Paul: And some of his friends that were also in honors like he was, that didn't get into the magnet, now they've gotten into magnet, you know, by reapplying. We didn't get in this year either. Well, I guess that's good because now we've got more points. And so, you know, it's like, gee, it's a win-win. I don't know.

Jenny: Yeah. We figure if he doesn't get in this final year, we'll have more points. And if he does, then it's easier to get into a magnet if you're already in a magnet. So we can't lose this year with him.

Paul: But it just seems another level of absurdity.

Paul and Jenny are benefiting from the overlapping structures and practices that coordinate Honors programs and magnet schools for gifted students within some of the district's schools. They see, only partially, how the school choices that their children enjoy are constructed around intersecting, and sometimes conflicting, district policies, making the process appear absurd instead of systematic.

Because my research took place over two years, parents whose children were entering middle school at the start of the study were already looking into high school by the end of the study. During my last meeting with them, Jenny and Paul knew the importance of getting information early and had already attended high school information nights for their son. They knew that if their son was not successful in the lottery for El Rancho Gifted Magnet for the coming year, he would then have 12 waiting list points. They figured that those may be enough for getting into a high school magnet. Attending the high school meetings, they were hearing that now that their son is at El Rancho, it should not be a problem for them to get him into a good high school:

Jenny: Some of the administrators, well, they'll say in various ways, you know, like when we were applying at El Rancho, they said, "Well, you know, if you need help, let us know." You know, in fact, at the high school night some of the people said, "Well, you know, if your kid really needs to get into this school, let us know." So there are sort of these back-door ways, I guess, that they all have up their sleeve. And I guess I believe that if you had some real sincere case or reason or whatever or just was the squeaky wheel, that you might just get what you really want.

Paul: I heard that differently. I read that as being a message that El Rancho has a reputation especially in the honors programs to have better kids. So if they're looking at kids from El Rancho versus kids from Madison, based on Madison's reputation, that they're more than happy to accommodate the El Rancho kids over the Madison kids .... And I think that was, you know, some of the comments that were made was, well El Rancho is an important feeder school for us. And, of course, Columbia High School said, "If your kid wants to come, we'll get you in. I'm sure they don't say that in every single city school, you know, but they said that at El Rancho.

One of the levels of analysis in an institutional ethnography is to explicate the complementary role of the local school and local school personnel in the social organization and coordination of parents' school choice options. Paul's and Jenny's experiences highlight how many of these schools are choosing parents along with parents choosing schools (Wells, 1993; Bowe et al., 1994; Ball, 1996). They suspect that schools are also selecting certain students over others. An administrator at El Rancho said something similar in the last chapter when talking about schools that are trying to keep or build their reputations as good schools; they know that one way to do that is to enroll the high achieving students. And clearly some parents are getting the message that administrators have some leeway in letting parents in on permits if options like open enrollment are closed off owing to lack of classroom space. While this revisits the equity concerns of the administrators in the departments that oversee these options, these concerns need to be focused on local administrative actions as well as on parents.

Manuel

In Chapter 1, one of the permit options described was the interdistrict permit. This is the permit that allows a student to attend a school in a district that is not their resident district. There are a few surrounding districts that have interdistrict transfer arrangements with the Deluca USD. Manuel's son participates in this kind of interdistrict transfer, and in fact had the opportunity to attend schools in two other districts. A district administrator explained to me how one of the interdistrict transfer arrangements that was available to Manuel's son came about. He told me that about 20 years ago a neighboring district, Rio Vista USD, wanted to integrate their district and the high school in particular. They also wanted access to some of the federal money that went along with integration plans. Rio Vista High School, which serves an affluent community, was originally given permission by Deluca to contact minority families at only one middle school in the district and offer parents the option to send their children to Rio Vista HS.

I learned informally that there were once a few high-ranking minority administrators in Deluca USD who had sons, daughters, nieces, and nephews who transferred to the particular middle school from which Rio Vista recruited so they would be eligible for selection to Rio Vista HS. Rio Vista only solicited the top minority students from the school, and the arrangement meant that many minority students, who otherwise would have matriculated to the local high school, never showed up. The arrangement was protected for several years, until parents from the middle school and local high school complained that rather than allowing Rio Vista to raid the bright minority students from one school, the district should open up the opportunity to students from all schools.

Today, Rio Vista selects from a particular few middle schools; El Rancho is one of them. The administrator further explained that Rio Vista has "permission from the district to contact the schools and to get the names of the students that they're interested in and then contact those students," and added, "It is a very biased program. They pick and choose the kids that they want to select from." I was told that there are other similar transfer programs between Deluca USD and neighboring districts and particular school communities, which are based more often on the receiving districts' needs for increasing their funding from the state than increasing the choice options for Deluca's students.

Manuel received a letter from El Rancho asking him if he was interested in enrolling his son at Rio Vista (and for his daughter the following year). He said:

Sí nos llega la información de la El Rancho. Pero lo que pasa es que, se me hace que [Rio Vista] es como para gente que es muy, muy alta. Y yo, pues allí llegan los hijos de los ricos en su limousina, y mi hijo va a llegar en el bus. Y yo no lo quiero hacer menos. Mejor que vaya Horizon.

We get information from El Rancho. But what happens is that I feel that [Rio Vista] is only for people who are really, really up there. And I, well there the children of the rich people come in their limousine, and my son is going to get there in the bus. And I don't want him to feel any less. It's better that he go to Horizon.

Horizon High School is located in another district and allows some students to transfer to the school on interdistrict permits and is where Manuel's son Victor was enrolled. If a district like Horizon has the classroom space, taking in students on transfers is advantageous because it increases the per-pupil funding they get from the state. Manuel had heard through his sister's friend that Horizon was a better school than his local high school, Davis. His son had a 3.0 grade point average at El Rancho and Manuel's sister suggested that they find a way for his son to attend Horizon. When I asked how he was able to get his son into Horizon he said:

Pues, yá ve que es uno muy mañoso (laughs). Bueno, mentiría. Yo le diría yo a los maestros, mi hijo esta bién y que yo necesito que por favor le den el chance pues de ir a esa escuela. Porque, sí, yá recu - cómo? Recurrimos una vez a esa oportunidad cuando de Victor [wanted to go to Horizon]. Dijimos que mi hermana que vivía o que tiene su trabajo por allí y que por eso que a mi hijo le quedaba bién la escuela. No, es pues, no piden muchos requisitos, simple y sencilla - mente que su puntuación. Sus grados estén bién y que alguien viva para que le dé una carta de que necesitan sus servicios. Por ejemplo de mi hermana, mi hermana trabajaba en la Ciudad Horizon y alli tenía un patrón, entonces su patrón le dió una carta donde ella tra - bajaba y que ella podía hacerse cargo de mi hijo cuando saliera de la escuela y cuando entrara.

Well, you see, that one is very tricky (laughs). Well, I would lie. I would tell the teachers, my son is good and that please, I need to have a chance for him to attend this school. Because, yes, we already did that — how? We did that before when Victor [wanted to go to Horizon]. We said that my sister lives or that she has her work over there and that's the reason why the school was convenient for my son. Well, what happens is that the school doesn't ask that much requirements, just about their grades. The grades must be good and also that someone lives in the area. For instance my sister works in the City of Horizon and she got a letter from her boss stating where she works and that she was able to be in charge of my son, bringing him and picking him up to and from the school.

Before being granted the permit, Victor had an interview with the principal in which he was asked questions about why he wanted to come to the school and how he heard about the school. He was asked to bring his grade transcripts.

Manuel is aware that grades make the difference in whether his children can benefit from the interdistrict transfer. Because his daughter had only a 2.0 grade point average, he did not try to enroll her at Horizon. She attended the nonmagnet program at Davis High School, the part of the school that some of the other parents in the study would not consider for their children because of the poor reputation and low test scores associated with the regular program at Davis. Manuel did not indicate that he knew of the low academic reputation of regular Davis, yet he compares what he has learned about Horizon to what he has learned about Davis and reached a conclusion similar to the other parents.

Pues yo te voy a decir que regularmente lo estoy aprendiendo lo de las escuelas porque ellos van pasando, ¿no? Por ejemplo, Victor yá paso en Hughes, yá pasó en El Rancho, ahora está en Horizon. Entonces yo voy seleccionando qué tipo de escuelas. Ahora para el próximo que va él (Fernando), que va ir él, prefiero Horizon porque allí vi la experiencia que con que es mejor con Victor que en Davis con Marisol. Y me lo han comprobado porque la vez pasada me llegó un reporte de la escuela donde él, su nivel estaba bajando y me mandan a decir que pasó. Entonces yo tengo entendido que es más estricta esa escuela de Horizon. Porque mi otra hija (Marisol) no me mandan nada. O sea no me mandan a decir.

Well I should tell you that usually what I learn from schools is through my children as they pass from one level to the other. For instance, Victor passed from Hughes, passed from El Rancho and now he's in Horizon. This is how I am making a choice about schools. Now the next level for him (his younger son, Fernando), he's going to be next, I'd rather choose Horizon because I could see the experience there is much better with Victor than Davis with Marisol. And they have proved it to me, because the last time I got a report from the school where he (Victor), his performance was decreasing, they [the teachers] ask me what happened. So I understand that Horizon is very strict. Because my other daughter (Marisol), they don't send me anything. I mean they don't let me know.

All four of Manuel's children attended their neighborhood elementary school, the same school which was the neighborhood school for Suzanne's children, a school to which she would not send her daughters. All of his children attended regular El Rancho and were not enrolled in the Honors program. Manuel mentioned in Chapter 2 how he had thrown out the magnet brochure he received in the mail in English. His school choice alternative was to use his family's cultural capital and social network to get his son into Horizon. The option was only possible because his son had good grades to begin with and because he was willing to lie.

Compared to the other parents in the study who are white and or wealthier, it is striking to see how little useful information and opportunity for choice within Deluca USD Manuel was provided by the schools his children attend. Yet, it seems it was easy for him to be contacted by the Rio Vista district for both his son and daughter as that district tried to diversify their campus.

I was not able to explore further the historical and political contexts of interdistrict transfers, but within the context of how Manuel accomplishes his choice are much broader issues extending from underenrolled districts trying to increase their state funding to whiter and wealthier districts increasing their diversity to qualify for federal funding. These dynamics are not something that Manuel can see; he sees only the importance of good grades as determinants of opportunity. But Manuel's story shows the potential for exploring, from the standpoint of an undocumented, single father, how broad social relations shape and determine the inequitable educational opportunities and outcomes his children receive in an urban public school district, opportunities and outcomes that are very different from those of the more privileged parents in the study.

OTHER WAYS INTO SCHOOLS OF CHOICE

In many cases the parents spend a great deal more time and do even more work to try other options that range from using political favors, child care permits, open enrollment options, and so on. These other options also operate to organize socially parents' experiences with choice, though in different ways. Presented here are four stories that capture the different ways some parents were able to secure a place for their child at a school other than their regularly assigned school when their preferred choice option did not work out. Suzanne asks her ex-husband to file papers documenting that he is one-fourth Native American so she can have their daughters' racial identity changed to Native American, thereby increasing their chances of getting into magnet schools. Linda finds out her son's application was kicked out of computer processing because of a school error and fights to have the problem corrected. Brenda describes paying someone she knew to use that person's address to enroll her daughter into El Rancho. And the continuous rejection that Robin experiences in trying to get her daughter into El Rancho and her son into a good elementary school results in her having to go over a principal's head to seek the help of a regional administrator in placing her son at a better school. In these accounts are sometimes more texts for parents to negotiate, more applications to complete, and letters to write.

The district's policies and implementation practices locate parents, mothers, within a complex student assignment system allocating a very small percentage of students to magnet schools. The remaining students in the district attend mostly regular nonmagnet schools, many of which are not perceived as good schools. Once again it is important to point out that the newly required NCLB school choice transfers will only further complicate the already inequitable school choice options that parents encounter.

The stories in this chapter already point to the ethical issues parents negotiate, whether manipulating waiting list points or lying in order to secure a transfer permit. Parents who have knowledge of alternative ways of getting into schools do not always use that knowledge without reflecting on those ethical issues. Because of the way choice is socially organized in Deluca USD, local school personnel are involved with ethical issues as well. One of the El Rancho administrators talked about the kinds of dilemmas parents find themselves in when they do not want to send their children to the neighborhood school:

> I got an interesting phone call from a parent a couple of weeks ago. And she said to me, "I want to talk to you." She said, "I don't know what to do. My child's graduating from the fifth grade from one of the local elementary schools. Most of the kids at that elementary school go to El Rancho, but where we live, they go to another school." And she said, "I would really like to send my child to that [other] school, but my daughter just finished there, and she really had three extremely difficult years." And so when I told her that they had a new administration there that I was very impressed with, and I thought that it was the right leadership and so forth, and I said, "You know, really, I think things will be different." And her answer to me was, essentially, "I can't wait three years. My child's starting the sixth grade next year." So she was faced with a dilemma. She obviously had people who she knew within this community who would provide quote, "The child care," unquote. She didn't feel comfortable doing that because

there are, obviously, ethical issues involved in doing that kind of stuff. At the same time, she has a real flesh and blood child that she wants to get the best education you can possibly get in a safe environment and a tough decision to have to make.

When parents are faced with these tough decisions, the decision they ultimately make is also going to affect another parent's child. I have tried to make clear that not just parents but the school district and administrators also have fostered perceptions that there are good schools and then there are all the rest of the schools. The administrator quoted above sees ethical issues for everyone involved when some schools are not doing a good job at teaching and learning saying:

What do you say to a parent who says what some of the parents have said to me, and you know it's true? Do I say to that parent, "Tough. The right thing to do is to put your child in a school where you think your child may very much suffer"? There are conflicting values there.

The administrator continued:

Now, if, on the other hand, I really felt that the other school had an equal program, I would have no problem saying, "Hey, go there. Because although there may be some differences, you know, they may be stronger in some areas, and we may be stronger in some areas. I think your child will do just fine and get a good education at that school, and that's what you should do."

Scholars have noted that the frustration educators and parents feel over public schools that are not equal and not successfully educating all students is real (Dehli, 1996). These statements by the El Rancho administrator also signal that there is a complementary role played by local schools, even if sympathetic to parents, in helping to construct how parents will experience the choice process. Another El Rancho administrator further makes this point when addressing the strategies parents use to get into the school. The administrator discussed openly and honestly what is taking place:

Not only am I aware, but sometimes I help parents. Sometimes I teach them about the child care permit. I have even assisted them in getting child care providers. Parents are desperate. It's a desperate situation, and sometimes parents who are new to the community, for example, it isn't just the mommy tom-tom. It's the college tom-tom. We have had many, many parents come to us saying they have been advised by their colleagues at the college that this is the only middle school that they should come to, this or Wilson. And frankly they live in the Madison area and they have been told by their colleagues, "Do not send your child to Madison, or to Foster, or even to Paul Smith."

One of the schools, Madison Middle School, happens to be the neighborhood school for Paul and Jenny, and has numerous parents requesting child care permits out of the school. The same El Rancho administrator also said, "Parents sincerely have a need. They want to come to this school. We can't end this tide of parents who are seeking better schools for their children. And if Madison ever decided to stop signing those [transfers], I think that there would be hell to pay. I don't think anybody wants that headache."

The administrators also described how the Korean community has found ways to get their children enrolled at El Rancho. One of the administrators said that for a long time many Korean students attended the gifted magnet at Kennedy Middle School, and recently the school administration changed. The new administrator did not reach out to the Korean community and "that word just spread like wildfire." As a result the Korean community "discovered" El Rancho. One of the El Rancho administrators explained:

We have a cottage industry that has developed where a Korean woman, who is a tutor, rents an apartment in our neighborhood so that she could provide after-school child care for the kids and tutor them. And then the parents pick them up after work, which is sometimes 6:00 and 7:00 o'clock in the evening. I mean, I saw this group of kids waiting in front of school one day, and this wasn't even that group, and I said, "What are you guys waiting for?" They're waiting for their van to pick them up. It's a whole group of Korean kids, Korean speakers. I don't know if they're American born, some of them are, some of them are newly arrived, have been here for three, and four, or five years. But they're waiting to go back to Koreatown. Somebody told me, in fact they brought in one of the local Chinese publications, and they have a list of schools that they recommended, and El Rancho was one of them. So there is that underground information system that occurs with the ethnic populations, and it's strong in the Asian community, very strong. That accounts for 2% growth, you know, 2% here is eighty kids. That's a lot of kids. That's a lot of Asian kids to increase. That's almost three classes of kids.

The administrator in Chapter 2, who discussed the changes to the magnet application brochure and how the choice process was designed to be in compliance with court-ordered desegregation, may not have been aware of the inequities created as a result of district's administrators' efforts to organize choice. And while I have no reason to doubt that they are well-intentioned, administrators are positioned differently from parents. The decisions they make from positions of power in the district bureaucracy help construct how parents and which parents will be able to accomplish school choice. As educators who made a career-long commitment to Deluca's urban schools, they tried to make sense of district policies, practices and goals given their local school culture.

However, in this investigation I want to move away from taking the perspective of controlling institutions and their agents and instead take up the standpoint of parents, beginning with their experiences in their everyday worlds with their children. Examining the administrators' statements, then, from the standpoint of parents of different racial and social class backgrounds, it is possible to see how the administrators' actions contribute to accommodating and privileging parents of more preferred students, in the case of El Rancho, for example, parents of the higher achieving, well-disciplined Asian students.

The following sections of this chapter offer a powerful contrast of stories from four parents, Suzanne, Linda, Brenda, and Robin. Their school choice processes differed, as did the outcomes of their choice work yet each story allows us to penetrate into the social relations that help to shape and organize the district's choice policies and practices.

Suzanne

Suzanne is a most resourceful parent when it comes to networking, and she does a great deal of research on the schools of choice she is considering. Suzanne has both her daughters in gifted programs. It would be easy to apply some of the critical literature on parents and paint her as a powerful, aggressive parent interested in only the best opportunities for her children. Yet that would not help us see *how it happens* that she is positioned to network the way she does, accomplish what she does, use her privilege the way she does. It would not help us see *how it happens* that she becomes a participant in the inequitable practices established by the schooling institution itself.

Like other elementary magnet parents, Suzanne learned about the magnet programs while her oldest daughter was in preschool and kindergarten:

At that time I was in a real panic, I was in the middle of a divorce, didn't know where I was going to be living, and I needed to find a place that was going to be appropriate for her. And they [the former school] told me about the magnet program and told me to call and get an *Opportunities* booklet and whatever. And they had said, "You know, for Michelle the place is the Spring Street School. That would be the place for her, but it's nearly impossible to get in."

Suzanne applied for Spring Street, Christopher Street, and Del Mar, gifted elementary magnet schools. At first, her daughter was accepted at Del Mar and Suzanne enrolled her at the school. Then Suzanne got a call saying that her daughter was accepted into Christopher Street School, too. As she was getting ready to enroll at Christopher Street, she got a call from the Spring Street elementary magnet school:

I get a call from the Spring Street School saying, "We're going to add another cluster, we're going to take another X number of kids and we need white kids and so she's in." And it was like, Yea! It was like the day before school was going to start. I was running around taking her folders and her immunization report, I mean from school to school. And it was like Yippee!, it was wonderful, so I got into Spring Street School and we were so fortunate, it was just kismet, we were very lucky.

Her daughter did well at Spring Street and was identified as gifted. In the meantime, Suzanne bought a home in the Hughes elementary school community so she could stay in the Deluca USD's attendance boundaries. When Suzanne's younger daughter was ready for elementary school, Suzanne applied for Spring Street again:

I just knew what kind of a wonderful education Michelle was getting over at the Spring Street School. I wanted Amy to have that as well. So we didn't get in, we were like on the bottom of page 17 of the waiting list even though she was a sibling. It's so hard to get in there. So I thought, what can I do? So I went and got her tested independently and at four years old she had like 144 IQ and you know which is phenomenal.

Deluca USD only accepts IQ tests for giftedness that are administered by their own psychologists, but Suzanne took the test score to the principal of Spring Street and asked her to look at them:

> Carol looked at them and said, "Oh my God," and I said so you can understand she's like Michelle and she cannot go to our local school. You have to understand that. She goes, "Oh, I understand that. What can we do?" She said, "Well, you know, we really need Native American kids here. Are your kids Native Americans, ha-ha-ha." I said, "Well as a matter of fact their dad is one-fourth Native American." And she went "Oh, my God. They should be here as Native Americans. They'd be in like Flynn." And I went, "Oh."

Her daughters' father had never identified himself as Native American. But after doing some research and completing the various forms, Suzanne and her ex-husband were able to come up with enough verification to satisfy Deluca USD that their daughters were Native American:

> So we're there now officially enrolled as Native Americans. I mean you do whatever you can, so we filled it out and as Native Americans [snap of her finger] and immediately the next spot she was in. So that's how, that's the truth of how Amy got into the Spring Street School and she got in right before school started .... Our Native American thing, I never would have thought in a million years about using that until Carol said, "Well if you're Native American" and I went, "Oh yeah! There was something about that. Arnie said something about that." And she was like, "Well, use it," you know.

This chapter presents the kind of work Suzanne did for secondary school choice. With her daughters able to list either white or Native American, Suzanne now knew to ask which racial group was needed more by the school before sending in the magnet application for high school choice:

> I was told by the magnet coordinators for high school, we need white kids. You know, 'cause I asked, "Would it be better for her to be Native American or white?" And they said, "We need white kids." But for elementary and for the middle school they wanted Native Americans. But this year Amy is Native American and Michelle is white. Whatever it takes! So I just ask them, because it's more important that they get in the right school and you

know, I don't think I'm doing anything illegal, it's just how do you play the game. What is the strategy for playing the game.

Learning about Suzanne's experiences, I could see how they were tied to the magnet elementary schools' needs to stay in compliance with the integration formulas. I could see how her economically privileged position allowed her to have her daughter tested by a private psychologist and certainly guaranteed her daughter would be also identified by the school district psychologist as well. Even the ability to pursue her daughter's Native American heritage was supported by class privilege, either because of her educational background, which gives her an edge on researching the necessary documentation, or because she could take time off from work to complete the paperwork. Moreover, local administrators' actions and textually-mediated practices oriented to institutional discourses are shaping the context in which Suzanne can act.

The advantages and privileges her daughters have been granted by the schools are evident again for high school choice. Suzanne applied for and got her daughter into the Davis Liberal Arts magnet. Near the end of her daughter's eighth grade year she received a letter in the mail "out of the blue" describing the new Advanced Community-Articulated Studies (ACAS) program that was starting at Wagner High School:

> They somehow went to the schools, and I guess they picked what schools they wanted to look at. They went to McNear. They went to El Rancho because of their program. And they contacted specific kids. Not everybody in this program got the letters. So everybody, I think, who was on the waiting list at Keyes got an invitation. But we didn't even apply to Keyes. But it also went to McNear and to El Rancho because they've had, you know, the talented kids and I guess, wanted some certain GPAs or whatever .... And they said, if you show up at this meeting and you want to go to this program after you hear our presentation, if you sign up that night, you will be accepted because they already sort of prequalified your kid.

Suzanne and her daughter liked what they heard about the program and liked the campus. This was a difficult decision to have to make on such short notice, especially since she had looked at a lot of other schools and felt the Davis magnet had one of the best programs:

> What we did was, we went and we toured the school, which I like the place there with all the trees and there were all kinds of

animals running around. We found cats. We saw squirrels. We looked at a turtle. And she likes that kind of natural environment. I knew that it would be academically challenging, which is what we were looking for. And, it was close enough for me to deal with driving there every day. And, so we went with it. And I figured if it doesn't work out we can always go try back to Davis next year, but I was afraid we'd lose our magnet pull, so that was a scary thought. We chose to go that night, and we got in …. You know, it was a very quick thing, and I didn't have a whole lot of time.

The ACAS program at Wagner High School did happen quickly. An administrator from Wagner explained that their principal had seen a letter announcing the new ACAS programs going into various school communities. Wagner was not on the list, yet the school had numerous Advanced Placement courses it offered its students and had a long-standing reputation of meeting the needs of high achieving students. After offering itself as a site for the ACAS, it was agreed by the administrator overseeing the program that Wagner could go forward and start contacting parents. Because it was so close to the end of the school year, the administrator from Wagner said decisions had to be made quickly in order to have the program ready for the start of school in the fall.

After her daughter started the school year, Suzanne was talking to friends and said that her daughter was going to go to Wagner High School. Her friends said, "Oh Wagner, the stealth magnet." She believes that parents in the community are finding out that Wagner, without being a magnet school, has always had a reputation for good programs for advanced students.

The district administrator who oversees the ACAS program told me that the program is supposed to be coordinated and articulated so that "elementary, middle school, senior high school people are working together. I wanna see them meet together, to know the programs of each other. I also want them, when people talk to them, to be able to say what they are doing that is differentiated" (Tomlinson, 2000). The administrator explained that this program will follow the district's integration guidelines and any other rules and regulations the district must meet and will enroll students on open enrollment transfers. The ACAS programs are designed to be based in neighborhood school matriculation patterns. The administrator said that this is because the ACAS

is not a magnet program option. It's the regular program option. But it is being driven by magnet parents though, who want more options for their children without the hassle of getting into a magnet school. And that's why with ACAS, it's not a magnet. It's a designation. And it's a designation and a commitment to flexibility.

I sensed many conflicts of interest by the different district level administrators in regards to the gifted magnet programs, the new ACAS program, and the open enrollment transfers ACAS would appropriate. There is no single department overseeing choice in Deluca USD, so these kinds of issues will be negotiated among the different district departments. Parents like Suzanne, regardless of privilege, are still going to be caught in the overlapping and conflicting goals of the different programs and have to make sense of what they should do on their own. Parents will inevitably be invited to participate in programs that continue to be connected to extended social relations beyond their everyday worlds, be it the rapidly growing student population and the lack of new school construction, or the disagreements between departments in the district over which students' needs are served when resources are scarce.

All of the parents in the study had some kind of plan about which schools they wanted their children to attend as a result of what they discovered from their own experiences with schooling and their children's. Suzanne describes it as a strategy for playing the game. This study shows it is a game organized outside of parents' everyday worlds.

In the next story, Linda comes into contact with a different aspect of the choice process when she finds out what happens when it is not a game anymore.

Linda

Like Mary and Bonnie, Linda was able to get both of her children into the elementary magnet without being placed on waiting lists. She did much more choice work when she was researching middle schools for her older daughter. Ultimately, the choice she made for her daughter was a private school. She had not liked El Rancho when she visited it for her daughter, but when she took her son to visit the school, he liked it and it was where his friends were going. Linda completed the magnet application on time and drove it to the district office in downtown Deluca. About a month later, she received a letter from the DSI saying that they did not have verification of her son's gifted status and could not process his application. Her son had been identified as gifted at Spring Street School in third grade so Linda took the letter to the principal:

And she said, "Don't worry. It's an oversight or something didn't happen, but we'll take care of it." I put it out of my mind. And then, I don't know, April or whenever the things come, we got a notice that Peter, because his gifted status never was sent to the district, was dropped from the list entirely. He didn't have a school to go to. It was as though he hadn't applied.

Linda was concerned that her son would lose all his magnet points and matriculation rights if he did not go to a middle school magnet and she was "furious" this had happened:

> So I went to Ellen [the principal] and I said, "Ellen, this is not good here." And so she said, "Oh Linda, I don't know what happened. Oh, my gosh, don't worry about it." And a week later she calls me and says, "I don't think I can do anything." And I said, "Well, I think you'd better do something." She said, "You know, I made a couple of calls and they tell me it's done and El Rancho is full." And then she said, "You know, I heard Kennedy isn't that bad." And I said, "Forget it, Ellen. No. No, this is not okay."

Apparently when Linda gave the letter to the principal, the principal then gave it to someone else to confirm Peter's gifted status and mail the verification back to the district. Linda said the phone must have rung or the paper got lost but the verification was never sent back to the DSI. Linda was not willing to send her son to their neighborhood school instead of El Rancho just because Spring Street School made an error. She continued to describe what happened:

> And I said, you know, "And I frankly am rather disappointed that, you know, Ellen, you've got a distinguished school award, you've got this, this. I know because I've gone with you to these district meetings. You have clout. And I see you waffling on this. He is not going to Kennedy [middle school]. There is no private school I can get him into at this point …. then he's getting in the magnet program. And it's going to be full court press."

She went to the central district office and felt that that they gave her the run-around. The DSI told her there was nothing that could be done. They then sent her to a regional office to see what they could do:

> You know, they just kept sending me different places. The regional office said, "Oh, well, you know, I don't know who you talked to down there." So I was getting very frustrated. And then Peter's teacher in fifth grade said, "Well, you know, I'm a resident in El

Rancho. One of the things we could do is Peter could just come to El Rancho, not in the magnet, on a child care permit, and I would sign a child care permit."

Once again, Linda said no. She wanted her son in the magnet program. She met with the principal from El Rancho and said that the principal had an interesting response to her problem. She said that he told her that he has the well-being of the entire school in mind. "And I think he realizes that there is this sort of, at least in the parents' minds, a perception that the magnet is better than the rest of the school, which is not something he wants to promote. So he was not really all that sympathetic with my obsession about having him in the magnet." She tried to explain to the principal that she was thinking of not only the middle school but the options for high school as well, since she knew magnet points were very important for high school choice:

And I said, "And also, it's the stupidity of this little thing that happened that can never be reversed, and he's lost all his magnet points. He's never been in a school that wasn't a magnet school, and now he doesn't have any magnet points." I said it's the principle here. I'm out for principle on this." He was like, Oh, God, another fanatical parent.

Linda also checked to see if Carnegie had any openings and they did not. The principal at El Rancho was reluctant to give her a child care permit. She went again to the DSI and was told most of the gifted magnets were full. Linda told me that eventually she found a sympathetic person in the department and described this as her big breakthrough in getting her son back in the magnet program. "Because everybody had told me it's impossible, you cannot reverse this decision. It doesn't matter that it was a clerical error, whatever. It's done. Once it goes through our computers we can't [change it]." Linda said she felt like she was running in circles and needed to find someone who would take the time to explain to her what she could do. When she finally landed help from an administrator at the DSI, Linda said, "Look, you know, this is ridiculous. Tell me what I need to do." The person said, "Here's the letter you need from Ellen. Here's what you need from the region office. Here's da-da-da-da, and I'll take it in." Describing what happened next, Linda said:

They told me exactly what Ellen should say in her letter and, you know, who to take it to at the region office and then get this and come back. It was more just this is the procedure that you have to do. It was all I did. It took me about three weeks almost full-time doing this.

Once Linda had the various letters and paperwork turned in, her son was placed on the waiting list for El Rancho. Linda found out that there were 280 students on the waiting list and 60 of the students had 15 points, which was still 3 points more than the 12 points students get from matriculation or playing the points game:

> And I went, oh, forget it, he's not going to get in. But ironically, I had to get him released from Kennedy, too. Kennedy is over-crowded. So he got an additional point because he was coming from Kennedy, so he had sixteen points. But it put him to the top …. So anyway, that's Peter's story. And so he got into El Rancho.

Her son did not officially get into El Rancho until the week before school started. As Linda reflected on the work she did to get her son enrolled in the school she said, "I really did not realize how bureaucratic it is. And you know, I can step back and realize why. It's huge." As a result, she wants to be prepared in case there is another problem at another time, saying, "I made copies of everything so that if anything ever happens again, I have every letter, everybody I spoke to, a phone log, everything. Because I realize, you know, who knows? Something else could happen, and you should really have documentation."

In some sense the fact that it was so difficult for Linda to get the process reversed for her son does speak to the efforts by the district to treat everyone the same. However frustrating it would be for anyone to have a clerical error result in so much additional work, especially given all the choice work that preceded mailing in the application, Linda's story does indicate that the district, initially, rejects all applications with errors the same. Linda's ability to spend the time, demand, and command the cooperation of administrators speaks to her class privilege, her cultural capital, and her confidence using it.

But Linda, in this context, was also somewhat powerless to help her son. His academic achievement, as represented on a piece of paper, or verified and put into computer records, was no longer working to give him advantage and privilege in the magnet program. Linda was able to use the gifted identification as a documentary record that justified her fight for her son to have access to the gifted magnet program available at El Rancho. Linda was working to keep her son from becoming one of the 90% or more of students who don't attend magnet schools. I know that she could have rebuilt her son's magnet points at regular El Rancho, just as Jenny and Paul were doing. But it was not the intention of this analysis to say "Oh, poor Linda" or "That's tough, Linda." The importance of Linda's story is that it helps our understanding of how the social organization of Deluca's school choice options works in different ways for different parents.

Linda is not alone among the parents in this study who use giftedness as a reason to access better school programs for their children. Giftedness emerged as an important factor in many of the parents' decisions about school choice. This practice brings considerable criticism to parents, particularly in the detracking literature (Kohn, 1998; Oakes, 1985; Wells and Serna, 1996). The gifted identification criteria have a distinct place in the *Opportunities for Success* application brochure. As parents of smart children, good children — perhaps gifted students all — they could interpret from the promotions in the brochure that the special environments for learning are intended for their children. When they pursue those environments for their children with an air of entitlement, criticism of their actions must be weighed carefully against the discourses in circulation within and around the district's magnet school programs.

WHEN CHOICE HURTS THOSE IT SHOULD HELP

Manuel's children attended the nonmagnet part of El Rancho and he made no statements that he ever considered changing middle schools for his children. The nonmagnet part of El Rancho is considered by many people to be a better school than neighboring regular middle schools. So even if a child was not able to go to the gifted magnet at El Rancho, for some parents, the regular school is still sought after as a school of choice. Such is the case for Brenda and Robin whose stories follow.

Brenda

Brenda, like Suzanne and some of the others, began looking at schools well in advance of the year she would have to make a choice for her daughter. She has four children, and as she learned about the district's magnet programs she was able to get two of her younger children into magnet schools. But much of what Brenda learned about school choice options came as a result of looking for a school for her oldest child, her daughter, who in the previous chapters was reported to be far below grade level in reading.

Brenda was not satisfied with the middle school to which her children were assigned as a result of the Carnegie College Preparatory magnet taking over the former Webb middle school campus that once served her neighborhood. She heard that El Rancho was a good middle school. Administrators at El Rancho noted the irony that among the problems that result from having a popular school is that their school must operate at full capacity. The school's size made it harder to implement middle school reforms and maintain the successful programs the school has built its reputation around. As Brenda looked into having her daughter attend El Rancho's regular school program, she experienced El Rancho's enrollment problems differently.

Brenda liked to visit schools independently of tours. She tried visiting El Rancho on her own but a staff member in the school's office asked her where she lived and told her that she needed to visit Foster Middle School where children from her neighborhood are assigned. Brenda was not allowed to walk through the campus or sit in on classes at El Rancho and was frustrated: "And so I couldn't get in to just look at the school, couldn't get in." Brenda left with the impression that the school was very concerned about who lived in "their territory." She followed up with a written note to the principal asking to see the school and was again told that El Rancho was not her resident school. She said, "I think we're the outcasts, you know. Anybody who lives outside their territory, like the children that are from my area, are not wanted."

El Rancho has both a regular program and a gifted magnet program on the same site. Appendix B shows the racial/ethnic differences in enrollment in the gifted and nongifted programs at the school. West notes, "Racial segregation within partial-sight magnet schools is particularly damaging to the minority students who constitute the nonmagnet portion of the school, because it labels them as inferior to the white transfer students who constitute the bulk of the magnet students within the program" (West, 1994, quoted in Staiger, 2004, p. 161). The El Rancho gifted magnet has a high percentage of white students compared to the predominately minority enrollment of the regular program. Brenda's comments capture the meanings parents and their children can draw from the resegregating practices of a program arrangement like El Rancho's.

It was discussed in the previous chapter that Brenda eventually was able to take an El Rancho tour and liked the school. When the time for submitting an application came, Brenda applied for magnet schools for her daughter, of which Carnegie was one. She told me:

> I forgot to put the grade for next year and because I did that they sent me a letter saying "No way," because I didn't complete the application. So she didn't get in but I sent in another one and I

asked for Carnegie which is still just right here, it's right here. And so it's a late application, and next year maybe, hopefully.

Brenda was frustrated with not getting a magnet spot for her daughter, and though she knew she would try again, she was aware of the difficulty of getting into Carnegie as she said, "I'm trying to figure out a way how to get around the magnet. I may go in there from now on and say I'm not Hispanic anymore. I may become French [laughter], you know." She planned on applying to Carnegie for her son, who was next in line to enter middle school and discussed her efforts to make sure he got accepted into the school. She asked a regional administrator who knew of her volunteer work at her children's elementary schools to put in a good word for her at Carnegie. One of the Carnegie administrators called her:

And she said, "Well, to tell you the truth Mrs. Figueroa, I really don't know if there's anything I can do for you. Mr. Hartman has talked about you, you know, Oh, what a great parent you are and you'd really be an asset to the school, but the magnet [department] is the one who makes the choice of who attends." And I said, "Well, do you know that you only have 9% Hispanics?" "Well, that's because of the language barrier," she said. And I said, "Well, my children don't have a problem with no language barrier because they can speak fluent English and Spanish." And she said, "Well, that's why we don't get a lot of Latino parents because, you know, it is English only. We don't teach ESL and so that's why we don't get that many." So I said, "Do you know Deluca is 60% Hispanic? And only 9% of us fit into your school?" And she had no answer, she had no answer. She said, "Well, I don't pick and choose who comes to this school and who doesn't." And she said, "Oh, we have to take it up with the magnet office." But next April if my son didn't get in to let her know. And I said, "As long as my son is on the list and you have an opening my son can get in because at Berry magnet that's what they did."

These comments match Brenda's previous concerns about how the children in her neighborhood are perceived by school personnel. Through her involvement in leadership roles at her children's different schools, Brenda was already aware of the low percentage of Latinos at Carnegie. Her comments about changing her racial identity supports a comment made in Chapter 1 by one of the administrators from the DSI that some other Latino parents are thinking the same thing. The broader context of Latino students comprising approximately 69% of the district's student population and only 35% of the magnet school population (at the time of my study), indicates not only the privileging of white students but how vastly underrepresented Latino students are in the magnet program. In the previous chapters, non-Latino parents and administrators offered explanations for why the Latino community itself may not choose to participate in school choice; Brenda understands that it has more to do with the opportunity provided (or not) to parents in her community.

Brenda has seen how magnet school administrators can jump students to the top of waiting lists; this happened with her son at his magnet school. And while she has the least amount of formal education, Brenda had one of the more critical perspectives on what she saw happening with school choice in the district. She also showed remarkable inventiveness in manipulating institutional documents and texts to help get her daughter into a better school environment.

Brenda still had to decide how to get her daughter enrolled at El Rancho, since she was certain she did not want her to go to Foster, the school to which the district buses children from her neighborhood. At our final interview when I asked her what happened with middle school choice for her daughter she said, "I forged everything to get into El Rancho."

The first thing Brenda did was to arrange for her daughter to be considered a matriculating student into El Rancho. She told me that a person in the office at Greenfield Elementary School, where her daughter was a fifth grade student, helped her get her daughter's name on the list of Greenfield students that lived in the attendance boundaries for El Rancho. This meant El Rancho would request matriculating information from the feeder elementary school and begin assigning her daughter classes.

Brenda was attending classes as part of California's GAIN program[1] and knew a woman who lived in the El Rancho area. She explained to me how she was using that friend's address for the El Rancho paperwork and that she had gone to the Department of Motor Vehicles to change her address on her driving license to the address of her friend. She used the change of address receipt to verify her address with the person in the enrollment office at El Rancho. When Brenda took the address verification form to the school to complete her daughter's enrollment processing, she described what happened:

> So she gave me this piece of paper and it said like under penalty of perjury, you know, and consciously I went, "Oh, my God, I'm

going to break the law," maybe two to three years in the state prison, you know. I think it was something the school wrote up, but on the bottom part, it made me really stop and think. I'm very religious. Yeah, I signed it, I signed it. I said, "Please, please forgive me, but I'm not going to send my daughter to Foster." And so I signed the paper.

After Brenda signed the address verification form, the person in the enrollment office at El Rancho told her that her friend had to come to the school and show proof of residence. Brenda brought in her friends and they brought in their bills establishing their legitimate residence at the address:

My friend and her husband, they testified that I lived there and then [the person in the enrollment office] said, "Well, this [other] girl lives there, too. Has she moved out?" .... She said, "Because I think there's a lot of things going on here that are not true."

Brenda said her friend responded, "Yes, [the other girl] moved out, she's gone, but now Brenda is staying with me and her daughter needs to attend school here." So the school enrolled Brenda's daughter. Then Brenda added:

Oh, and the paper they give, you have to list two neighbors. Two neighbors who would say you live there. Fortunately, one of the parents in my class, which, the lady who let me use her address was a parent in my class also, lives like two apartment buildings up from her, so I used her as one of the neighbors. And then I got one of her neighbors and gave her some money to say that I lived there. And she [person in the enrollment office] said, "So if we go down and we knock on their door they'll say you live there." And they said, "'Yeah, we will." Because I knew the one parent because she had came here and her child was in our classroom, and the other one, well, because I paid her.

Brenda was worried about what she had done and I asked her if she talked with anyone about it. She said she had told a district administrator and the administrator didn't seem surprised at Brenda's actions:

I talked to her because I was real concerned about filing that piece of paper. It upset me. I was really worried, you know, and I said what happened if they come out and they knock on these doors because it's like an apartment complex like this and I only asked the one neighbor for the reference, not all of them so what if they do and she said, "Don't worry about it, they're not going to do that." And I said, "What if they?" And she said, "They don't have time to do that." Then she said, "Did you sign the paper? Don't worry about it. They're not going to come out." And I went like "O.K." And I said "You work for this school district, so please don't turn me in." She just said, "Don't go around advertising it to too many administrators," but the principal at [Greenfield] I think pretty much knew. I mean she never acknowledged it or said anything, but she knew and the office staff helped me, yeah, helped me. So we're all going to jail together.

When the school looked on the district's computerized student information system, they told Brenda only part of the information they needed was there. She recalled, "Well, I had to bring back the immunization card and I had to bring back the birth certificate because they said only bits and pieces were on the computer. And they had put Sandra in regular classes and she can't cope." Because of her low reading level, Brenda's daughter had been given an Individual Education Plan (IEP) for special education services during fifth grade.

I asked them if they could place her in resource. "Well, we have a waiting list." And she was placed in regular, so I kept going back, "How long is the waiting list and how do I get on, who can I talk to get her through there?" you know. So I did go back several times.

On one trip to El Rancho, an African American city police officer was there trying to enroll his child at the school. He too lived in the Foster attendance area and was told he could not automatically enroll at El Rancho. Brenda said,

I felt like, you know, and I can't remember her name for the life of me, but I felt that the lady in the office, you know, she was talking down to me, like she was acting down to me. She treated the police officer much differently, you know, and tried to help him find other ways of getting in, saying like what if he had child care in this area. She didn't offer that information to me. But I didn't go and tell her where I actually lived because I wanted to make it sure that Sandra got in.

Once enrolled at El Rancho and on the waiting list for the school's resource program, Brenda said the school still needed additional records from the elementary school:

Well, the papers had my address here but since [Greenfield] had botched, you know, her enrollment altogether, they didn't have it. So what I did was I fixed it so if they got it and looked at it they could say, you know, she always lived at 2425 Clarandon. I'm not going to give them a paper that said I lived at Greenfield and then ruin it, you know, because these are dated documents so I wasn't taking any chances that they could throw me out.

Brenda got copies of all the records, which she knew she was entitled to have as a parent. Before taking copies of the records to El Rancho, she cut out all references to her address and made new copies with the address of her friend inserted. "Instead of bringing them the original, I cut them up and I changed the address and everything and I said they're not going to catch me. And so I had no problems."

After all the work Brenda did researching schools for her daughter, she no longer was willing to let the district bus her daughter to a school she did not believe was a good school. And as an administrator said earlier in this chapter, people from the "college tom-tom" would not send their children to Foster either.[2] Even though she sensed children like hers were not as welcomed at El Rancho, using her own resourcefulness, and engaging in activities that may not seem ethical, Brenda made sure her daughter got into El Rancho:

You do whatever you can, you do whatever you can. And I could have applied for open enrollment, but I don't know what that process is. If someone in the back room throws them up in the air and says, "Hey, these people get in and those that don't, don't." I don't know, you know, what that process is. Just like I don't know what the magnet process is. I don't understand that either, you know, so I didn't want to chance it. And the baby-sitting thing was out because I don't work full time. So I was willing to make sure my foot was in the door, so I'd have my foot in the door. Now I went to extremes, to extremes, but any person could've done this, any person could. Any parent who has a copy of their child's records could copy it, could change it, could fix it …. They might be expelled from school if they found out that you don't actually live there, but any person could have done it. Now [the principal] may not approve and may throw me out altogether, but I'm not going to just let it go because now I know what she can be getting and I'm not willing to settle for less anymore.

Both Manuel and Brenda admit to lying in order to get their children into better schools. The advisor from the Latino community said that there are many parents using other parents' addresses:

Those that are more sophisticated parents, they know the ways how to use the system, because they are the parents that have gone there and tried or maybe later on they will. Or their own kids they say, okay, I know this so-and-so and they are using this address, so why don't we do the same thing? In fact, I know this one guy that chose to be the legal guardian, and he was no relative, he was no family, but he was saying it's legal after all, it's legal.

A person I spoke with in the district's permit department said that the district and local schools "don't have the resources, the people, the time to check everything," and as a result, they have to accept everything at face value unless something arouses their suspicion:

For example, when people come in and say they're working. And if they're a domestic worker, they might bring in a little letter that says they work, you know, part time for someone for cash. And they bring in a series of letters where someone just wrote it out that "So-and-so works for me one day a week and I pay her in cash." It may be a handwritten letter, but we have to accept that.

The district is aware that in many situations, people do lie and manipulate the permit option; it is a real dilemma. One way the district is trying to handle the problem is to train people working at the local schools on how to spot potential fraud and how to use common sense approaches when enrolling a child in a school because that is the time to catch parents who are not truthful. One administrator said, "We are driven by state and federal law …. And once they're enrolled, you catch hell if you try to get them out." The administrator believes that when parents exercise their choice and manipulate the system these ways, "they're only cheating another child who may be forced to get on a bus because there's no space at the school because someone lied and cheated to get into the school."

The administrator's perspective does not include the experiences of parents like Brenda who is also forced to put her child on a bus. What Brenda sees is that more privileged parents get to send their children to an excellent school like Carnegie, which is right down the street from where she lives: right down the street from where Robin lives, the mother featured in the next section.

Robin

Robin has three children. Her oldest daughter was in college and no longer lived at home when I met Robin. She was raising her two younger children, was receiving public assistance as her only income, and lived in a Section 8 apartment unit.

The Transportation for Participating Schools (TPS) program is part of the district's voluntary integration program and was described briefly in Chapter 1. Participation in the TPS program has been declining each year. One administrator told me it is a program mostly serving African American students and other students of color. The district assigns students to schools in the TPS program; parents do not choose a school. None of the parents considered the TPS program as a choice option but it ended up the choice program in which Robin's daughter would participate.

While Robin's daughter was attending Greenfield Elementary School, she was identified as gifted. Greenfield had a poor reputation, and Robin learned that other parents were getting their children into better schools through open enrollment. She applied for an open enrollment transfer to Brookhaven Elementary School:

> I kept calling and I kept calling, and I wasn't going to give up, and a friend of mine's little girl was going there and she said "Call, Robin." She said, "Maybe," you know .... I said, "I've been at Greenfield for two years and I would like to have her at this school [Brookhaven]. And she's a fourth grader and I believe she deserves to be in the GATE [Gifted and Talented Education] program," so forth and so on. "Please let me know if there's any opening." And so I just kept calling so finally she said, "Well, Mrs. Jackson, we have an opening and come on over and get the open enrollment form."

Robin went over to Brookhaven and introduced herself at the school office. She asked for more information about the school, looked around the school and "gave it the check." She enrolled her daughter and got involved as a parent volunteer at the school, saying, "I worked for that school. I helped raise money. I did fund-raisers. I did everything. So it's not like just dumping my kid off." She said that her daughter, Caroline, was delighted to go to Brookhaven and did very well. Knowing that her daughter was identified as gifted and seeing how well she was doing at Brookhaven, Robin wanted her daughter to go into a magnet program for middle school. As with Brenda, there is no neighborhood middle school in her community for her children to attend. Her daughter would be bused to Foster. In both of my interviews with Robin, we talked about the magnet application process. Of all the parents in the study, she appeared most confused by the application process. She said:

> I chose all the better schools, the magnet schools, the best schools I could get her, and they put her in lower schools. And my understanding was I don't think she had enough points or something like that because they hadn't been adding them up. I'd been applying ever since she was little. They didn't do anything for my baby. I don't even know how many points she got now.

She insisted that her first choice had always been Carnegie because the school is so close to where they live. Her next choice was El Rancho because she knew the students from Brookhaven matriculated to El Rancho and many of them went into the gifted magnet, which her daughter was qualified to attend as well.

I believe that Robin may have been confused about the difference between the magnet program and the TPS program and inadvertently checked the TPS option. At one point she pointed to the application and said she had checked transportation because she doesn't have a car. The box for transportation is the TPS program. Her daughter did not get into a magnet program and was assigned to Wilson Middle School, which is not a zone school for her neighborhood. Like El Rancho, Wilson also has a magnet program on its campus, yet Caroline was assigned to the nonmagnet school at Wilson, which historically has enrolled a considerable number of TPS students. "That was for the transportation TPS, I didn't know what TPS was. So I didn't know how far Wilson was and they sent me this thing to go there once I got the choice made and it's way too far to travel." Caroline wanted to go with her friends to El Rancho and Robin decided they would "go to Plan B."

Robin filled out an open enrollment application for El Rancho but Caroline's name was not pulled from the lottery drawing. Robin was then told she could get in through a child care permit. For several years the YMCA has provided space and assistance to welfare parents who need child care while they take classes to enter the workforce, and since Robin was in classes at a community college, she was eligible for the child care program the YMCA operates at El Rancho. She contacted the YMCA child care provider at the school site and was granted a reduced fee. "I qualified and had everything done. They made me do all this running around. They said Caroline could get into the program through child care, and that's what approved her. And they still did not accept her. I was left in awe about it." Robin and her daughter were disappointed. She asked the school why her daughter was not accepted to El Rancho and was told that, in fact, she did not qualify for a child care permit because she was not working and could care for her children herself.

This prompted Robin to write a letter to the principal of El Rancho. Robin gave me copies of the letter she wrote and the letter she received back from the principal. It was the end of the school year when she wrote her letter to the principal, which she hand delivered. In her letter she says she had received a call from his staff telling her she needed to be in school full-time to get a child care permit. She was upset at the way the person had spoken to her and felt she had been insulted because she was on welfare. Her letter says she felt entitled to an apology. Her letter makes statements that accuse the school of judging her by her low income and therefore implying she and her daughter are not qualified to go the school. In the letter she describes herself as an involved parent as well as a welfare recipient. She asks the principal to reconsider her daughter's application and gives the name and phone number of her college counselor. The following quote captures the tone and grammatical content of Robin's letter which she had typed at a rented computer terminal at a local Kinko's:

> Your school is just less than fifteen minutes away from where I live, I have signed the appropriate forms for child care and I cannot attend school or work unless my child is in school child care … I did not know parents are judged by their income to attend certain schools, I have been a welfare recipient for a number of years and I have volunteered thousands of hours to Deluca USD. I need your help, why do you want to break my child's heart, does it give you pleasure to offend parents of low income or do you think I and my daughter are not qualified enough to attend El Rancho. The school needs my help and if I or my daughter does not come there it will be your terrible loss, therefore I am asking you to reconsider Caroline and that she be able to attend El Rancho so I can go to college and get my degree and eventually get off welfare, time is running out.

In two days, the principal wrote back and supported the actions of the staff member. He said he had reviewed the paperwork prior to the staff member calling Robin. He stated that at the time, Robin was not employed full time or in school full time and that the child care permit rules state that a person must be enrolled full time to obtain a child care permit. He mentions that he called the college counselor to verify her school status and that he was told she was a part-time student. He also called the elementary principal and found out that at Brookhaven her daughter had been on open enrollment permit, not a child care permit. He did say in the letter that should she enroll in classes full time, she could resubmit her application. Robin felt the full-time rule was unfair:

> I don't know how they figured that, because I was in school full time. I was going day and night, and I had lab. I was taking nine units. They go by units. They can't really go by that, because when you're in school you're in school full time. You got the reports. You know, they go by the units, but they don't realize it's extra work to be done. Don't they see that? Don't they see that you're not just sitting doing nine units of work? Don't they know you're working to get those grades and those credits? And I'm not a dropout. I complete my courses. All they should have looked at, I was in school making an effort to get my degree, and that was what's important.

Robin also did not understand why the school didn't respond more positively to her letter, "And I wrote the letter so nicely, typed them up and took time to bring them and was coming and just pleading to them, you know, 'Can you help me?' And didn't seem like the help was there. They denied me instead of helping me." Robin believes she had done all the proper paperwork: "I had done the paperwork for ten days. I mean, I was running around. I just went back and forth to that school. Everything was signed. They said, 'Go sign this.' I did whatever was asked of me, and still." The experience left her questioning whether the talk about helping parents like herself was genuine:

> They say go to the schools and we've got people that will help you. Just come on over. But when you come and they look at you and they see that you're trying to make a difference, seems as though they're not hearing you. Seems for some reason when you're black and trying to make it better for yourself they don't hear you. For some reason they will meet you with open arms and say, "Well, I'll tell you what I'm going to do. I'm going to send you to so-and-so and so-and-so, and he can help your daughter so-and-so and

so. And we're going to help you get started." But for some reason they're sitting there all just not willing to really share anything with you.

When it comes to child care permits, an administrator at El Rancho said, "You have to prove to the school you're leaving that you have [child care]. See, they're the ones who have to sign off on it. Once it gets signed off at the other school, then it's not for us to say it's not legitimate. They're the ones that have to hold the line to make sure that what people are doing is legitimate." The administrator went on to explain what verification is needed at El Rancho to complete the child care permit application:

> You have to bring in the proof that you're working full time. If it's two members of a family, then both working full time. You have to have proof that the person who's providing the child care actually lives within this community. But, you know, theoretically, I suppose if they had the personnel time, they could go out and investigate to see whether or not that child's actually going there every day after school or not. But, I mean, nobody has the time or the inclination to do that, anyhow.

The administrator at the permit department told me that the district "doesn't hold fast on the full time issue," because state law does not define full time. Therefore, each district determines full time on its own. The administrator said that Deluca USD uses a minimum of 25 hours per week to count as working full time, adding, "Of course, they would always have to have some documentation for that." Any kind of child care permit would need proof of employment or training, and if a parent claimed to work at home, a permit likely would be denied on the assumption that a parent could pick up a child from school.

As already described in Chapter 1, child care permits are good for only one year at a time. The administrator said that even though district policy states that permits are not to be canceled because of poor grades or behavior, principals who wish to get rid of a child could do an investigation: "They can start checking out the parents: who picks up the kid after school; are they really working; do they have the documentation. And if you do that little investigation, you can basically show that the parent is not eligible, that something is wrong."

One can look at Robin's experiences and understand how the application brochure may have so confused her that she might have selected the wrong program, resulting in her daughter getting assigned to faraway Wilson, a school hardly accessible by public transportation. With the high percentage of white students at El Rancho it is hard to imagine that Caroline's name would not have been quite high on the waiting list if Robin had in fact selected the magnet program, not TPS. Robin, like other parents, tried a couple of options to get into El Rancho. And it seems that although an administrator from El Rancho said that they do not have the time or inclination to investigate all permits, someone did find the time, quickly, to do an "investigation" on Robin. And ironically and sadly, whereas the YMCA had policies and practices to assist parents like Robin, the school's response to her and the principal's authority to deny a permit, took away one of the few benefits of which she could take advantage.

In the end, her daughter had to go to Wilson, and Robin made sure she was in Honors classes. But she did say, "There's nothing I could do to just try to remedy the situation." Robin talked to her daughter and said, "Let's just try it and see. You will adjust to it. You may not like it at first, but you've got to go to some school." Robin added that, "I took her over there. She resented it. She did not want to go, and, now, she loves it over there."

At the same time Robin was trying to get her daughter into El Rancho, she was trying to get her son Reggie into kindergarten at Brookhaven. She said, "Caroline was graduating, and Reggie would have went right in, but for some reason the principal just thought that he shouldn't come there." Robin thought there was "no reason why he shouldn't have been able to go to Brookhaven." She told me the school had given her recognition letters and awards for working and volunteering at the school. She said, "I was real upset about that. I said, 'You know, I really worked hard for this school when I came in. I've done so much for the school. I paid $30 a year to be with Friends of Brookhaven. Now, you know, Reggie's name is on the waiting list.' Which I think is totally unfair." She was told the school didn't have any additional room:

> So I didn't want to go and beg for my baby to go to no school. I just said, "Okay." He was on the list. They didn't call me, contact me, or anything. They didn't say anything, and I didn't really bother to fight about it. My baby just didn't have a chance to get in. They were saying that they were full up. There was no [space for] siblings. They gave me all kinds of excuses.

Robin was able to enroll Reggie in kindergarten on an interdistrict permit to another school district where she could also get child care. To take him to school each day, travel on to the community college for her classes and tutoring, and pick him up after school, required her to take two different public buses and transfer twice. She told me she was very tired throughout that year.

Her neighborhood school was Greenfield Elementary School; it was overcrowded, and she did not want Reggie to attend the school for first grade. She decided to try to get him into a neighboring elementary school, Main Street, which Caroline had attended when she was in primary grades. She was unable to enroll Reggie through open enrollment, or on a child care permit. The same principal was at Main Street School from when her daughter attended the school. But Robin felt the school, the principal, the rules, had all changed since she was there last. Not able to get into the school, Robin went to a region administrator and asked for help. She tells how she was finally able to get Reggie into Main Street Elementary School:

> He got in on a — they call it a region permit. Which is something that doesn't even exist. The parents write up the region permits. We're to write up how our child is going to go to their school and then the region [administrator] signs it. In other words he puts us at risk and the child, too, so if we deviate from what we've written out, oh, God. I went through hell, I'll tell you. I had to write a letter to the region stating that I would not make him late, and that I would follow the rules and that he would be a good student and I had to just make an oath. I had to make an oath. 'I swear that Reggie Jackson will do A, B, C, D, E, F, G, H, I, J, K, L, M, N, O, P, Q, R, S, T, U, V,' and if he didn't — if I didn't hold to those standards he would be put back to his home school.

One of the district administrators I spoke with explained that there are region permits and parents do call the region with requests to move their child from one school to another. The administrator said that, usually, parents are told that they need to write a letter and state their reasons for a transfer. To grant a transfer or a permit, region administrators need a reason to "hook it on" and then from the region level they can try to do something for the parent:

> But to give you an example. What if there's a woman who is very active or goes out of the way to come to me. I try to help every parent who has the wherewithal to come to me and say, "Look, I don't want my kid going to this local school because it stinks," and I know that local school stinks, you know. I really try to help lever them in. I give them the whole song and dance first. And

parents have some responsibilities, too. And sometimes I'm terribly disappointed because they're taking a kid out of a situation because of safety and what have you, but the kid's a no-goodnik and causes problems over at the new school.

Once at Main Street School, Reggie was having some difficulties in his reading skills and with some of the other children in the school. Robin had to meet with the classroom teacher and the principal. I sensed from what Robin shared with me during the interviews that the principal was not happy that Robin got her son into the school by going over the principal's head. Robin said:

She seems to be uncomfortable around me, and it makes the other parents kind of wonder what's going on with the principal and you know, everybody is looking at me like I'm some idiot, like I just dropped off the moon from space .... and I'm not good enough to be part of that school. She's always telling me, "Well, you're not working, you don't work, and you're outside of the school boundaries." .... So, therefore, I'm not as good as the parents that work, and the parents that can give more or do more or pay their $10 dues or what have you.

Robin was able to graduate with her AA degree and was trying to find a job. She hoped to find child care for Reggie so she could have more time to look for work. The school has a child care program, but by the time Robin got Reggie's region permit, that program was full. Although, she noticed that:

Other parents get to find out other things before I do. But I'm always reading the newsletter that comes home. I will ask to find out on my own and say, "You know, I think the kids are here after school after 2:30. Is there a way I can get my child in this program?" or, "How much is it for this and such?" She says, well, "You can register Reggie. There's no charge. This is the after school program." And I said, "Oh." And it's been two months I've been picking Reggie up everyday at 2:30, and now he stays until 3:30 or 4:00, and that gives me time to look for a job.

Robin was aware that the school may not have wanted to offer her much help. She added, "And they know I can't look for a job waggling a six-year-old around with me. So this gives me a little more time. But what's so bad about it is, they don't want to be up front with the parents or either, a parent like me."

As a former public school teacher, I can imagine how negatively Robin's letter about Caroline was received by school personnel at El Rancho. She also hinted that her relationship with the principal at Brookhaven was strained at times. I suspect that since El Rancho and Brookhaven schools enroll many middle class students, how Robin presented herself and her concerns and opinions, particularly if delivered in the form of a letter, was off-putting to the administrators at the schools.

Robin's story about getting Reggie into Main Street indicates that she was learning how to use her letter writing more effectively to get her child into a better school. But getting into the better school did not come without qualifications. As was shown with Manuel, and can be assumed to be the case with Brenda, the poorer parents, who are also parents of color, cannot let their children's performance or behavior become suspect or their enrollment at the school of choice will be jeopardized.

The frustration Robin feels in trying to make a school choice other than her assigned neighborhood schools was evident when she said:

And even if you've got everything the way they say you have to have it, and I have — this has gone on time after time. I have done everything they have requested, dotted every i, I've crossed every t, and still they have given me problems. Because I go with my baby. Where she go I'm going to be. And that is a hurtful, resentful thing from the district and the people that are supposed to be in power to help us. Because they're not letting me have access to the information to get my foot in the door, or to get my child's foot in the door so to speak.

She continues with her own thoughtful critique:

Well, parents have a choice based on their children's smartness, knowledge. That's the only choice it is. Other than geographically, you ain't got no choice. You got to go to the school in your area whether it's downgraded, falling apart, who cares. Unless you can show that your child has some sort of disability or your child is smart enough to get on a program, that's how you can have a little bit more of a choice. And that's where you still have to get this point system. I don't like that. You know, points? We're talking about these kids' learning. It takes years to get those points, and who knows whose counting the points accurately? So the choice is — it's very limited, very limited choice. But the parents I've talked to, they tend to agree they don't have no choice. We get together

and we talk, and I say, "What do you think about so-and-so" ...
They're not too pleased. The self-esteem in the community is low.

Both Robin and Brenda spoke of school choice outcomes quite differently from most of the other parents. Robin expresses this when she says, "You know, it's a cocky system we got. It's a maze and just getting through to the end is just one heck of a job." Both mothers saw more fully some of the social relations that help to shape and determine their choice work and the choice opportunities for their children. Their neighborhood elementary school has a very poor reputation. The predominately minority community in which they live is home to many working-class families and families receiving some form of public assistance. The magnet program that was designed to address the harms of racial isolation as part of the district's voluntary integration, in effect may have reinforced those harms in these mothers' experiences and of probably many other mothers choosing schools for their children.

DISCUSSION

The past two chapters have shown that getting into good schools requires work. As the parents in this study entered the school choice process, there was a larger context organizing and containing their choice practices. There were differences in how the different mothers in this chapter were treated by local and district level administrations as they tried to get their children into better schools. For example, Linda's social and cultural capital got her into El Rancho, whereas Brenda felt like an outcast and unwelcome at the same school. Brenda's story generates concern as to why the district still seems unable to resolve the lack of proportional representation of Latino students in the schools of choice in the Davis High School complex. Brenda made a point of that in this chapter. But one of the administrators interviewed for the study has noticed some change in Latino parents' interest in choosing schools and made this comment:

One could argue that there's always been a special group of parents, the parents who had the wherewithal and the knowledge. For the first time this year I got buttonholed at some Title I parent meeting by some Latino parents, "Can we come speak to you in your office?" They came over in my office and told me that they had picked out the schools that they wanted, the middle school and the high school where they wanted their kids to go, and could I help them, and da — da — da. It was kind of interesting. I had never in my career been approached by Latino parents with that kind of request. Had I been approached by Koreans? Oh, yeah. African Americans? Oh, yeah. Whites? Oh, yeah. Chinese? Oh, yeah. But never the Latino parents. So what that means is, you know, and I've talked to others who are getting these same kinds of requests, the message got across. They have figured out that there are some schools who are a more productive climate for their kids, okay? Notice I didn't use the word 'better,' okay? They're more productive, and they know which ones they are now.

The mothers in this study were all active and involved parents at their children's schools, and most received some kind of special attention as a result. Mimi is a good example of the benefits that come from being an involved parent who brought much needed language skills to the school community. As the chapter shows, the parents' experiences and choice work differed by choice of school, grade level of schooling, what problems they encountered, and the solutions they found. Their experiences differed by how they were positioned by the race relations and class relations operating in the district. Natalie and Mimi are nonwhite middle class parents, and their experiences of getting into the magnet program were very different from those of Brenda and Robin, who are poor women of color. To get their children into good schools, the poorer parents cashed in their chips with administrators or others with the means to help them. Brenda and Robin went to the region office for help, like the parents mentioned in the quote above, and Manuel's sister got her employer to write her a letter for Manuel's son. In some ways it did not matter whether the parents were white or black, Asian or Latino, because all the parents took their choice work seriously; they believed that their children's educations and futures were at stake.

The difference in the experiences of these parents as each of them did their choice work opens up important new issues for examining how the institutional organization and coordination of public school choice continues to work in the interests of those with more power. Comparing stories allows us to see the institution's role in supporting racial and class privilege. We see also the bureaucratic politics between district departments and local administrators. We see how the technicalities of school choice policy and practice work differently for some vs. others.

Suzanne accomplished choice with the help of district policies and practices. The information from her principal about the need for students of a particular racial group was connected to the racial formulas used in the district's voluntary integration plan. The district accepted her claim that her daughters' one-eighth Native American heritage should allow them to be enrolled in the district as Native Americans. Given the integration formula established by the court, we can imagine the situation switched where Robin or Brenda asked about getting their children into a school and the principal said: "We need white students. If you could use that you were white, you'd be in like Flynn." The institutional rules about race and the rules about access may change for each mother's situation, but we can clearly see how the rules are centered around the benefits associated with white privilege (Wildman, 1996).

When Robin's daughter went to Brookhaven Elementary School, her involvement was welcomed at the school. When it was time for her son to attend the school, there wasn't space for him, while there was space for Paul and Jenny's daughter. Brookhaven had 58% white students and only 11% black students. If the principal was trying to achieve more diversity at the school as the district's integration guidelines require, Robin's son should have been enrolled. Instead, Reggie was put on a waiting list. If Robin's involvement at the school was appreciated, as her awards seem to indicate, then, like Mimi, she should have had some clout to get her son enrolled on a permit in the same school from which her daughter had just graduated. It didn't happen that way for Robin. Chapter 1 showed that once a student was on a waiting list or seeking a permit at a local school, local administrators had considerable authority to control who would be granted enrollment and who would not.

Recall the administrator at El Rancho who admitted to helping parents from the mommy and college tom-toms. Brenda was not being sent to El Rancho with references from the college tom-tom, she was coming from the Greenfield school community. She was not given the same help offered to parents with more cultural and material resources. But Brenda received the cooperation of someone in the office at Greenfield Elementary School to add her daughter's name to the list of students matriculating to El Rancho. Using the knowledge she obtained from her network of friends in the community, she was then able to deliver the necessary proof that her family lived within El Rancho's attendance boundaries. Because the Greenfield office did not send the remaining records and the El Rancho office allowed her to bring over copies of the files they needed, she had the opportunity to change her daughter's records. Brenda was innovative and resourceful in using the help to which she had access. However we feel about the way Brenda altered the paperwork, she was ironically aided in her efforts by the district's difficulties transferring student records from one school to another.

The need of the district to be in compliance with integration guidelines worked to Suzanne's advantage when she chose schools for her daughters, but it did not work that way for Robin. Brenda and Robin were forced to deal with the context created by the closure of the neighborhood middle school for the Carnegie Preparatory magnet school and a local elementary school that struggled to meet the needs of its poor and minority student population. These situations were not under the control of the mothers yet helped to construct the choice options they had. Understanding the historical and institutional context helps us understand the decisions they made. Brenda resorted to forging papers to get her daughter into El Rancho. After repeated failure using various choice options, Robin went over a principal's head and got a region administrator to grant a permit for her son to attend elementary school, but she and her son were put on a behavior contract in exchange. Suzanne may have been within her right to use her daughters' father's Native American heritage, but since he did not actively identify with being Native American, she as a white woman used her daughters' racial identities as a performance and a convenience.

The conceptual framework that I described in the introduction asks us to view our public school choice policies and practices from the standpoint of parents making choices. By beginning in the everyday lived experiences of these parents, I was able to explore the extended social relations, discourses, and organizational practices that help to construct these parents' choice work and choice work outcomes. I was also able to explicate how each step of the choice process is related to the next and to the parents' goals of getting their children into good schools. Texts were an active part of the organization and coordination of school choice and were constantly part of parents' negotiations and manipulations. From the standpoint of these parents, I map in Figure 5 what I saw happening in their work for choice so that we can see how their actions and experiences were tied to the bureaucratic processes and texts that coordinated the parents' activities with those of other parents.

At each stage of the institutional ethnography, I saw how social relations and textually-mediated organizational practices allowed some parents to go farther in the magnet choice process than others, leaving some parents to take a less preferred path into a good school. Figure 5 illustrates this. The parents in this study varied in how successfully they negotiated the social organization of school choice in the district. The parents' children, though, eventually got into good schools, but not all got into the magnet schools.

The parents' stories teach us about the work involved for parents who choose schools and the ways that they are privileged or disadvantaged by

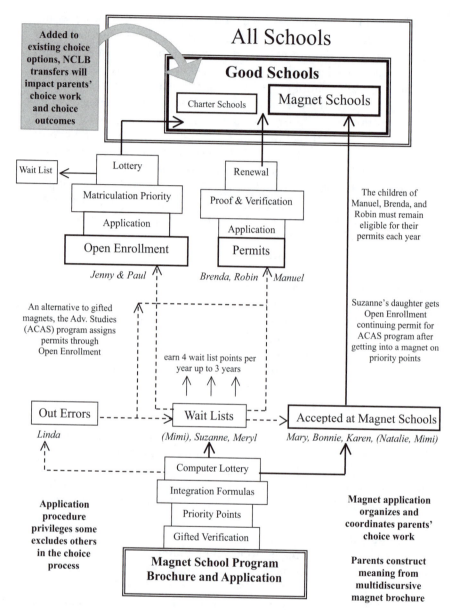

Figure 5. The Bureaucratic Organization of Parents' Choice Work

the policies and practices of the district. As we reflect on their choices and the decisions they made, we should be troubled by their individual school choice practices, by the way the local school and the district helped to shape and determine their participation in the school choice process, and by the failure of our judicial and political systems to provide equal and equitable educational opportunity for each of these parents' children.

Critical Race Theory reminds us to focus on who benefits from institutions' rules about race and access and who does not (Crenshaw et al., 1995). This means that, as readers, we may need to set aside our personal feelings about what the parents did as part of their involvement in their children's education and direct our critique at what is wrong with the institutional system. Disaggregated test score data or the racial breakdown of the student population at a Deluca USD school will hide the kind of work that the parents, mothers mostly, did on behalf of their children. Critical feminist theories remind us that women's work raising their children and participation in their children's education is objectified in many of our representations of the family-school relationship. Drawing on insight gained from theories grounded in critical analysis of institutions can help us understand how parents are complicit in the historical inequalities. But they also push us to ask how could they not be.

There are parents like the parents whose stories are captured here in many of our urban school communities doing the hard work of raising their children while trying to make smart decisions about their children's schooling. All of the parents in the study had some kind of plan about which schools they wanted their children to attend as a result of what they discovered from their own and their children's experiences with schooling. Their plans included that they first try to get their children into a magnet school. Suzanne describes the process as "a strategy for playing the game." This study shows it is a game organized outside of parents' everyday worlds and that the rules of the game are different for minority and/or poorer parents like Brenda and Robin.

The literature presented in the introduction suggests that we look within institutions to search for where privilege and exclusion happens (Griffith, 1992; Haney Lopez, 2000; Larson and Ovando, 2001; Smith, 1998). As the parents in this study entered the school choice process, there was a larger context organizing and coordinating their choice practices, which in part can be traced back to the courts as I made apparent in Chapters 1 and 2. Crenshaw and her colleagues have stated that "the law is shown to be thoroughly involved in constructing the rules of the game, in selecting the eligible players, and in choosing the field on which the game must be played" (Crenshaw et al., 1995).

Because the district is only 10.5% white, and yet requires by court order wherever possible a 30% white student population in the magnet schools, the advantage for getting into magnets goes to white applicants. The combination of court-ordered racial balance formulas favoring white families and a magnet lottery system that is coordinated with those formulas generated privilege and racial advantage for some families over others.

It is now possible to see how it happens that the organization and coordination of parents' school choice processes continues to implicate parents, mothers, in the district's historical pattern of inequitable access to good schools for all students. The district's allocation of the scarce resource of classroom space in good schools reinforces Wellman's (1993) position that institutions structure racial advantage through struggles over scarce resources. Consequently, institutions discriminate against those with less privilege and less social, cultural, or political capital. In this study, parents used any kind of advantage or privilege they had. But they are only a small group of parents that were successful. Certainly, there are thousands of other parents in the district who were less successful, and as this chapter shows, it would be safe to suggest that the less successful parents are going to be the poorer parents or parents of color.

If the experiences of the middle-class African American mother, Natalie, and the Korean mother, Mimi, are suggestive of similar experiences for other middle-class or wealthier minority families in the district, as some of the district people interviewed implied, then class relations among the minority communities participating in magnet school choice should also be addressed. Winant speaks about the impact of the class transformations taking place among minority communities in a social order that is still highly structured by race. He says, "The 'increasing significance of class' does not, therefore suggest a 'declining significance of race' .... We need a way, in other words, to grasp the increasing significance of class for African Americans and other racially identified groups that does not deny the centrality of race in the formation of identity and everyday experience" (Winant, 1994). I add that we need better ways of understanding the opportunities denied those members of racial or ethnic groups not benefiting from the class transformations as well.

I'd like to end this chapter with a quote from Natalie, because in many ways it reflects a view of the social order that I believe underlies why parents are doing this choice work. In the best ways these parents know how, they are trying to make certain their children will be prepared for their adult lives. In the quote below, Natalie describes talking to her son about the importance of education in a world that offers opportunity to far too few:

That's how discrimination works. It's all about leaving out. I tried to explain this to my son. I said, "Imagine this. You're an employer.

You have one job." I said, "How many people can you interview for that one job?" I said, "There's the whole world. Eight billion people." I said, "You're gonna interview eight billion people to find the right person for the job?" He goes, "No." I said, "So how are you gonna tell people don't even bother to apply?" He goes, "I don't know." I said, "The first thing you say is don't bother to apply if you don't have a high school diploma. That's carves a bunch of people out. Then you tell them don't bother to apply if you haven't had two years of college. Don't bother to apply if you haven't graduated from college. Don't bother to apply if you — " I said, "And you just narrow it down until you get a manageable load of people that you're going to interview." I said, "That's how the world works. It's based on discrimination. You don't have time to be interviewing everybody." I said, "And you just got to make sure that you have all those qualifications so you don't get shifted out too early." You know. I said, "Until there's enough of everything for everybody, you got to make sure that you are always prepared to meet the last criteria." And that's why he hates to talk to me, but oh, my God.

5

WHAT WE KNOW OTHERWISE:
HOW BROWN AND NCLB HIT HOME

There are no existing organizational structures in public schooling that guide students through both a quality and an equitable K–12 educational career path; that difficult task is the work of parents, and mostly mothers. There are conflicting messages coming from educational literature on what parents' roles in their children's schooling should be. In exchange for better opportunities, educational institutions still expect parents to support the work of schools as part of their everyday lives and responsibilities raising their children. When parents make choosing schools a part of their work coordinating their children's educations, they necessarily become entangled in the existing inequitable schooling structures and practices historically related to race and class relations. Clearly, there are grounds for reexamining educational policy and policy effects from the position in which parents find themselves when they choose schools for their children.

Parents have their own experiences with schooling that will determine their perspectives, how they see schooling, and the meanings they draw from their experiences. When parents enter the educational system with their children, it is the second time around for them. Their own schooling experiences combined with the social context of their own lives, their work, and their children's activities, locate them in an everyday world with real interests. Parents' experiences are located in what Smith has called a bifurcated consciousness. One dimension locates parents in a local material world, their everyday world; the other dimension includes their experiences in a world organized for abstract goals in and among extended relations beyond parents' everyday thinking and doing (Smith, 1987). However educational institutions or schools structure and organize school choice policies and processes, whether to meet the abstract goals of the economy (e.g., market based choice proposals) or simply to stay in compliance with court orders, (*i.e., Brown v. Board of Education*) there is this other location where parents know otherwise, their real world with their children: loving, caring, feeding, worrying about getting them to school on time, their friendships, and their futures (Griffith and Smith, 2004; Smith, 1987).

STAYING TRUE TO PARENTS' EVERYDAY WORLDS

Focusing on the different parents' personal experiences and choice work helps ground this book in parents' everyday world without moving the overall analysis away from how educational institutional structures, practices, and discourses help constitute parents' experiences with schooling and the meanings they draw about quality education and good schools. Before we can understand how urban public school parents become complicit in inequitable educational opportunity through school choice, we must know them in their everyday lives.

I do not want to claim that all parents spend as much time worrying about their children's schooling as the parents with whom I spoke, but I do think that the work and attention that most parents devote to sending their children off to school, day in and day out, is not fully understood. As I look back over the stories that parents shared, I remember the mothers like Bonnie and Suzanne who openly and honestly stated that their bottom line is that they want the best education possible for their children, but these sentiments were implied by all the parents. I know that the ways in which the district's school choice programs were structured for parent participation was influenced by many of the same social relations and discourses, yet the parents' experiences and how they drew meaning from those relations and discourses differed. I saw how parents' comments continued to expose their limited and sometimes contradictory understandings of the race and class dynamics that are historically part of schooling. In this final chapter I want to bring forth the parents' voices one more time as I discuss how the mothers and fathers are multiply positioned within and by the social world and the institutional ruling relations of education. I will start by returning to an idea I mention above: when parents enroll their children in school it is like going through school all over again.

Schooling the Second Time Around

Searching for school environments for her four children was important to Natalie, not just because they are African American or because (as her quote from the previous chapter indicates) she is well-aware of the struggles they will encounter in our society as people of color. Natalie based her search for a good school for her children on her own public school experiences.

> I had an outstanding education. I had all kinds of teachers. I had men. I had women. I had black. I had white. I had Asian. I had young. I had old. I just had a wonderful variety of teachers. I grew up in a town where — I want to say there wasn't any prejudice — but I will say that I didn't experience any because everyone had everything. I believe prejudice is based on economics, and so if everyone has the same thing there's nothing to be resentful of what other people have or think that anyone's trying to take anything away from you. Everyone lived in a house. Everyone had a car. Everyone had a good job …. Everybody had the same thing. So the expectations when you walk in the classroom were the same. No one looked at you and decided you would probably do better than this kid. They were serious about education. They said you will all learn or you won't leave here, and they were serious about the kind of person you were. So public school education is just like phenomenal for me …. And they taught me how to read, write, and Latin roots, and how to get past the SAT, and what it's going to be like in college, and how to write a term paper, I mean everything, just everything.

Mimi had two very different experiences with schooling. Mimi came to the U.S. when she was thirteen and like many immigrant students in our public schools she had to adjust to a different educational system. She described the merit-based national curriculum in her native country:

> All children are challenged equally in all grades. Whether you lived in metropolis Seoul capital, or you lived in remote island of six students, every single grade — the first grade will all have the same textbook — no matter where you are in the country. The second grade will have the same. It goes all the way through high school and in the end everything will be ranked accordingly. Every classroom will be ranked, and the entire grade will be ranked. So, you know, it's pretty clear who's the top student and

who's not. Coming from Korea, you know, we've always been challenged — rigorous academics — so that was just a way of life. And everyone's expected to go to school and study very hard. The whole atmosphere is driven to that. So if you're not a good student, you are automatically stigmatized as a bad student so, uh, not much choice there.

Mimi added that when she began school in the U.S., "I was feeling like, 'Oh, my God, I don't know what was happening in school.' Because my mother didn't speak English, and my parents didn't know the school structure so I basically went through the system, and I felt like many times, I fell through the cracks." She felt that is was her educational experiences in Korea that carried her through high school and college here in the U.S.

Brenda was born in central California, the only daughter in a farm laborer family. At two years old she was sent to Mexico to be raised by family members and returned to California when she was fifteen. Entering school as a Spanish-speaking student, she was placed in a lower grade, eighth grade, so she could learn English.

I felt very uncomfortable because nobody there was my age, but I took it and I put up with it. I wanted to learn English. I wanted to be able to defend myself. I wanted to be able to understand what was being said and I wanted to be able to say, you know, "This is what I think" Well, like in ninth grade I went through all my classes and I did very well, so when I got into eleventh grade I was thinking like, you know, "Can you guys like move it along? I want to go to college. I want to do some other things with my life." And they said, "Well, you have to wait, you have to have so many credits" and stuff like that. So I left. I went to Job Corps and I got my GED within 45 days.

Shortly after that, Brenda met her children's father when he came from Mexico to work as a seasonal farm laborer. They moved to the city of Deluca when he began working as a landscaper.

When speaking with me about their own schooling, Mimi and Brenda acknowledged that they benefited more from their educations in Korea and Mexico than from their schooling in the U.S. A good educational experience can lead a parent like Natalie to believe that the kind of educational structures and practices that gave rise to her experiences are related to the quality schooling that she received. The institutional practices, discourses, and social relations that help construct parents' own schooling experiences also help shape and determine what parents could know about quality education, who gets access to quality education and who does not, and why that is so.

Looking at parents' experiences as one source of their knowledge about education helps us to understand better how they see the social order in their children's schools at work systematically. It allows us, and sometimes, them, to see the saliency of the class and race relations (as well as immigration issues) operating in their everyday worlds as they think about, help with, and plan for their children's education. The fact that it is mostly mothers' experiences being shaped and helping to shape these relations, shows the saliency of gender as well.

Doing Mothers' Work

Though gender issues were seldom mentioned specifically in reference to choice work and for the most part remained *unseen* by the parents and district personnel, gender relations were still very much an issue. The gender relations coordinating and constructing parents' work for their children's schooling becomes visible as we listen to their comments:

> Meryl: I was married for almost ten years before I had my first one, so I went through school and college and worked for ten years. And then when my daughter was born, I decided that I was going to stay home and basically become a school advocate and work with my children. And that is my job is to be in the public school system as a school volunteer. The way it works with my husband and I, ever since elementary school, it has been my role to work in the schools. And basically it is my job to find out all the information and to do all the legwork, and that's the way I like it, too.

> *Manuel: Aunque a ellos, no — yo no me puedo quejar — no? Sí, sí porque como, pues los quiere uno mucho, al contrario, siempre está uno llamádoles la atención que hagan eso, que levántense, que báñense, que váyanse a la escuela, todo. No, no. Yo yá — o sea al contrario. Me siento a gusto así con mis hijos así; que yo cocino, que yo veo sus tareas — todo — todo.*

> Manuel: Well, I can't complain. Yes, because I love them very much. I'm always calling their attention, to do this, to get up, take a shower, go to school and everything. No, no, it doesn't bother me, it's totally the opposite. I feel alright like that, the way I am

with my children — I cook, I see their homework — everything — everything.

Natalie: I try to get them out at 8:30 because I work feverishly from 8:30 to 2:00. And then I try to give them the afternoons because what's the point of having a mother at home if you come home and she's not accessible to you in the afternoon. So I give them from 2:30 till — well, 3:00 till 5:30 is pretty much the time I give to them that, yes, you can ask me questions, yes, you can sit on my lap, yes, I will watch this stupid program with you, and, yes, I will explain multiplication yet another time to another child. After that I'm in the kitchen cooking, and then about 8:00 o'clock I'm done being a mother. I'm the kind of person that, okay, I've had enough of being a mother, and now I want to be an only child again, which I am, so I need my own time. From 8:00 to like 9:00 I kind of chill, and then I try to be a wife from 9:00 to 11:00.

Mimi: I've always been a career woman, and I've supported myself since college. And I had very good careers. It was a conscious choice for me to stay home until my son went to kindergarten which was six years. And that was probably the biggest sacrifice because, I think, working is probably ten times easier and you make more money, and have all kinds of gratification. But somehow, I said to myself, "You know what? I'd better do this right because my mom didn't do it right with me." Now looking back, she did a lot of things right, but I still was, at that stage, "Oh, my God. You know. My mom's really screwed up being a mother. So I'd better do it right."

Suzanne: I expect that my girls will be working. I want them to have a good satisfying career, and I tell them that they have to do well in school to get into a good college to get training so they have a good career. Thank God I got a good education because I ended up having to, you know, support myself and my kids, which I'm perfectly happy to do. That suits me just fine. But, if I had relied upon a man, heaven help us all. As it turned out I ended up marrying two men that I am more successful in making money than they are. You know, I hope they find some wonderful man, and they're in love and they stay that way or a partner, whether it be a man or not. But, never to rely upon another person. I want them to be able to be self-sufficient. And their education is the key for that.

I believe that it is easy for policy makers and educators to forget how much "mothering work" is involved raising school-age children (Griffith and Smith, 2004). We think of other parents' children as simply students in our classrooms. When the parents talked about what they actually did as mothers or fathers, it reminded me of the importance to remain faithful to the full life they share with their children (Harding, 1991). The parents understood that their children are students in school for only part of their lives and were deeply committed to ensuring that their children's education prepares them for the future. Robin captures this well as she explains what she said to her daughter:

> As long as I'm living mommy's going to help open some doors for them. So you better go do what mommy tell you, because one day mommy's going to be old and tired and sick, and I may not be able to fight for you, so while I'm a go-getter now, listen to me. Just listen to me, Caroline, and study. Find the avenues, the way that you can get in. Stay with the kids that are moving and going places, you know? Don't look for the easy way out. It's going to be hard. Look for the best. Go for the best. Don't just settle for the mediocre. Just try to get in. Just do it — if you feel something is working, go there. Go where it's working. Go where you feel you have a chance. And this is what I tell Caroline. Caroline say, "Well, mom, I want to get on the basketball team. I want to get me a scholarship." She's twelve. And she's hearing things, where the good stuff is. She wants to go where there's winners.

With mothers doing much of the choice work, critical and feminist research can problematize the relationship of choice work to mothers' work. Though Collins (1994) reminds us that feminist theorizing on motherhood can only offer partial perspectives, stories of mothering presented in studies such as those by Griffith (1995) and Graue and Kroeger (2001) capture how much of mothers' work on behalf of their children's education is context bound and part of the normative standardizing relations of schooling (Griffith and Smith, 1987).

In her research with mothers, Hays (1996) noted that none of the mothers seemed to understand their intensive child-rearing efforts as an unjust burden or a task imposed on them by those in more powerful roles. Analyzing the contradiction this implies about women's participation in support of patriarchal institutional practices, she states that:

> Arguments about "equal opportunity" and "individual responsibility" for one's social position, in these terms, are simply ideological mechanisms meant to disguise systemic injustice. So, too, is the ideology of intensive mothering. It operates to convince

women that they want (or at least should want) to commit themselves to a task that, in fact, ultimately serves those with the power
to manipulate and control ideas. The ideology of intensive child
rearing, then, is both the result of and a form of *disguising* domi-
nation (1996, p.165, italics hers).

Bringing together these various analyses on mothers and schooling,
we can start to understand how "mothers' work" can put some mothers
in the position of supporting the normative practices of schooling
while they remain subordinate to the relations of power that construct
those practices.

The insights from feminists who have addressed the tensions and
contradictions of women's work as mothers along with the critical
studies on parents' roles in their children's schooling help advance
more thoughtful analysis on how parents, and mothers in particular,
are positioned within and by school choice processes. Reay points out
that parents' decisions about school choice are but an "apex of a hidden
pyramid of choices" mothers make on a daily basis (Reay, 1996).
Reay also notes that choosing schools is a far riskier business for working-class parents than for middle-class parents who benefit from the
normative assumptions in school choice discourse. She writes:

> They are engaging in a totally different process to the middle-class
> parents; one which holds dangers as well as promises .... when
> working-class families make a greater investment in their child's
> academic achievement, through choosing a school which empha-
> sizes academic excellence, they are also piling up far greater
> psychological and emotional stakes to lose in a game where the
> odds lie elsewhere (Reay, 1996, pp. 591–592).

Therefore when I apply feminist standpoint theorizing to an analysis
of public school choice in the context of mothers' everyday lived experiences, it becomes possible to ask, How can we learn from parents',
mothers' understandings of what it takes to get into a "good" school
when they are choosing among the historically unequal schools in a
large urban school district? What choices look reasonable to parents
given the changing nature of education today?

Choosing Schools Is Socially Situated

The parents in this study were doing their choosing among a relatively
small number of district magnet schools and other schools perceived to
be good schools. Not surprisingly, the parents in the study who had
more material resources did far better in this struggle. Studying parents

and school choice in England, Reay stated that school choice cannot be conceptualized in isolation from localized issues of history and geography and the influences of differential access to social power and material resources (Reay, 1996).

Whether the parents rent or own their home; live far from work and schools; receive income from jobs or welfare; or interact with a multiplicity of people in private and public organizations, these social locations are all part of the extended relations shaping the context in which they choose schools. The families' residences may connect them to the broader social relations in which their lives are situated (Holme, 2002; Varady and Raffel, 1995), but where parents lived, like the parents' own personal experiences with good or not-so-good schooling, was not always divided along social class or racial lines. It is not easy to draw clear distinctions about their participation in choice based on these factors. For example, Natalie owns a home with her husband in a middle-class, racially diverse community. Bonnie lives in a duplex apartment several blocks away from Brenda's and Robin's apartments, two mothers who receive subsidized housing benefits. What these parents had in common was that among the different neighborhood schools to which their children were assigned, at least one of the schools was not perceived to be a good school by them, nor by some of the district's administrators and teachers themselves. The parents, while choosing to live in diverse communities, were not sending their children to the neighborhood schools in their own communities.

The parents were hard at work trying to get their children enrolled in "good" schools in a school district perceived to have far more "not-so-good" schools. How we should interpret the intensity with which these parents, mothers, worked to get their children into good schools is seldom addressed in studies of parents' roles in their children's schooling. It is hard to attach labels to these parents, and in particular, the white and middle-class parents, because they were clearly trying to get the most out of living and working and doing school with their children in a diverse city. Linda seems to capture this when she says:

> I want my child to be a citizen of the world. I think that's very important and I want them to know people from all walks of life. I want them to have as many experiences as possible and I want them to get a good education. So how all that gets married together is a big question mark, I don't know.

None of these families lived in segregated (by race or income) suburban communities. They lived in the city, traveled heavily trafficked city streets, listened daily to city noises, and adjusted to the hectic pace of a large urban metropolis. While many of the parents lived in the more liberal (and whiter) parts of the city, I could not walk or drive around any of these families' neighborhoods, parks, markets, and restaurants and not appreciate the diversity of peoples with whom they share their daily lives. That many of these parents were privileged by society and by schooling institutions is nonetheless apparent. However their subjective experiences and knowledge differed, all these parents understood that schools are about achievement, and achievement happens at good schools; this is what seemed to be driving their choice work. Hence the increasing salience of an achievement discourse.

THE BUREAUCRATIC STRUGGLE TO PROVIDE CHOICE

Uncovering parents' different experiences with schooling, by itself, does not help us understand how parents, mothers, as a result of choosing schools for their own children, are complicit in the inequitable educational opportunities for other parents' children. Moving analysis to the institutional context and looking deeper into district organizational practices provides a more detailed and nuanced understanding of school choice in Deluca USD.

The district faced major problems in providing school choice options for parents within the guidelines of its voluntary integration programs. First, the classroom space needed for an ever increasing student population made any kind of choice option ultimately an issue of allocation of scarce resources; in this district, the scarce resource was a seat in a classroom at a magnet school or another "good school." Second, the large bureaucratic structure of the district and the different departments overseeing choice options complicated the organization and delivery of school choice for all but the most devoted and/or sophisticated parent applicants. Third, district policies and practices have historically privileged white participants in the district's integration program and consequently help to shape the race and class relations contributing to the inequities seen in the parents' choice processes and outcomes.

The Inevitability of Resegregation and Privilege

The parents in this study took their choice work seriously. They researched schools and did everything that was expected of them. They chose the schools they wanted their children to attend. When they didn't get into the schools they wanted, they found other ways in. The parents have told us that there are only so many good schools, there is such limited choice, and the stakes are high. The frustration they felt was captured by Jenny:

Well, I think what's changed, you know, it's true that we have unequal schools and we've always had unequal schools. What's happened is the game has changed. That it used to be that people bought their way into better schools by where they lived. And it doesn't work anymore. And it doesn't even work to escape to private schools because if you can afford them, you can't necessarily get into them. So what's happened is instead of people buying, you know, a home in a place where they would be assured of a better education, they have to play the game. And so the end result is we still haven't done anything about making all schools better for everybody. Because if all schools were good, then we wouldn't have to do all this game playing and monkeying around and our kids could go to Ross or to James Madison and not think anything of it.

By the very fact that Bonnie, Brenda, Karen, Linda, Manuel, Mary, Meryl, Mimi, Natalie, Paul and Jenny, Robin, and Suzanne were actively at work trying to choose good schools for their children, they became participants in inequitable educational opportunities for other parents' children. It is here where their complicity is located. But it was not all their doing.

The district administrators clearly were not prepared to see how closely the new local structures and practices that came with voluntary integration were tied into class relations, whether their own, parents', and those historically part of schooling (G. Smith, 1990). How they institutionalized the voluntary integration program fitted right into already existing textually-mediated, socially organized "ruling relations" (Smith, 1987) of children and their parents (standardized test scores, grades, discipline contracts, etc.). The previous chapters examined the various social relations, institutional practices, and texts helping to shape and determine the knowledge and resources parents need to get their children into good schools. Deluca USD has organized and coordinated parents' choice work, which is primarily mothers' work, to the district's own needs and interests through its use of these structures, practices, and texts. Additionally, the bureaucratic organization of school choice options reinforced some of the historical inequities that result from parents' participation in the school choice process by increasing the saliency of class relations in getting into good schools and masking the exclusion taking place while only a small percentage of the district's students get access to the diversity and academic achievement available in some of the schools in the district's voluntary integration program. The decisions by the court and the district administration that implemented the court order failed to address how the racial integration formulas continued to support white privilege. The design of the priority points system and new application text made matters worse.

All the various data I collected — interviews with administrators, a letter from the State Controller's office, the magnet brochure, and various district bulletins — indicated or strongly implied that the district is still under an active court order to integrate its schools (for example, see Figures 2 and 3). However, Deluca USD's voluntary integration plan is no longer being monitored by the court. Usually when court orders are issued, a court-appointed monitor reviews a district's compliance with any plans approved by the court. In the case of Deluca, the court gave final approval to the district's voluntary plan in 1988 and then terminated jurisdiction over the case. The court does not have an appointed monitor for Deluca USD. This means the court order approving the district's last submitted plan stays in effect indefinitely unless that plan is challenged with new litigation. It also means the district can enjoy some autonomy in its policy formation and implementation of the voluntary integration program. I do not want to suggest that the district believes it can operate independently. To the contrary, to continue to receive the millions of dollars it gets from the state to operate its integration programs, the district must respond to annual state audits.

Nonintegrated Magnet Programs

Given the racial and class advantage some families have in the magnet school application process and the exclusion the process creates for other families, the district could modify the racial formula used in the priority points system that allocates students to magnet schools. I believe this is, in fact, happening. When Brenda and I discussed that the purpose of magnet schools was to integrate the district's schools, she said:

> Does anybody check and see if that's true though? If they have integrated, because in my daughter's classroom, she's in magnet school, and there's eleven African Americans, O.K.? There's one Korean and there's three Hispanics. Now is that integration, because if it is, she can go to Greenfield for that, you know. That's not integration.

The data for Berry Elementary magnet, where her younger daughter attends school (see Appendix B), establishes that Brenda was right. There are no white students in that magnet school. I investigated further and found examples of other district magnet schools that did not have the required 30% white students. So while numerous sources in the district stated the district must use the racial integration formulas established by the court, apparently that is not always the case.

Following the guidelines of the court-ordered formula should not absolve administrators from considering the consequences of the decisions they make — decisions that draw parents into school choice processes and practices that they know are inequitable. Nor can the school district administration remain unaware of the resegregation that is taking place. While placing blame on parents for their unknowing participation in the historical inequities of school choice is of no help in bringing about more equitable procedures and practices, this study does not seek to place blame on particular administrators. I, in fact, think many administrators are aware of the resegregation taking place in the district, as the comment by one administrator indicates:

> Well, when you call it resegregation, it's resegregation of a different type. You' re talking about a resegregation — and what we don't like to talk about in this country that's on a social-economic level .... we never deal with true issues in desegregation, true issues of this country. We designed [desegregation] to fail, and it is failing. We programmed it to fail by putting — and we don't say this — different socioeconomic levels together in the same school and then expect them to compete, when one kid has got a yacht at home and one kid hasn't got a boat to put in the bathtub with him .... But the magnets though, because the magnet parents have similar interests, they're going to help their kids. Parents may not be in the same socioeconomic level in terms of dollars and cents but they still have the same interest in terms of their children. And that's why they're successful in the magnets. They'll get in there and work and make sure that they get those children the support they need.

Frankenberg and colleagues (2003) point out that since 1974, the Supreme Court has been either limiting desegregation or dismantling existing plans. They note that racial segregation has been ignored in the two major educational innovations of the past twenty years — standards-based reform and school choice. While they are concerned that policy makers may assume that civil rights goals have been achieved, that separate schools can be equal, or that race does not matter, they disagree strongly with the suggestions that desegregation failed — that it was a goal that could not be achieved (Frankenberg et al., 2003). Reforms like NCLB that focus on choice and quality schools "can foil integration efforts" — the implication being that integration is no longer a primary goal of education while increasing minority student achievement is (powell, 2001, p. 686).

FROM INTEGRATION TO INCREASED ACHIEVEMENT

Early in this book, I stated my concern that voluntary integration programs and the desegregation goals they were designed to address may be overtaken by market-based choice options. Perhaps the gains made in the neoliberal agenda for an open market of choice are happening because choice advocates have been able to tie public school choice to student achievement rather than student integration. At the time of my research, district administrators were under pressure to demonstrate that they could raise student achievement. Decisions by local administrators to enroll students that aided those goals were an inevitable outcome. The accountability requirements of NCLB place even greater demands on local administrators as they try to manage school-wide improvement.

Seeing the Discourse Change

Deluca USD's experience with voluntary integration and school choice is an example of how an integration program can become vulnerable to discursive shifts from desegregation to integration to choice to achievement as discourses common in neoliberal proposals for to choice are taken up in an effort to close the achievement gap between white students and underrepresented minority students. In the introduction, I described two key discourses — an integration discourse and an achievement discourse — identified in the district's school choice policies and practices by examining the texts that shape and construct parents' choice work. Throughout the book I have paid close attention to the details of parents' and school people's actions around school choice texts. In Figure 5, I illustrated how the magnet brochure, application, and application procedures for nonmagnet school choice options actually put parents to work as they sought better schools for their children. In Figure 6, I try to capture more of the textually-mediated organization and coordination of parents' choice work and how the integration and achievement discourses are embedded in the choice process. Mapping the textual links that may originate in the courts, in Congress, or in the state legislature and following those links to the implementation policies and practices of the district's central offices, help us see across the texts that are part of the choice process. It makes it possible to illuminate the social relations and the often-invisible "doings" and work of many

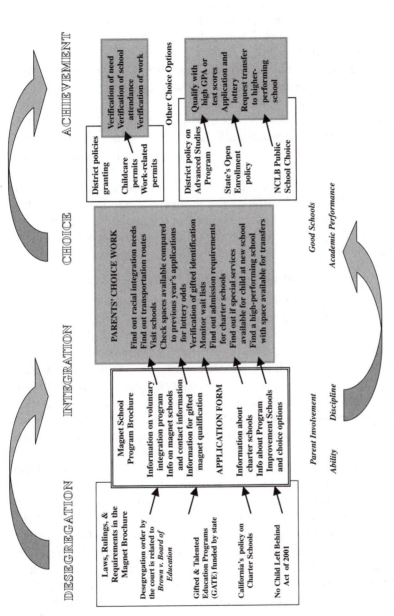

DESEGREGATION   INTEGRATION   CHOICE   ACHIEVEMENT

Laws, Rulings, & Requirements in the Magnet Brochure

Desegregation order by the court is related to *Brown v. Board of Education*

Gifted & Talented Education Programs (GATE) funded by state

California's policy on Charter Schools

No Child Left Behind Act of 2001

Magnet School Program Brochure

Information on voluntary integration program

Info on magnet schools and contact information

Information for gifted magnet qualification

APPLICATION FORM

Information about charter schools

Info about Program Improvement Schools and choice options

PARENTS' CHOICE WORK

Find out racial integration needs

Find out transportation routes

Visit schools

Check spaces available compared to previous year's applications for lottery odds

Verification of gifted identification

Monitor wait lists

Find out admission requirements for charter schools

Find out if special services available for child at new school

Find a high-performing school with space available for transfers

District policies granting

Childcare permits

Work-related permits

Verification of need
Verification of school attendance
Verification of work

Other Choice Options

District policy on Advanced Studies Program

State's Open Enrollment policy

NCLB Public School Choice

Qualify with high GPA or test scores
Application and lottery
Request transfer to higher-performing school

Parent Involvement   *Good Schools*

Ability   *Discipline*   *Academic Performance*

Figure 6. Change in Discursive Orientations of Public School Choice

people who are behind or between textual procedures and are, one way or another, connected with and by the texts.

Seeing this institutional organization and coordination visually, we get a better understanding of how the discursive shift from desegregation to integration to choice to achievement could take place in the district's school choice programs. Understanding how parents' and school people's actions are hooked into notions of ability, discipline, and parent involvement, we can see how an orientation to an achievement discourse and a belief that achievement happens at good schools (or as NCLB promotes, schools with high test scores) could overtake school integration priorities. We can locate various social relations coordinating activities in multiple sites as parents' choice work is linked via texts to the work of others — work that may be oriented to one or multiple discourses. If the stories of parents choosing schools in Deluca USD are read with this framework in mind, I think we will be better equipped to critique the impact of the neoliberal turn in public school choice policy and how it may affect federal support for desegregation efforts.

Well-Intentioned Reform, Oppressive Effects

Parents believe strongly that they have a responsibility to ensure the best opportunities for their children (Graue and Kroeger, 2001). They are working hard for their children's educations (Smith, 1987). Still, the advantage to being a white or wealthier parent ends up limiting the opportunity to achieve greater equity for other parents' sons and daughters. It is important that researchers question just how this happens to parents as they do the work of raising and schooling their children. Research also reminds us that reforms to help schools become better at educating children are continuous. Privileged white and middle-class parents as well as poor and minority parents get caught up in trying to understand these reforms and what they mean for their children's educations. Little research has been done to explore fully parents' subordinate status in educational institutions. There is more than sufficient work by critical scholars to support the argument that educational institutions maintain oppressive structures for students of diverse racial, gender, class, and linguistic backgrounds (Hinchey, 1998; McLaren, 1995; Valenzuela, 1999); we can expect them to be the same for many parents. Poor parents and parents of color will increasingly come to understand how institutional structures help to further their oppressions. It stands to reason, then, that educational institutions have played a role in shaping and determining parents' participation in inequitable educational practices. Fine reaches a similar conclusion:

> It is frightening to consider that public schools claim universal inclusion yet invent highly exclusive boundaries to control who is actually in and out and then represent these boundaries as protecting the common good. While the notions of merit, choice, and tradition may appear to be liberal and benign ideologies of public schools, they actually provide a cover for moral exclusion, and they carry sweeping consequences for those excluded and even damage those who are ostensibly protected (Fine, 1992, p. 114).

Therefore it is important that we continue to explore how the work parents are expected to do in choosing schools ends up serving the race-, class-, and gender-based oppressions of a capitalist society, especially at a time of increasing marketization of public education.

The neoliberal market-based models of school choice assume parents will act a certain way under the market conditions that choice plans create. Although it did not surface with the parents in my study, a strong level of competition among parents is expected in the school choice process. Parents generally did not feel they were competing against one another, and if anything, they were competing against, as Suzanne said to me, the "choice system." With the new NCLB school choice transfer requirements, any remaining school choice options in Deluca USD soon will be gone. This could impact the networking and sharing of information among parent groups, further privileging those parents already advantaged in the process. It is important to point out that the schools of choice in this study were so popular that they consequently operated at full capacity. Schools like El Rancho and Carnegie had the definite advantage of being perceived as good schools against a general perception that many schools in the district are not-so-good. While the magnet schools benefited from attracting the better students, they also seemed to welcome parents going elsewhere, changing the dynamics normally predicted by market models of school choice. The allocation of scarce classroom space in a good school will bring to light the less-than-positive side of a market economy; families will be turned away. Moreover, the connection of any increased public school choice options to future state or federal funding apportionments makes larger political and economic contexts important as well.

The Importance of Tracing the Local to the Global

Issues of privilege and exclusion, such as those impacting public school choice in the district, can be understood in more depth when analyzed with the tools of critical and feminist theories (Marshall, 1997). While a major focus of such an analysis should include issues of power and politics, more than that is needed, as the following quote by Foucault suggests:

> In the Western industrialized societies, the questions "Who exercises power? How? On Whom?" are certainly the questions that people feel most strongly about .... On the other hand: Who makes decisions for me? Who is preventing me from doing this and telling me to do that? Who is programming my movements and activities? Who is forcing me to live in a particular place when I work in another? How are these decisions on which my life is completely articulated taken? All these questions seem to me to be fundamental ones today. And I don't believe that this question of "Who exercises power?" can be resolved unless the other question "How does it happen?" is resolved at the same time (Foucault, 1995, pp. 41–42).

Foucault's question of "How does it happen?" is an important one for researching in our school organizations and institutions just how exclusion and privilege does happen. Textual analysis helps us see the social relations that organize and coordinate a parent's local activities with the workings of educational institutions supporting reform implementation, compliance mandates, and political and economic agendas. Texts mediate, regulate, and authorize the activities of many different people at work in educational institutions, in government, and in the marketplace.

Recall from the introduction Harding's analogy about the stick in the pond and Smith's response that she is interested in discovering the shape of the pond. And recall also Crenshaw and colleagues' analogy from Chapter 4 that the law is involved in constructing the rules of the game and choosing the field on which the game is played. These analogies are helpful as we try to move our analyses from the lived realities of parents into the institutional contexts and ruling relations helping to shape their lives and the outcomes of their choice work. Adapted from Pense[1] (2002), Figure 7 illustrates a trajectory useful for linking our understanding of parents' everyday worlds to the relations of ruling that help to shape and coordinate parents' activities on behalf of their families. Parents' mothering work and choice work is taken up into and between institutional sites and organized according to the regulating entities controlling and ordering social and legal relations to state, national, and global economic contexts. By following the diagram in Figure 7, it is possible to see how parents are drawn into ruling relations

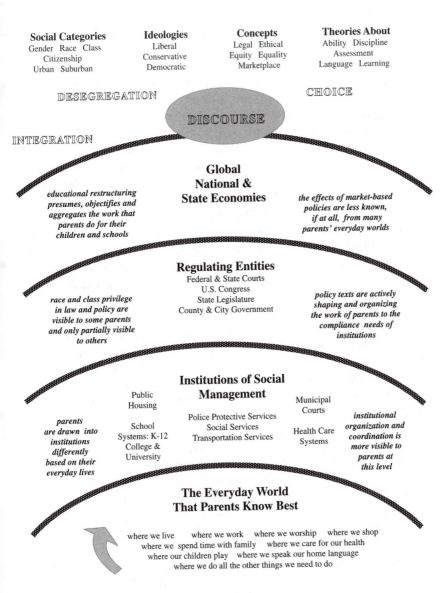

Figure 7. Mapping Social and Institutional Relations

through institutional polices, practices, and texts that organize and coordinate the outcomes of their different children's schooling in ways that parents may or may not be aware. The way in which global, national and state economies are related to inequitable structures and practices and unequal educational opportunities is not fully visible to all parents.

Through our research and analysis, we can *see* how a mother like Suzanne is afforded a privileged position in the social order of schooling and institutional relations compared to mothers like Brenda or Robin who must navigate ruling relations from their everyday worlds as women of color, who do not have access to the same social and material resources. For example, consider that Suzanne's drive from her own home to work is not a difficult commute. She also has a carpool with other mothers from her children's schools. Suzanne earns a good income as a professional and has a broad-based information network. Suzanne's daughters were advantaged in the magnet school lottery by the District's integration formula and their high achievement qualifies them for the Advanced Studies Program, as well. Her daughters are well-prepared for competitive university admission processes. Robin, on the other hand, is under pressure to enter the workforce as her welfare support is reduced. Her apartment rent is subsidized by vouchers provided by the Housing Authority. Robin understands that she needs a college degree to earn a salary that can adequately support her family but her poor grades keep her from continuing in school. Robin was not successful in the magnet school application process and her daughter was assigned to a school by the district far from her home. As a result, Robin's two children attended schools miles apart hardly accessible to her by public transportation. Now compare Brenda's everyday world with Suzanne's. Like Robin's children, Brenda's children qualify for the district's Free & Reduced-price Meals Program. Brenda's daughter was not accepted into the magnet school to which she applied — a school with only 11% Latino students in a district with a large Latino student majority. Two of Brenda's other children attend a magnet school with no white students. The family receives food stamps and lives in Section 8 housing. Brenda volunteers regularly at her four children's schools. The father of Brenda's children, a day laborer, lives the reality of global workforce demands as he travels to and from Mexico.

Using the diagram in Figure 7 to analyze the different mothers' stories, it is now possible to see the trajectory of how parents, from their everyday world, are drawn into institutional ruling relations differently depending on their gender, racial, and class identities. But however differently they may be positioned, they will be subject to dominant discourses nonetheless, and this will influence how they experience and understand the schooling their children receive. The changes that parents are encountering in school choice programs (as well as with school curriculum, instruction, and assessment practices) result from reforms like NCLB that have been driven in large part by neoliberal and neoconservative discourses. By mapping parents' experiences with school choice policies, processes and practices through and between institutional locations, I can extend the analytical trajectory into national and global economic contexts in ways that may not be visible to parents themselves.

To some, this extended analysis may appear too far removed from studying the practical realities of parents and people in schools. But I agree with Dehli that this kind of "conceptual labour" about how parents are positioned between the state and the market "is important because without it, it is difficult to make (feminist) sense of how New Right and Neo-Liberal interventions in and discourses of education operate, how they differ and where they overlap, and how they are (apparently) able to appeal to widespread discontent with public or state schooling" (Dehli, 1996, p. 374). While critiquing public education institutions, neoconservative and neoliberal policies have supported the restructuring of education to the needs of the workforce. Insomuch as economic conditions and restructuring policies are related to the inequitable structures and practices and unequal educational opportunities in our educational institutions, the influence of neoconservative and neoliberal policies is less visible to all parents. This makes it harder for parents (and many educators) to understand that schooling could be institutionalized in more democratic ways (Apple, 2003).

Douglas says, "The most profound decisions about justice are not made by individuals as such, but by individuals thinking within and on behalf of institutions. The only way that a system of justice exists is by its everyday fulfillment of institutional needs" (Douglas, 1986). Keeping in mind the work of critical theorists, it is necessary to find ways to illustrate just how government actions, including those of the courts, privilege those who are white and those with more material resources, while further burdening those who are nonwhite and poor (Haney Lopez, 2000). I said at the outset of the book that I want to know where in and among institutional structures and practices exclusions and privileges take place. I have begun to map some of these locations in Figures 5 and 6.

As I extend analysis into broader social relations, it is necessary to move from the everyday world of parents into local and state level institutional structures and then into the more abstract levels of the economy, where neoliberal and neoconservative discourses, ideologies, and conceptual practices reside. Figure 7 illustrates only one such trajectory as part of my institutional ethnographic account of parents and public school choice. Mapping social organization and institutional relations can enlarge our perspectives beyond what can be learned if we were to limit our studies only to parents' participation in their everyday worlds. By beginning in the actual coordination and organization of parents' work on behalf of their children's schooling we can discover the concepts, theories, and discourses that are included in that coordination, and bring to light the social relations implicit in the organization of parents' experiences and public education (Smith, 2002).

THE NEXUS OF VOLUNTARY INTEGRATION AND PUBLIC SCHOOL CHOICE

Policy makers and educators need to know how discourses and social relations construct and constitute their work. As policy-makers consider the next decade's efforts to address racial and class segregation taking place in urban schools, perhaps they can learn more from similar studies about how districts themselves sustain the existing privileges and exclusions of public schooling through what they communicate to parents. The kinds of educational practices uncovered in this study need to be explored in greater detail, because too often our research on educational policy skirts both a more nuanced understanding of district organization that contributes to inequity and inequality and a similar understanding about how global educational restructuring impacts the work of educators and parents in schools. We need to know much more about *how it happens* that some parents' children are privileged over others' in our public schooling institutions and the role schooling institutions play in helping to determine that that is so. As Dobson notes,

> the "structures" seemingly over and against us, such as "institutional" decisions, rendering us apparently powerless, are in fact the creation of people in definite relations. We are the ones who achieve organization together; organization does not exist "out there" as structures or buildings or even texts but rather as a social relation that was put together by people and continues to be so (Dobson, 2001).

Investigating from parents' everyday activities in support of their children's schooling to learn how those activities are shaped by institutional policies, practices, and texts put in place by people and coordinated across many people's doings can begin the needed exploration and explication of the social relations, and the textual relations, that continue to sustain inequitable and unequal educational opportunities.

Equity-Based School Choice

In the 2000 statewide election, Proposition 38 put before California voters a voucher plan that would have offered every school child in California a fixed dollar amount they could use to attend private or religious schools. The initiative suffered an overwhelming defeat because voters did not believe it was fair to give such benefits to the already wealthy or to drain money from public schools (Wolfe, 2003). A market-based-only approach to choice, one that relies on freedom of choice and self-interest arguments, has choice advocates recognizing the need to focus on providing school choice opportunities for racial minorities and the poor. The rhetoric around choice has changed from market-based choice to emphasis on equity-based choice (Macedo, 2003; Wolfe, 2003). Advocates of market-based models of choice continue to refine their proposals and plans to address these very issues (National Working Commission on Choice in K–12 Education, 2003), but the broader use of vouchers will not likely happen soon because of voters' concerns about equity (Macedo, 2003).

Equity concerns are addressed in NCLB. The act requires that school accountability systems disaggregate achievement data. Unfortunately, the emerging data shows what desegregation scholars continuously report: that there are disparate outcomes for minority students in poorly resourced urban schools compared to students attending middle-class, white, or integrated schools (Orfield, 2001; Orfield and Lee, 2004). Boger's analysis of the convergence of the high-stakes accountability measures of NCLB with the increased racial segregation taking place in North Carolina argues that those forces — what Boger calls the "perfect storm" — threaten to worsen the plight of schools with a disproportionate amount of poor and nonwhite students (Boger, 2003). It appears that the new practices established by NCLB do not work for all students and all families, and integration efforts aimed at achieving greater equality and equity are even undermined by the new organizational structures and practices the federal act creates. Orfield states that past failure to develop policies that could deal with the realities of metropolitan communities and the large demographic transformation the country faces is a "crisis of law, policy, and demography" (Orfield, 2001, p. 15). To address the developing crisis of which Orfield and Boger speak, we must know how resegregation by race and class *happens* in local district contexts. A closer look at the workings of districts that are trying to address the race-based and class-based resegregation in their schools — in those areas where districts are succeeding and where they are not — is crucial for advancing more equitable education policies that can penetrate all levels of our schooling institutions.

LEARNING FROM PARENTS' STANDPOINT

I have shown that when we explore the context of public school choice from the standpoint of parents' experiences, we add to our existing knowledge new perspectives of how voluntary integration programs work alongside other choice options and good and not-so-good neighborhood schools. Some school choice advocates believe that, by continuing to provide more choice options for parents, we will improve the conditions of urban schools while not adversely impacting school integration efforts. The data from this study suggests that such arguments are simplistic and leave unaddressed the salient issue of how race and class really operate in educational institutions.

Years after *Brown* and years after the court that had jurisdiction over Deluca USD's voluntary integration plan established the integration formula, we are brought into the context in which the parents in this study chose schools. There now are new questions we need to ask if we are to understand how these parents' stories match up to the intent of *Brown* and to the state and federal legislation that has expanded public school choice options.

This book began with a reflection on why, 50 years after the *Brown* decision, we still find schools resegregating by race and class. I believe that my study shows how the court rulings, while intending to address racial inequalities for poor and minority students, did not anticipate how the local structures and practices institutionalized with magnet school programs and the school choice programs that followed would remain so closely tied not only to race and class but also to gender relations as well.

The need of school districts to meet desegregation mandates set in place a pattern of capitalizing on parents' desires to secure the best possible education for their children. Texts and discourses were produced to attract parents to school integration programs and the special environments for learning that magnet schools provide. Perhaps this kind of coercion of parents, which was meant to achieve more equitable and democratic goals, was necessary given the inequalities associated with residential segregation and the political needs at the time. But since mothers have historically done the work associated with parent involvement practices, and similarly so with school choice, those mothers who engage with educational institutions are forced to struggle with whether their children will be among the haves rather than the have nots.

Today, the school choice provisions of the NCLB are added to the options the district must offer parents. In addition to existing choices, students attending Title I schools that are not meeting their Adequate Yearly Progress (AYP) targets and that have been designated as Program

Improvement Schools must be allowed transfers to higher achieving schools. Parents, mothers mostly, are again going to be drawn into a competitive scramble to find good schools for their children to attend.

Since completing the research presented in this book, Foster Middle School, having failed to meet its AYP targets for three years, is now designated a Program Improvement School under NCLB. Foster is the school that was Brenda and Robin's "resident" school because the Carnegie Preparatory magnet school took over the site of what was once their neighborhood middle school. Were Brenda and Robin choosing schools today, they would first be told that their children were being bused to Foster, because that is the school to which the district has assigned them, and then they would have to be told that that Foster is a school out of which they are entitled to transfer. But where would they go? What choices would they really have? Before NCLB was the law, Robin already understood what such a situation could mean:

> I'm in region 5. Okay, I'm like in this box. I'm in a geographic box. I can't go outside of where I live to send my children to school. I have to deal with the schools that are already there — it's a matter of whether or not I have a choice to send my kids to this school or that school. They're cutting us off. That's what I see. I'm cut off on the east, west, north, and south. I'm stuck here on Prescott Drive, and I have very few choices, and the choices I have they're even telling me those choices aren't good. I can't go fifty miles. My baby can't be going an hour, two hours to school, and I surely can't drive her way, way out there, you know?

California has over 6 million K–12 students. The Department of Education recently released the number of schools identified as Program Improvement schools under NCLB for the school year 2004–2005. Over 900 Title I schools are in their second year of Program Improvements (PI), which means that the parents of the lowest-performing students in those schools can request a public school transfer. How many students will that be? A couple hundred thousand, I presume (California Department of Education, October 13, 2004).

This scenario is more than a ridiculous outcome of overlapping school choice policies; it is now reality for many parents. And it is an unfortunate testament to how different courses of action, coordinated and organized over time, while not initiated by or directly attributed to any single individual in a district or any single judge's ruling, have had the concerted effect of sustaining power and privilege for those parents who are white, middle class, and whose children perform at high academic levels (Haney Lopez, 2000; Smith, 1990). It is a scenario about how some parents' children are indeed gifted at the expense of the children of poorer parents and parents of color. Maybe in light of what we know about their experiences, we could understand that, if Brenda or Robin were offered a voucher for private school, they would likely consider using it. And perhaps the high achieving children of parents like Bonnie or Suzanne or some of the other parents will continue to be granted privileges in our system of schooling, and their parents will justify the privileges as earned and their children as deserving (McIntosh, 1989).

CONCLUSION

The current context in which former court-ordered desegregation plans are being dismantled or converted into voluntary integration programs, coupled with school districts' efforts to accommodate NCLB choice requirements, suggests that we need a closer look at the local practices that have developed around existing public school choice programs. Local district policies and managerial procedures that have been in operation for many years can provide us with important insight into how public school choice will be organized for parental participation in these new times.

Critiques of privileged parents and their actions will not be enough to bring about social change. Parents must be real and equal participants in the dialogues about education if there is going to be any possibility for them to act in ways that support quality, diverse, and equitable education for all students. While many parent activists, like myself, have long envisioned truly democratic participation by parents in public education, this kind of dialogue just has not been sustained (or even taken place) in the past. The public also needs to be reengaged in dialogue on segregation and exclusion, but not at the expense of targeting any one racial or ethnic group, or economically disadvantaged groups. There are harms to the racial segregation and overinclusion and privileging of whites that need to be part of the public dialogue as well.

Additionally, an important question for scholars who study school choice should be whether, given our rapidly changing urban school communities and renewed political support for a return to neighborhood schools, voluntary integration and public school choice can be implemented in ways that will achieve *Brown's* goal of integrated schools. It might be the case that local schooling institutions think that they can carefully design structures and practices to bring about social change through a variety of public school choice programs, but today's context may require a more careful look at how these programs are really implemented in school communities. Perhaps a closer examination will show that the rules and processes that districts institutionalize to bring about access, equity, and equality may serve to hide the very real ways that race and class still support exclusion in our schools. I hope that the project shared in these pages will encourage more research on why it is that when some parents make what they believe is the best decision for their children and family they end up complicit in the unequal outcomes for other parents' children. But I believe it is even more important that the research we undertake in the future helps us to understand better how it happens that our institutional policies and practices themselves make this so. This means moving our analyses beyond the experiential scope of individuals to the more abstract but very present ruling relations that organize and coordinate much of the action that leads to the injustices and inequalities we seek to end.

The literature on parent involvement is too often written from the perspective of schooling and people in schools — what helps students' educational outcomes and what schools need parents to do. I have shown that there is a parental standpoint from which to research educational institutions and parent involvement practices. From this standpoint, we saw how the various school choice and voluntary integration policies and practices of the district placed some parents in privileged positions while the same policies and practices positioned the poor parents of color differently. The parents in this study moved their children to better schools, leaving behind the parents and children who would still attend their not-so-good neighborhood schools. I do recognize that in many ways the parental standpoint presented in this one analysis is not inclusive enough. There are many parental voices and stories left unstudied that if heard would add to an even deeper understanding of our educational institutions. Our educational institutions have been stubborn about addressing the differences in the everyday worlds of diverse urban parents and their experiences with the schools their children attend. Clearly, more research that steps back from blaming parents for the ways in which they do or do not participate in their children's schooling is needed.

It is time that our studies of the family-school relationship begin with gendered parents with real lives, particularly with mothers who bear the major responsibility for the work of schooling. Research focusing on parents needs to consider the varied contexts in which parents themselves were educated and how educational institutions socially constructed what parents came to know about schooling. We must recognize that mothers and fathers experience the effects of fragmented and overlapping policies, numerous reform efforts, and over 50 different educators cumulatively influencing their children's lives through ever-changing pedagogies and curricula during 13 years of schooling. The schooling context that parents encounter is not easy to negotiate, and parents can become easy targets for powerful discourses that undermine efforts to make schools more socially and economically just. Our studies must openly examine how parents' race and social class intersect with their gendered roles so we can better understand how some parents' children become privileged over others'. Therefore our research must not lose sight of how material positions, racial privilege, and dominance matter in the outcomes of schooling for all parents' children. If the desired result of critical policy research is to change the inequitable educational outcomes of urban public school students, the changes will be more effective if we learn not only why, but also how, parents, mothers, end up making the decisions they do and in which ways schooling institutions are helping to shape those decisions.

And while I offer my study as one effort aimed at helping us see how parents become participants in inequitable schooling outcomes, the work of equity-minded researchers must not stop here. We need investigations that probe deeper into our educational institutions through the very texts that help to shape and organize what people in institutions do so that we can strategically transform *how it happens* into how it could happen differently. It is my hope that this book will help critical and feminist scholars to continue to build evidence in support of the changes needed in state and national educational policies implemented within the subordinating structures of public school bureaucracies. I also hope it will encourage others to take on the challenges and the complexities of studying diverse parents, diverse mothers, as they work to raise their children among the intersecting and overlapping race, class, and gender relations operating in urban public schools, exploring with them the world they know otherwise so that we can do otherwise.

APPENDIX A

Parents	Children	Race	Schools
Bonnie	Sabrina Jessica	White	Christopher St. Magnet Elem., Carnegie HS, El Rancho Gifted MS, Davis Liberal Arts HS
Brenda	Andy Carlos Sandra Elena	Latino	Greenfield Elem., Berry Magnet Elem., El Rancho Regular MS
Karen	Jayne Lynne Neema	White Biracial: White-Black	Christopher St. Magnet Elem., Kennedy MS, El Rancho Gifted MS, Carnegie HS
Linda	Julienne Peter	White	Columbus Elem., Spring St. Magnet Elem., El Rancho Gifted MS, Private
Manuel	Rosa Fernando Marisol Victor	Latino	Hughes Elem., El Rancho Regular MS, Davis Reg. HS, Horizon HS
Mary	Eric Michael	White	Christopher St. Magnet Elem., Carnegie HS

(continued)

(continued)

Parents	Children	Race	Schools
Meryl	George Claudia	White	Ridgecrest Elem., El Rancho Gifted MS, Davis Liberal Arts HS
Mimi	Gracie Myung	Korean	Christopher St. Magnet, Highland Gifted Magnet Elem.
Natalie	Daniel Derrick Renée Joseph	Black	Christopher St. Magnet Elem., Private
Paul & Jenny	David Cathy	White	Brookhaven Elem., El Rancho Regular MS
Robin	Kristin Caroline Reggie	Black	Greenfield Elem., Brookhaven Elem., Main St. Elem., Wilson MS
Suzanne	Michelle Amy	White	Spring St. Magnet Elem., El Rancho Gifted MS, Wagner HS

APPENDIX B

Appendix B.1

Data* for Children's Schools	Total Enrollment	% Asian	% Black	% Latino	% White	% Other	Math Test Percentiles	Reading Test Percentiles	Expected Openings	Magnet Applications
Elementary schools							—			
Christopher Street Magnet	360	31.1	25.3	6.1	35.8	1.8	66	63	40	689
Main Street	322	4.3	44.1	27.3	21.4	2.8	49	45	—	—
Hughes	554	13.5	18.8	49.6	16.1	2.0	35	39	—	—
Ridgecrest	658	7.8	23.6	36.3	30.1	2.3	51	52	—	—
Greenfield	899	0.3	37.6	60.0	1.0	1.1	21	20	—	—
Brookhaven	541	11.6	10.7	18.5	57.7	1.5	68	70	—	—
Spring Street Magnet	368	18.8	18.8	20.4	39.7	2.4	62	67	40	809
Berry Magnet	141	2.8	34.8	62.4	0	0	29	22	41	73
Middle schools										
El Rancho	1349	8.5	34.8	35.0	19.1	1.9	37	38	—	—
El Rancho Gifted	451	29.9	19.3	7.3	41.2	2.3	84	82	156	521
Foster	988	1.1	21.6	67.0	9.0	1.2	32	29	—	—
Wilson	1329	6.6	17.4	22.3	52.1	1.6	66	65	—	—
Madison	1073	1.8	38.3	55.6	3.4	0.9	26	21	—	—

(continued)

Appendix B.1 *(continued)*

Data* for Children's Schools	Total Enrollment	% Asian	% Black	% Latino	% White	% Other	Math Test Percentiles	Reading Test Percentiles	Expected Openings	Magnet Applications
High schools										
Carnegie College Prep. Magnet (6–12)	1489	12.1	42.8	10.8	32.2	2.2	70	68	300	1681
Davis	1659	3.9	42.9	44.5	6.8	2.0	27	20	—	—
Davis Fine Arts Magnet	877	6.0	35.9	15.6	40.0	2.3	55	50	225	540
Davis Liberal Arts Magnet	327	3.7	34.6	22.6	37.3	1.8	68	63	110	242
Wagner	2311	12.2	17.4	40.8	27.7	2.0	47	34	—	—

* Enrollment data and Stanford 9 test scores are from 1998. The test scores of the parents' children are aggregated in these scores.

Appendix B.2

Gifted Data* for Children's Schools	Total Enrollment	Total Gifted Enrollment	% Asian of Total Enrollment	% Asian of Gifted Enrollment	% Black of Total Enrollment	% Black of Gifted Enrollment	% Latino of Total Enrollment	%Latino of Gifted Enrollment	% White of Total Enrollment	% White of Gifted Enrollment
Middle schools										
El Rancho	1349	109	8.5	9.2	34.8	12.8	35.0	18.3	19.1	58.7
El Rancho Gifted	451	333	29.9	30.6	19.3	11.7	7.3	10.2	41.2	46.5
Foster	988	75	1.1	0	21.6	18.7	67.0	61.3	9.0	18.7
Wilson	1329	222	6.6	8.1	17.4	6.3	22.3	6.8	52.1	78.8
Madison	1073	42	1.8	9.5	38.3	33.3	55.6	45.2	3.4	4.8
High schools										
Carnegie College Prep. Magnet (6–12)	1489	573	12.1	17.6	42.8	34.2	10.8	9.2	32.2	38.2
Davis	1659	112	3.9	11.6	42.9	25.0	44.5	14.2	6.8	43.8

(continued)

Appendix B.2 *(continued)*

Gifted Data* for Children's Schools	Total Enrollment	Total Gifted Enrollment	% Asian of Total Enrollment	% Asian of Gifted Enrollment	% Black of Total Enrollment	% Black of Gifted Enrollment	% Latino of Total Enrollment	%Latino of Gifted Enrollment	% White of Total Enrollment	% White of Gifted Enrollment
Davis Fine Arts Magnet	877	295	6.0	7.8	35.9	24.4	15.6	13.6	40.0	52.2
Davis Liberal Arts Magnet	327	191	3.7	9.4	34.6	22.7	22.6	12.6	37.3	49.2
Wagner	2311	456	12.2	25.9	17.4	9.4	40.8	18.2	27.7	43.4

* Data are from 1996. The race/ethnicity and gifted status of some of the parents' children are aggregated in these scores.

NOTES

Notes to the Introduction

1. What cultural knowledge one has of the larger, dominant society, and how one knows how to use that knowledge, is the part of the habitus that Bourdieu calls "cultural capital." The habitus system, as Bourdieu calls it, plays an important part in determining an individual's practice or actions within the structures of the social as well as economic world. Drawing attention to the vastly different forms and availabilities of cultural capital between the social classes, Bourdieu and Passeron (1979) extended the theory into the structures and organization of the educational system to demonstrate how students from different social classes are reproduced into their same social strata as a result of their education.

2. Grillo's description of intersectionality is helpful for understanding the concept.

> Each of us in the world sits at the intersection of many categories: she is Latino, woman, short, other, lesbian, daughter, brown-eyed, long-haired, quick-witted, short tempered, worker, stubborn. At any one moment in time and space, some of theses categories are central to her being and her ability to act in the world. Others matter not at all. Some categories such as race, gender, class, and sexual orientation, are important most of the time. Others are rarely important. When something or someone highlights one of her categories and brings it to the fore, she may be a dominant person, or an oppressor of others. Other times, even most of the time, she may be oppressed herself. She may take lessons she has learned while in a subordinated status and apply them for good or ill when her dominant categories are highlighted. For example, having been mistreated as a child, she may either be a carefully respectful or an abusive parent (Grillo, 1995, quoted in Knight, 1998).

3. Dorothy Smith uses terms such as 'social relations,' 'social organization' and 'socially organized' .... "to recover those forms of concerting people's activities that are regularly reproduced." Social relations does not refer to relationships such as instructor–student, parent–child, and so on. Rather, "it directs attention to, and takes up analytically, how what people are doing and experiencing in a given local site is hooked into sequences of action implicating and coordinating multiple local sites where others are active" (Smith, 1999, p. 7).

4. CRT takes an oppositional view of racial injustice. Critical race theorists do not believe that color-blindness will eliminate racism and do believe, on the contrary, that a progressive and transformative race consciousness is needed. They insist on an anti-subordination stance and systematic analysis of the structures of subordination. Their work is similar to that of Collins (1997), in that they suggest an analysis that is inter-sectional or multidimensional, taking into account other social forces and complex individual and group identities (Valdes et al., 2002, p. 2).

5. Haney Lopez proposes in his theory of institutional racism that individuals may lack any conscious discriminatory intent. He states,

> Institutional racism theory stresses how racial institutions, whether followed in script or path form, operate as taken-for-granted understandings of the social context that actors must adopt to make sense of the world, as well as to be accepted as bona fide members of that milieu. Under the sway of institutional racism, persons fail to recognize their reliance on racial notions and indeed may stridently insist that no such reliance exists, even while acting in a manner that furthers racial status hierarchy (Haney Lopez, 2000, p. 1827).

6. Parts of this project have been previously published in André-Bechely (2004, 2005).

7. The study did not focus on charter schools or vouchers during data collection, although the district did have some charter schools at the time of the study.

8. With many parents interviewed twice, the total interview time for each parent ranged from 2 to 4 hours.

9. It was Brenda's preference to be identified as Hispanic.

10. All tape-recorded interviews were transcribed and analyzed consistent with qualitative research traditions (Merriam, 1998; Patton, 2002; Yin, 1989) and institutional ethnographic inquiry (DeVault and McCoy, 2001). Throughout the study, various texts and documents referred to by parents or school district personnel were collected. Demographic data on neighborhood schools and the schools of choice referred to by parents was collected, and field observations were made at schools. Various policy bulletins and documents related to the different school choice options offered by the district were collected and analyzed. The district also produces videos each year about the magnet school programs and airs these on local cable television. Three years of videos were collected, transcribed, and analyzed.

11. Interviews ranged from 45 minutes to 2 hours. Two of the community advisors were African American and one was Latino. The two principals were white. Among the six district-level administrators, three were African American, one was Asian, and two were white.

Notes to Chapter 1

1. I have chosen not to identify the district in this study. I do this for three reasons. One reason is to maintain the confidentiality of the participants. Another is that this book contributes to our understanding of the implementation of voluntary integration programs and other public school choice programs primarily by sharing the experiences of parents. Finally, if I disclosed the name of the district, attention might be diverted to the unique context of the district rather than to how the bureaucratic organization and coordination of choice in the district help to shape parents' understanding and participation in the choice process. Therefore, all identifiable references have been changed, and pseudonyms have been assigned to the district, people, programs, departments, etc.

2. References are on file with the author.

Notes to Chapter 2

1. Standardized test scores are norm-referenced, and the tests are designed to distribute those taking the tests across the full range of possible scores from 0 to 100%. A score reporting procedure is used so that students' scores are converted to a nine-point scale score. The nine-point scale scores are formed by dividing the baseline of the normal distribution curve into nine parts. Each of the nine scale scores is called a stanine (a term created from "standard" and "nine").

2. The administrator is indicating how the two different formulas create an integration ratio range for the school, which is why his description does not add up to 100%.

3. If a student's sending school improves, districts no longer have to provide transportation, and students could be stuck without transportation to the school to which they may have successfully adjusted and at which they would like to remain.

4. The No Child Left Behind Act identifies a quality public school choice plan as embodying the following principles: choice is an important opportunity for parents and children; choice is an important component of the overall district educational improvement plan; an overriding goal is to provide students with access to quality instruction; communication with parents is timely and thorough; and *information on choices is provided to parents and students in a format that is easy to understand*" (U.S. Department of Education, 2004; italics mine). Based on the district's magnet brochure, this certainly is an important principle to promote in the newly mandated federal choice provision.

Notes to Chapter 3

1. For example, the California Department of Education publishes a pamphlet titled: How to Pick Your Child's School (1994). It is only available for purchase in bulk quantities.

2. The magnet schools discussed in the book are not meant to be representative of all magnet schools in the district, nor I am implying that what goes on in this study would go on in all cases in the district.

3. See, for example, the work of David et al. (1994) and Gewirtz et al. (1995).

Notes to Chapter 4

1. GAIN, Greater Avenues for Independence, is the welfare-to-work program in California.

2. The administrator who used this term talked about how parents shared information among themselves, passing along their knowledge about different schools through various family, religious, and social networks. I interpret her use of "tom-tom" as a reference to what she may perceive as a steady "drum beat" of information that parents (and college professors) share about schools.

Note to Chapter 5

1. The diagram is adapted with permission from Ellen Pense and is drawn from her presentation at the Institutional Ethnography Network Conference, "Putting Institutional Ethnography into Practice," University of Victoria, Victoria, Canada in June 2002. Pense and colleagues use the diagram in presentations and as part of their advocacy work incorporating institutional ethnographic inquiry. Information about Ellen Pense's work is available at: http://www.praxisinternational.org.

REFERENCES

Aasen, P. (2003). What happened to social-democratic progressivism in Scandinavia? Restructuring education in Sweden and Norway in the 1990s. In M. Apple, ed. *The State and the Politics of Knowledge*. New York: RoutledgeFalmer, pp. 109–148.

André-Bechely, L. (2004). The goals of a voluntary integration program and the problems of access: A closer look at a magnet school application brochure. *Equity and Excellence in Education* 37(3), 302–315.

André-Bechely, L. (2005). Public school choice at the intersection of voluntary integration and not-so-good neighborhood schools: Lessons from parents' experiences. *Educational Administration Quarterly,* 41(2), 267–305.

Anyon, J. (1997). *Ghetto Schooling: A Political Economy of Urban Educational Reform.* New York: Teachers College Press.

Apple, M.W. (1996). Power, meaning, and identity: Critical sociology of education in the United States. *British Journal of Sociology of Education,* 17(2), 125–144.

Apple, M. (2001). *Educating the "Right" Way: Markets, Standards, God, and Inequality.* New York: Routledge.

Apple, M.W. (2003). The state and the politics of knowledge. In M.W. Apple, ed. *The State and the Politics of Knowledge*. New York: RoutledgeFalmer, pp. 1–24.

Balkin, J.M., ed. (2001). *What Brown v. Board of Education Should Have Said.* New York: New York University Press.

Ball, S.J. (1990). Introducing Monsieur Foucault. In S.J. Ball, ed. *Foucault and Education: Disciplines and Knowledge*. New York: Routledge, pp. 1–8.

Ball, S. J. (1993). Education markets, choice and social class: The market as a class strategy in the UK and the USA. *British Journal of Sociology of Education,* 14(1), 3-19.

Ball, S.J. (1994). *Education Reform: A Critical and Post-Structural Approach.* Philadelphia: Open University Press.

Ball, S.J., Bowe, R., and Gewirtz, S. (1996). School choice, social class and distinction: The realization of social advantage in education. *Journal of Education Policy,* 11(1), 89–112.

Blank, R.K., Levine, R.E., and Steel, L. (1996). After fifteen years: magnet schools in urban education. In B. Fuller and R.F. Elmore, eds. *Who Chooses? Who Loses? Culture, Institutions, and the Unequal Effects of School Choice*. New York: Teachers College Press, pp. 154–172.

Boger, J.C. (2003). Education's "Perfect Storm"? Racial resegregation, high stakes testing, and school resource inequities: the case of North Carolina. *North Carolina Law Review,* 81, 1375–1462.

225

Bowe, R., Ball, S.J., and Gewirtz, S. (1994). 'Parental choice', consumption and social theory: The operation of micro-markets in education. *British Journal of Educational Studies*, 42(1), 38–52.

Brantlinger, E. (2003). *Dividing classes: How the Middle Class Negotiates and Rationalizes School Advantage.* New York: RoutledgeFalmer.

Brantlinger, E., Majd-Jabbari, M., and Guskin, S.L. (1996). Self-interest and liberal educational discourse: How ideology works for middle-class mothers. *American Educational Research Journal*, 33(3), 571–597.

Brown, C.G., Piché, D.M., and Taylor, W.L. (2004). Choosing Better Schools: A Report on Student Transfers Under the No Child Left Behind Act. Washington, DC: Citizen's Commission on Civil Rights.

Brown v. Board of Education (1954). 347 U.S. 483.

California Department of Education (2004). O'Connell releases list of schools and school districts identified for federal program improvement. Accessed from: http://www.cde.ca.gov/nr/ne/yr04/yr04re188.as.

California Department of Education (1994). How to Pick Your Child's School. Sacramento: Bureau of Publications.

Campbell, M., & Manicom, A. (1995a). Introduction. In M. Campbell & A. Manicom (Eds.), *Knowledge, Experience, and Ruling Relations: Studies in the Social Organization of Knowledge* (pp. 3-17). Toronto: University of Toronto Press.

Campbell, M., & Manicom, A. (Ed.). (1995b). Knowledge, Experience, and Ruling Relations: Studies in the Social Organization of Knowledge. Toronto: University of Toronto Press.

Campbell, M. and Gregor, F. (2002). *Mapping Social Relations: A Primer in Doing Institutional Ethnography.* Aurora, ON, Canada: Garamond Press.

Cashin, S. (2004). *The Failures of Integration: How Race and Class Are Undermining the American Dream.* New York: Public Affairs Books at Perseus Books Group.

Chubb, J. E., & Moe, T. M. (1990). *Politics, Markets, and America's Schools.* Washington, DC: The Brookings Institution.

Collins, P. H. (1992). Transforming the inner circle: Dorothy Smith's challenge to sociological theory. *Sociological Theory*, 10(1), 73-80.

Collins, P. H. (1997). On West and Fenstermaker's "Doing Difference". In M. R. Walsh (Eds.), *Women, Men, and Gender: Ongoing Debates.* New Haven, CT: Yale University Press, pp. 73–75.

Clotfelter, C.T. (2004). *After Brown: The Rise and Retreat of School Desegregation.* Princeton, NJ: Princeton University Press.

Crenshaw, K., Gotanda, N., Peller, G., and Thomas, K., eds. (1995). *Critical Race Theory: The Key Writings That Formed the Movement.* New York: The New Press.

Dale, R. (1997). Educational markets and school choice. *British Journal of Sociology of Education*, 18(3), 451–468.

David, M., West, A., and Ribbens, J. (1994). *Mother's Intuition? Choosing Secondary Schools.* Bristol, PA: Falmer Press, Taylor and Francis.

Dehli, K. (1996). Between 'market' and 'state'? Engendering education change in the 1990's. *Discourse: Studies in the Cultural Politics of Education*, 17(3), 363–376.

DeVault, M. (1999). Institutional ethnography: a strategy for feminist inquiry. In *Liberating Method: Feminism and Social Research.* Philadelphia: Temple University Press, pp. 46–54.

DeVault, M. and McCoy, L. (2001). Institutional ethnography: using interviews to investigate ruling relations. In *Handbook of Interview Research: Context and Method.* Thousand Oaks, CA: Sage Publishers, pp. 751–775.

Dobson, S. (2001). Introduction: institutional ethnography as method. *Studies in Cultures, Organizations, and Societies*, 7, 147–158.

Dodd, A.W. and Konzal, J.L. (1999). *Making Our High Schools Better: How Parents and Teachers Can Work Together.* New York: St. Martin's Press.

Douglas, M. (1986). *How Institutions Think.* Syracuse, NY: Syracuse University Press.

Elmore, R.F. (1982). Implementation of federal educational policy: Research and analysis. *Research in Sociology of Education and Socialization,* 3, 97–119.

Elmore, R.F. and Fuller, B. (1996). Empirical research on educational choice: What are the implications for policy-makers? In B. Fuller and R.F. Elmore, eds. *Who Chooses? Who Loses?* New York: Teachers College Press, pp. 187–202.

Epstein, J.L. (1995). School/family/community partnerships: Caring for the children we share. *Phi Delta Kappan,* 76(9), 701–712.

Fantini, M. and Young, M. (1970). *Designing Education for Tomorrow's Cities.* New York: Holt Rinehart.

Fine, M. (1992). *Disruptive Voices: The Possibilities of Feminist Research.* Ann Arbor, MI: University of Michigan Press.

Foucault, M. (1995). Strategies of power. In W.T. Anderson, ed. *The Truth about the Truth: De-confusing and Re-constructing the Postmodern World.* New York: Tarcher/G.P. Putnam's Sons, pp. 40–45.

Frankenberg, E., Lee, C., and Orfield, G. (2003). *A Multiracial Society with Segregated Schools: Are We Losing the Dream?* Cambridge, MA: The Civil Rights Project, Harvard University.

Fuller, B. and Elmore, R.F., eds. (1996). *Who Chooses? Who Loses? Culture, Institutions, and the Unequal Effects of School Choice.* New York: Teachers College Press.

Gandin, L.A. and Apple, M. (2003). Educating the state, democratizing knowledge: The Citizen School Project in Porto Alegre, Brazil. In M. Apple, ed. *The State and the Politics of Knowledge.* New York: RoutledgeFalmer, pp. 193–220.

Gee, J.P. (1990). *Social linguistics and literacies.* London: Falmer Press.

Gee, J.P. (1999). *An Introduction to Discourse Analysis: Theory and Method.* New York: Routledge.

Gewirtz, S., Ball, S.J., and Bowe, R. (1995). *Markets, Choice and Equity in Education.* Philadelphia: Open University Press.

Good, T.L. and Braden, J.S. (2000). *The Great School Debate: Choice, Vouchers, and Charters.* Mahwah, NJ: Lawrence Erlbaum Associates.

Gordon, W.M. (1994). The implementation of desegregation plans since Brown. *Journal of Negro Education,* 63(3), 310–322.

Graue, M.E. and Kroeger, J. (2001). A Bakhtinian analysis of particular home–school relations. *American Educational Research Journal,* 38(3), 467–498.

Griffith, A.I. (1992). Educational policy as text and action. *Educational Policy,* 6(4), 415–428.

Griffith, A.I. (1995). Mothering, schooling, and children's development. In M. Campbell and A. Manicom, eds. *Knowledge, Experience, and Ruling Relations: Studies in the Social Organization of Knowledge.* Toronto: University of Toronto Press, pp. 108–121.

Griffith, A.I. and Smith, D.E. (1987). Constructing cultural knowledge: Mothering as discourse. In J.S. Gaskell and A.T. McLaren, eds. *Women and Education: A Canadian Perspective.* Calgary: Detselig, pp. 87–103.

Griffith, A. I., and Smith, D., E. (1990). "What did you do in school today?": Mothering, schooling, and social class. *Perspectives on Social Problems,* 2, 3-24.

Griffith, A.I. and Smith, D.E. (2004). *Mothering for Schooling.* New York, RoutledgeFalmer.

Grillo, T. (1995). Anti-essentialism and intersectionality: Tools to dismantle the master's house. *Berkeley Women's Law Journal,* 10, 16–30.

Haney Lopez, I.F. (2000). Institutional racism: Judicial conduct and a new theory of racial discrimination. *Yale Law Journal,* 109, 1717–1884.

Harding, S. (1991). *Whose Science? Whose Knowledge? Thinking from Women's Lives.* Ithaca, NY: Cornell University Press.

Harding, S. (2004). A socially relevant philosophy of science? Resources from standpoint theory's controversiality. *Hypatia*, 19(1), 25–47.

Hays, S. (1996). *The Cultural Contradictions of Motherhood*. New Haven, CT: Yale University Press.

Henderson, A.T. and Berla, N. (1995). Introduction. In A.T. Henderson and N. Berla, eds. *A New Generation of Evidence: The Family is Critical to Student Achievement*. Washington, DC: Center for Law and Education, pp. 1–20.

Hendrie, C. (2004). In U.S. schools, race still counts. *Education Week*, January 21, 2004, *Vol.* 23(19), pp. 1, 16-19.

Henig, J. (1996). The local dynamics of choice: Ethnic preferences and institutional responses. In B. Fuller and R.F. Elmore, eds. *Who Chooses? Who Loses?* New York: Teachers College Press, pp. 95–117.

Henig, J.R. (1994). *Rethinking School Choice: Limits of the Market Metaphor*. Princeton, NJ: Princeton University Press.

Hinchey, P.H. (1998). *Finding Freedom in the Classroom: A Practical Introduction to Critical Theory*. New York: Peter Lang.

Holme, J.J. (2002). Buying homes, buying schools: School choice and the social construction of school quality. *Harvard Educational Review*, 72(2), 177–205.

Jordan, S. and Yeomans, D. (1995). Critical ethnography: Problems in contemporary theory and practice. *British Journal of Sociology of Education*, 16(3), 389–408.

Katznelson, I., & Weir, M. (1985). *Schooling for All: Class, Race, and the Decline of the Democratic Ideal*. Berkeley, CA: University of California Press, Basic Books, Inc.

Knight, M.G. (1998). Unearthing the Muted Voices of Transformative Professionals: A Qualitative Study of African-American Candidates Learning to Teach Children from Diverse Student Populations in Urban Schools. Unpublished dissertation, University of California, Los Angeles.

Kohn, A. (1998). Only for *my* kid: How privileged parents undermine school reform. *Phi Delta Kappan*, 79(8), 568–577.

Ladson-Billings, G. (1995). Toward a theory of culturally relevant pedagogy. *American Education Research Journal*, 32(3), 465–491.

Ladson-Billings, G. (1999). Just what is critical race theory and what's it doing in a nice field like education? In L. Parker, D. Deyhle, and S. Villenas, eds. *Race Is. Race Isn't: Critical Race Theory and Qualitative Studies in Education*. Boulder, CO: Westview Press, pp. 7–30.

Ladson-Billings, G. (2003). It's your world, I'm just trying to explain it: Understanding our epistemological and methodological challenges. *Qualitative Inquiry*, 9(1), 5–12.

Ladson-Billings, G. and Tate, W.F. (1995). Toward a critical race theory of education. *Teachers College Record*, 97(1), 47–68.

Lareau, A. (2003). *Unequal Childhoods: Class, Race, and Family Life*. Berkeley, CA: University of California Press.

Lareau, A. and Horvat, E.M. (1999). Moments of social inclusion and exclusion: Race, class, and cultural capital in family-school relationships. *Sociology of Education*, 72, 37–53.

Larson, C.L. and Ovando, C.J. (2001). *The Color of Bureaucracy: The Politics of Equity in Multicultural School Communities*. Stamford, CT: Wadsworth.

Lemke, J.L. (1995). *Textual Politics: Discourse and Social Dynamics*. London: Taylor and Francis.

Lightfoot, S.L. (1978). *Worlds Apart, Relationships Between Families and Schools*. New York: Basic Books.

Lightfoot, S.L. (1983). *The Good High School*. New York: Basic Books.

Lopez, G.R. (2001). The value of hard work: Lessons on parent involvement from an (im)migrant household. *Harvard Educational Review*, 71(3), 416–437.

Lopez, G. R. (2003). The (racially neutral) politics of education: A critical race theory perspective. *Educational Administration Quarterly* 39(1): 68-94.

Love, B.J. (2004). Brown plus 50 counter-storytelling: A critical race theory analysis of the "majoritarian achievement gap" story. *Equity and Excellence in Education,* 37(3), 227–246.

Luke, A. (1996). Text and discourse in education: An introduction to critical discourse analysis. In M. Apple, ed. *Review of Research in Education,* Vol. 21. Washington, DC: American Educational Research Association, pp. 3–48.

Macedo, S. (2003). Equity and school choice: How can we bridge the gap between ideals and realities? In A. Wolfe, ed. *School Choice: The Moral Debate.* Princeton, NJ: Princeton University Press, pp. 51–69.

MacLure, M. (2003). *Discourse in Educational and Social Research.* Philadelphia: Open University Press.

Manicom, A. (1995). What's health got to do with it? Class, gender, and teachers' work. In M. Campbell and A. Manicom, eds. *Knowledge, Experience and Ruling Relations.* Toronto: University of Toronto Press, pp. 133–148.

Marschall, M. (2000). The role of information and institutional arrangements in stemming the stratifying effects of school choice. *Journal of Urban Affairs,* 22(3), 333–350.

Marshall, C. (1997). Dismantling and reconstructing policy analysis. In C. Marshall, ed. *Feminist Critical Policy Analysis I: A Perspective From Primary and Secondary Schooling.* Washington, DC: Falmer Press, pp. 1–39.

McCarthy, M. (2000). Privatization of education: Marketplace models. In B.A. Jones, ed. *Educational Leadership: Policy Dimensions in the 21st Century.* Stamford, CT: Ablex, pp. 21–40.

McIntosh, P. (1989). White privilege: Unpacking the invisible knapsack. *Peace and Freedom,* July/August, 10–12.

McLaren, P. (1995). *Critical Pedagogy and Predatory Culture.* London: Routledge.

McNeil, L.M. (2000). *Contradictions of School Reform: Educational Costs of Standardized Testing.* New York: Routledge.

Meeks, L.F., Meeks, W.A., and Warren, C.A. (2000). Racial desegregation: Magnet schools, vouchers, privatization, and home schooling. *Education and Urban Society,* 33(1), 88–101.

Mehan, H. (1978). Structuring school structure. *Harvard Education Review,* 48(1), 32-64.

Meier, K.J. and Stewart, J., Jr. (1991). *The Politics of Hispanic Education: Un paso pa'lante y dos pa'tras.* Albany, NY: State University of New York Press.

Meier, K.J., Stewart, J., Jr., and England, R.E. (1989). *Race, Class, and Education: The Politics of Second-Generation Discrimination.* Madison, WI: University of Wisconsin Press.

Merriam, S.B. (1998). *Qualitative Research and Case Study Applications in Education.* San Francisco: Jossey-Bass.

Metz, M. (1986). *Different By Design: The Context and Character of Three Magnet Schools.* New York: Routledge.

Naples, N.A. (2003). Epistemology, feminist methodology, and the politics of method. In *Feminism and Method: Ethnography, Discourse Analysis and Activist Research* New York: Routledge, pp. 13–35.

National Working Commission on Choice in K-12 Education (2003). School Choice: Doing it the Right Way Makes a Difference. Brown Center on Education Policy, Washington DC: The Brookings Institution.

No Child Left Behind Act of 2001. (2002). Pub. L. No. 107–110, 115 Stat.1425, 20 U.S.C. 6301 et seq.

Oakes, J. (1985). *Keeping Track: How Schools Structure Inequality.* New Haven, CT: Yale University Press.

Oakes, J., Quartz, K.H., Lipton, M., and Ryan, S. (2000). *Becoming Good American Schools: The Struggle for Civic Virtue in Education Reform.* San Francisco: Jossey-Bass.

Orfield, G. (2001). *Schools More Separate: Consequences of a Decade of Resegregation.* Cambridge, MA: The Civil Rights Project at Harvard University.

Orfield, G. (2004). *Introduction: Inspiring Vision, Disappointing Results: Four Studies on Implementing the No Child Left Behind Act.* Cambridge, MA: The Civil Rights Project at Harvard University.

Orfield, G. and Eaton, S.E. (1996). *Dismantling Desegregation: The Quiet Reversal of Brown v. Board of Education.* New York: The New Press.

Orfield, G. and Lee, C. (2004). *Brown at 50: King's Dream or Plessy's Nightmare?* Cambridge, MA: The Civil Rights Project at Harvard University.

Patton, M.Q. (2002). *Qualitative Research and Evaluation Methods.* 3rd ed. Thousand Oaks, CA: Sage Publishers.

Pense, E. (2002). Putting Institutional Ethnography into Practice. Presentation at the Institutional Ethnography Network Conference, University of Victoria, Victoria, Canada (June, 2002).

powell, j.a. (2001a). Integration is not cultural assimilation. In C. Hartman, ed. *Challenges to Equality: Poverty and Race in America.* Armonk, NY: M.E. Sharpe, pp. 141–148.

powell, j.a. (2001b). The tensions between integration and school reform. *Hastings Constitutional Law Quarterly,* 28(Spring), 655–697.

Raywid, M. A. (1985). Family choice arrangements in public schools: A review of the literature. *Review of Educational Research,* 55(4), 435-367.

Reay, D. (1996). Contextualizing choice: Social power and parental involvement. *British Educational Research Journal,* 22(5), 581–596.

Rossell, C.H. (1990). *The Carrot or the Stick for School Desegregation Policy: Magnet Schools or Forced Busing.* Philadelphia: Temple University Press.

Rossell, C.H., Armor, D.J., and Walberg, H.J., eds. (2002). *School Desegregation in the 21st Century.* Westport: CN, Praeger.

Rudalevige, A. (2003). No Child Left Behind: Forging a congressional compromise. In P.E. Peterson and M.R. West, eds. *No Child Left Behind? The Politics and Practice of School Accountability.* Washington, DC: Brookings Institution, pp. 23–54.

Sapon-Shevin, M. (1994). *Playing Favorites: Gifted Education and the Disruption of Community.* Albany, NY: State University of New York Press.

Saporito, S. and Lareau, A. (1999). School choice as a process: The multiple dimensions of race in framing educational choice. *Social Problems,* 46(3), 418–439.

Sarason, S.B. (1990). *The Predictable Failure of Educational Reform.* San Francisco: Jossey-Bass.

Sissel, P.A. (2000). *Staff, Parents, and Politics in Head Start: A Case Study in Unequal Power, Knowledge, and Material Resources.* New York: Falmer Press.

Smith, D. (1998). The underside of schooling: Restructuring, privatization, and women's unpaid work. *Journal for a Just and Caring Education,* 4(1), 11–29.

Smith, D.E. (1987). *The Everyday World as Problematic: A Feminist Sociology.* Boston: Northeastern University Press.

Smith, D.E. (1990). *Texts, Facts, and Femininity: Exploring the Relations of Ruling.* New York: Routledge.

Smith, D.E. (1999). *Writing the Social: Critique, Theory, and Investigations.* Toronto: University of Toronto Press.

Smith, D.E. (2001). Texts and the ontology of organizations and institutions. *Studies in Cultures, Organizations, and Societies,* 7, 159–198.

Smith, D.E. (2002). Institutional ethnography. In T. May, ed. *Qualitative Research in Action.* Thousand Oaks, CA: Sage Publishers, pp. 17-52.

Smith, D.E. and Griffith, A.I. (1990). Coordinating the uncoordinated: Mothering, schooling and the family wage. *Perspectives on Social Problems*, 2, 25–43.

Smith, G.W. (1990). Political activist as ethnographer. *Social Problems*, 37(4), 629–648.

Smith, M.L., with Miller-Kahn, L., Heinecke, W., and Jarvis, P.F. (2004). *Political Spectacle and the Fate of American Schools*. New York: RoutledgeFalmer.

Smrekar, C., and Goldring, E. (1999). *School Choice in Urban America: Magnet Schools and the Pursuit of Equity*. New York: Teachers College Press.

Solórzano, D.G. and Ornelas, A. (2002). A critical race analysis of advanced placement classes: A case of educational inequality. *Journal of Latinos and Education*, 1(4), 215–229.

Staiger, A. (2004). Whiteness as giftedness: Racial formation at an urban high school. *Social Problems*, 51(2), 161–181.

Steinhorn, L. (2001). Response to "Is integration possible?" symposium. In C. Hartman, ed. *Challenges to Equality: Poverty and Race in America*. Armonk, NY: M.E. Sharpe, pp. 84–87.

Tate, W.F. (1997). Critical race theory and education: History, theory, and implications. *Review of Research in Education*, 22, 195–247.

Tate, W.F. (1999). Conclusion. In L. Parker, D. Deyhle, and S. Villenas, eds. *Race Is. Race Isn't: Critical Race Theory and Qualitative Studies in Education*. Boulder, CO: Westview Press, pp. 251–272.

Tate, W.F., Ladson-Billings, G., and Grant, C.A. (1996). The Brown decision revisited: Mathematizing a social problem. In M.J. Shujaa, ed. *Beyond Desegregation: The Politics of Quality in African American Schooling*. Thousand Oaks, CA: Corwin Press, pp. 29–49.

Taylor, W.L. (2003). Title I as an instrument for achieving desegregation and equal opportunity. *North Carolina Law Review*, 81, 1751–1770.

Tomlinson, C.A. (2000). Reconcilable differences? Standards-based teaching and differentiation. *Educational Leadership* (September), 6–11.

Tyack, D. B. (1974). *The One Best System, A History of American Urban Education*. Cambridge, MA: Harvard University Press.

Tyack, D. (1992). Can we build a system of choice that is not just a "sorting machine" or a market-based "free-for-all"? *Equity and Choice*, 9(1), 13–17.

Tyack, D. and Cuban, L. (1995). *Tinkering Toward Utopia: A Century of Public School Reform*. Cambridge, MA: Harvard University Press.

U.S. Department of Education (February 6, 2004). Public school choice: Draft non-regulatory guidance. Accessed at http://www.ed.gov/policy/elsec/guid/schoolchoiceguid.doc.

Valdes, F., Culp, J.M., and Harris, A.P. (2002). Battles waged, won, and lost: Critical Race Theory at the turn of the millennium. In F. Valdes, J.M. Culp, and A.P. Harris, eds. *Crossroads, Directions, and a New Critical Race Theory*. Philadelphia: Temple University Press, pp. 1–6.

Valenzuela, A. (1999). *Subtractive Schooling: U.S.–Mexican Youth and the Politics of Caring*. Albany, NY: State University of New York Press.

Varady, D.P. and Raffel, J.A. (1995). *Selling Cities: Attracting Homebuyers Through Schools and Housing Programs*. Albany, NY: State University of New York Press.

Weedon, C. (1997). *Feminist Practice and Poststructuralist Theory*. 2nd ed. Cambridge, UK: Blackwell.

Weis, L. (1995). Qualitative research in sociology of education: Reflections on the 1970's and beyond. In W. T. Pink & G. W. Noblit (Eds.), *Continuity and Contradiction: The Futures of the Sociology of Education* (pp. 157-73). Cresskill, NJ: Hampton Press, Inc.

Wellman, D. T. (1993). *Portraits of White Racism*. Cambridge, UK: Cambridge University Press.

Wells, A.S. (1991). Choice in education: Examining the evidence on equity. *Teachers College Record*, 93(1), 137–155.

Wells, A.S. (1993a). The sociology of school choice: Why some win and others lose in the educational marketplace. In E. Rasell and R. Rothstein, eds. *School Choice: Examining the Evidence*. Washington, DC: Economic Policy Institute, pp. 29–48.

Wells, A.S. (1993b). *Time to Choose, America at the Crossroads of School Choice Policy*. New York: Hill and Wang.

Wells, A.S. (1997). *Stepping over the Colorline*. New Haven, CT: Yale University Press.

Wells, A.S., and Serna, I. (1996). The politics of culture: Understanding local political resistance to detracking in racially mixed schools. *Harvard Educational Review*, 66(1), 93–118.

Wells, A.S., Lopez, A., Scott, J., and Holme, J.J. (1999). Charter schools as postmodern paradox: rethinking social stratification in an age of deregulated school choice. *Harvard Education Review*, 69(2), 172–204.

West, K.C. (1994). A desegregation tool that backfired: Magnet schools and classroom segregation. *Yale Law Journal*, 103, 2567–2592.

Winant, H. (1994). *Racial Conditions*. Minneapolis, MN: University of Minnesota Press.

Wildman, S.M. (1996). *Privilege Revealed: How Invisible Preference Undermines America*. New York: New York University Press.

Wolfe, A. (2003). The irony of school choice: Liberals, conservatives, and the new politics of race. In A. Wolfe, ed. *School Choice: The Moral Debate*. Princeton, NJ: Princeton University Press, pp. 31–50.

Yin, R.K. (1989). *Case Study Research: Design and Methods* (Vol. 5). Newbury Park, CA: Sage Publishers.

Zelman et al. v. Simmons-Harris et al. (2002). 536 U.S. 639, 122 S.Ct. 2460, 153 L.Ed.2d 604.

INDEX

Page references followed by f indicate a figure
Page references followed by t indicate a table

A

B